An Introduction to AutoCAD Release 13

A. Yarwood

Autodesk.
Registered Developer

D0103184

LONGMAN

Longman Group Limited
Longman House, Burnt Mill, Harlow
Essex CM20 2JE, England
and Associated Companies throughout the world

First published 1995

British Library Cataloguing in Publication Data
A catalogue entry for this title is available from the British Library

ISBN 0-582-27450-8

Set by 24 in 10/13pt Melior
Produced by Longman Singapore Publishers (Pte) Ltd
Printed in Singapore

Contents

List of plates   ix
Preface   xi
Acknowledgements   xiii

1 AutoCAD R13 for Windows   1
    Introduction   1
    The AutoCAD 13 graphics window   2
    Configuring AutoCAD R13   4
    Dialogue, warning and message boxes   6
    Toolbars, tools and tool tips   11
    Entering commands at the command line   13
    Questions   13

2 AutoCAD R13 for DOS   15
    Introduction   15
    AutoCAD R13 for DOS pull-down menus   17
    AutoCAD R13 for DOS on-screen menus   17
    Entering commands at the command line   21
    Windows and DOS drawings compared   21
    Questions   22

3 Using AutoCAD R13 for Windows   23
    Introduction   23
    Why use computer-aided design software?   24
    The Preferences dialogue box   26
    The AutoCAD coordinate system   29
    Setting up a metric A3 R13 window   29
    Toolbars   32
    Prompts   34
    Practice drawing using Line, Polyline, Circle and Arc   34
    Questions   39
    Exercises   40

4   Accurate construction of drawings   43
Introduction   43
Using absolute coordinates   43
Using relative coordinates   48
Other tools in the Draw toolbar   50
Object Snap   52
Help   55
Keyboard short-cuts   57
Questions   58
Exercises   58

5   Setting up a prototype drawing file   62
Introduction   62
Starting a new drawing   62
Layers   63
A suggested prototype drawing file   65
Tool abbreviations   70
Questions   71

6   The 2D Modify tools   73
Introduction   73
The Modify toolbar   74
Using the Modify and Select Objects tools   74
Notes on the modify tool   91
Questions   92
Exercises   92

7   2D drawing   98
Introduction   98
Basic drawing tools   99
Basic handling tools   107
Saving your work   113
Questions   114
Exercises   115

8   Text styles and types of drawing   118
Text Styles   118
Adding text to a drawing   119
Spelling checker   121
Types of drawing   122
Isometric drawing   131
Questions   137
Exercises   138

9   Hatching   142
The Hatch tool   142
Hatch from the Command Line   144
Explode   146
Text within a hatched area   146
Questions   146
Exercises   147

10   Dimensions   152
Introduction   152
Examples of dimensions   155
The %%symbol calls   159
Questions   160
Exercises   160

11   The Edit menu and file types   163
Introduction   163
Undo and Redo   163
Object linking and embedding   164
Examples of OLE and pasting   165
The Edit menu commands   166
File types   169
Other types of file   172
Questions   173

12   Blocks and Insertions   174
Introduction   174
Libraries of symbols   174
Electric and electronic circuit diagram drawings   178
Other examples of libraries   179
Questions   181
Exercises   181

13   The Surfaces toolbar   184
Introduction   184
Methods of drawing   184
Using the Surfaces tools   187
3D surface meshes   191
Further 3D tools   196
Questions   200
Exercises   200

14   The UCS and the Solids toolbar   208
   Introduction   208
   The user coordinate system (UCS)   208
   The Solids toolbar   212
   The Boolean operators – Union, Subtract and Intersection   217
   Some 3D solid model exercises   220
   More advanced examples of 3D models   223
   Questions   226
   Exercises   226

15   More about 3D model construction   229
   Introduction   229
   Model Space and Paper Space   229
   3D model construct in four viewports   230
   Solid model drawing tools   234
   Further use of the Slice and Section tools   238
   The tool AME Convert   240
   Other solid model tools   240
   Questions   242
   Exercises   243

16   The Render toolbar   247
   Introduction   247
   Use of the Render tools   247
   The Shade tool   253
   Questions   257
   Exercises   257

Appendix A – Printing and Plotting   258
   Introduction   258
   Printing from AutoCAD R13   258

Appendix B – Some of the new features in R13   261
   Introduction   261
   Drawings previewed in the Select File dialogue box   261
   Customising a toolbar   262
   Groups   262
   The Purge tool   265
   Saving in AutoCAD R12 format   266

Appendix C – Glossary   267

Index   273

List of plates

Colour plates are between pages 146 and 147

Plate I   Selecting the **AutoCAD R13** icon from within the **Program Manager** window

Plate II   The **AutoCAD** window that first appears when **AutoCAD R13** is launched

Plate III   Selecting a drawing to open in the **Select File** dialogue box

Plate IV   The **Aerial View** window showing which part of the drawing has been magnified using **Zoom**

Plate V   The **Boundary Hatch** dialogue box; AutoCAD is configured here to display an on-screen menu and no toolboxes

Plate VI   A **Help** window

Plate VII   A 3D model in a distance perspective view (**Dview**)

Plate VIII   A 3D model displayed in a four-viewport graphics window

Plate IX   The 3D model in Plate VIII displayed in a single viewport with the **Clipboard Viewer**

Plate X   A rendering of the 3D model shown in Plate VIII

Plate XI   A 3D model after the tool **Shade** has been selected and applied

Plate XII   The 3D model shown in Plate XI rendered in several materials

Plate XIII   The same rendering as in Plate XII displayed with a different screen colour configuration

Plate XIV   An exploded view of a part from a pump device after rendering

Plate XV   A rendering of an exploded 3D model

Plate XVI   A rendering in coloured materials

Preface

This book was written for the use of students in colleges and for those in industry who are beginning to learn how to use AutoCAD® Release 13 installed on a PC. Although the book's contents are designed for those using the software installed on a PC, it will be found that it will be just as suitable for those who are working with AutoCAD R13 installed on other platforms. Although both a DOS version and a Windows version of Release 13 are available, the contents of this book are mainly confined to methods of using the Windows version, although a short chapter has been devoted to a description of the DOS version.

The methods of working described throughout the book have been written on the assumption that the reader will be using a computer on which AutoCAD R13 has been installed, and that the computer has been properly configured to run the software. Because of this assumption, details of features such as the configuration of the screen, digitiser and printer ready for constructing drawings have been left to a bare minimum. The description of settings of the numerous AutoCAD variables necessary for accurate drawing have also been largely ignored, assuming that the loaded software will be mainly set to the default settings. Details of the various languages, such as AutoLisp and the AutoCAD Development System (ADS) and others which can be used in conjunction with AutoCAD are not mentioned, being outside the scope of a book of this nature.

AutoCAD, in its various releases, is the most widely used CAD system in the world, with over 50% of all CAD workstations being equipped with the software. The publication of this latest release of AutoCAD (13), with its numerous enhancements over previous releases will undoubtedly allow the software to maintain its dominance in the CAD world. Despite these enhancements, an operator coming new to Release 13 from an earlier release will find that the basic methods of calling commands and constructing drawings, which have become established in earlier versions, can still be used when working with this latest release. This retention of earlier methods of working will allow those new to Release 13 to start constructing drawings with its aid and to commence becoming conversant with the enhancements it offers.

Early chapters deal with two-dimensional (2D) drawing. These early chapters are followed by chapters dealing with methods of constructing 3D solid model drawings, first using Surface tools, then using the Solid tools. A final short chapter deals with the rendering of solid models described in earlier chapters. Appendices follow, the first on printing or plotting and a second containing explanations of some of the enhancements found in Release 13. A final Appendix is a short glossary of terms used in computing, with particular reference to CAD.

No description of the use of the rendering software AutoVision™ Release 2, which can be used within AutoCAD R13 for the production of first class renderings of AutoCAD 3D solid models, has been included. The description of renderings given here is confined to the Render program within AutoCAD R13. AutoVison Release 2 could command a book of this nature in its own right.

All drawings throughout the pages of the book were constructed with the aid of a Windows version of Release 13. The illustrations of screens are from bitmaps of dumps produced with the aid of the Inset software program Hijaak Pro 3.0. The original page layouts were made up in the Aldus desk top publisher PageMaker 5.0 and the final page designs produced from my PageMaker files on disk. The computer used with these software programmes was a DX2, running at 66 MHz, with a large hard disk, a couple of floppy disk drives and a CD-ROM drive. This computer was made up to my specification by Dart Computers of Romsey Hampshire.

Finally it should be noted here that a book of this size can only be seen as an introductory book to such a complex software package as AutoCAD R13. It is hoped that the reader will learn from this book how to construct simple drawings with the aid of the software and, as a result become interested in the possibilities of advanced drawing which the software has to offer. This interest should then lead the reader to research further into CAD with the aid of AutoCAD.

Salisbury 1995   A. Yarwood.

Acknowledgements

The author wishes to acknowledge with grateful thanks the help given to him by members of the staff at Autodesk Ltd.

Trademarks

The following trademarks are registered in the US Patent and Trademark Office by Autodesk Inc:

Autodesk®, AutoCAD®, AutoSketch®, Advanced Modelling Extension® (AME).

The following are trademarks of Autodesk Inc:

ACAD™, DXF™, AutoCAD Device Interface™ (ADI), AutoCAD Development System™ (ADS).

IBM® is a registered trademark of the International Business Machines Corporation.

MS-DOS® is a registered trademark, and Windows™ is a trademark of the Microsoft Corporation.

A. Yarwood is a Registered Developer with Autodesk Ltd.

Registered Developer

CHAPTER 1

AutoCAD 13 for Windows

Introduction

This chapter is an outline of the method of starting and working with AutoCAD Release 13 for Windows. Chapter 2 outlines the methods of starting and working within AutoCAD Release 13 for DOS. From Chapter 3 onwards, this book deals exclusively with the Windows version of the software. However, it will be found that some of the methods of working are common to both versions.

Terms

The following terms will be used throughout this book:

Cursor: Two types of cursor are commonly used in AutoCAD – an arrow cursor and a pair of hair lines intersecting at a point often referred to as a **pick point**.

Drag: Move the cursor on to a feature on screen, hold down the left-hand mouse button and move the mouse. The feature moves in relation to the mouse movement.

Left-click: Place the cursors, under mouse control, on to a feature and press the left-hand mouse button.

Right-click: Place the cursors, under mouse control, on to a feature and press the right-hand mouse button.

Double-click: Place the cursor(s), under mouse control, on to a feature and press the left-hand mouse button twice in rapid succession.

Enter: Type the given letters or words at the keyboard.

Return: Press the Return or Enter key of the keyboard; except when stated a *right-click* has the same result.

Pick: Move the cursor(s) under mouse control on to a feature, followed by a *left-click*. Or, position the **pick box** under mouse control on a feature, followed by a *left-click*.

Pick box: A square box either at the intersection of the cursor hairs or on its own under the control of the mouse. As will be seen later (page 54), the **pick box** can be varied in size.

Fig. 1.1 The AutoCAD Release
13 for Windows icon

Starting AutoCAD Release 13 in Windows

To start up AutoCAD Release 13 for Windows, *double-click* on the
R13 icon (Fig. 1.1) in the **AutoCAD R13** window of the **Program
Manager** window (Fig. 1.2). After a short period of time the AutoCAD
graphic window (Fig. 1.3) opens.

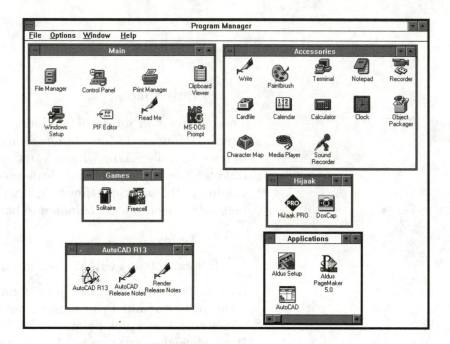

Fig.1.2 The **AutoCAD R13**
icon in the Windows **Program
Manager**

The AutoCAD 13 graphics window

Depending upon how the opening drawing file **acad.dwg** or **acadiso.dwg**
has been configured, the AutoCAD R13 graphics window will open
with a format similar to the one illustrated in Fig. 1.3. That shown
is one configured for a metric A3 drawing sheet and with certain
toolbars positioned along the top, left-hand and right-hand sides.
Note the following features:

Menu bar: Displays the names of a number of pull-down menus. A *left-
click* on any one of the names brings down the relevant pull-down
menu. Fig. 1.4 shows the resulting **Options** pull-down menu when
the name **Options** is selected from the menu bar.

The Object Properties toolbar: Includes the layer icons. These icons
represent the state of the current layer – on, off, frozen, thawed.
More about these icons in a later chapter (Chapter 3). Other icons
are included in the **Object Properties** toolbar.

Current drawing filename: In the given example no filename has so far
been given to the drawing, hence its **UNNAMED** title.

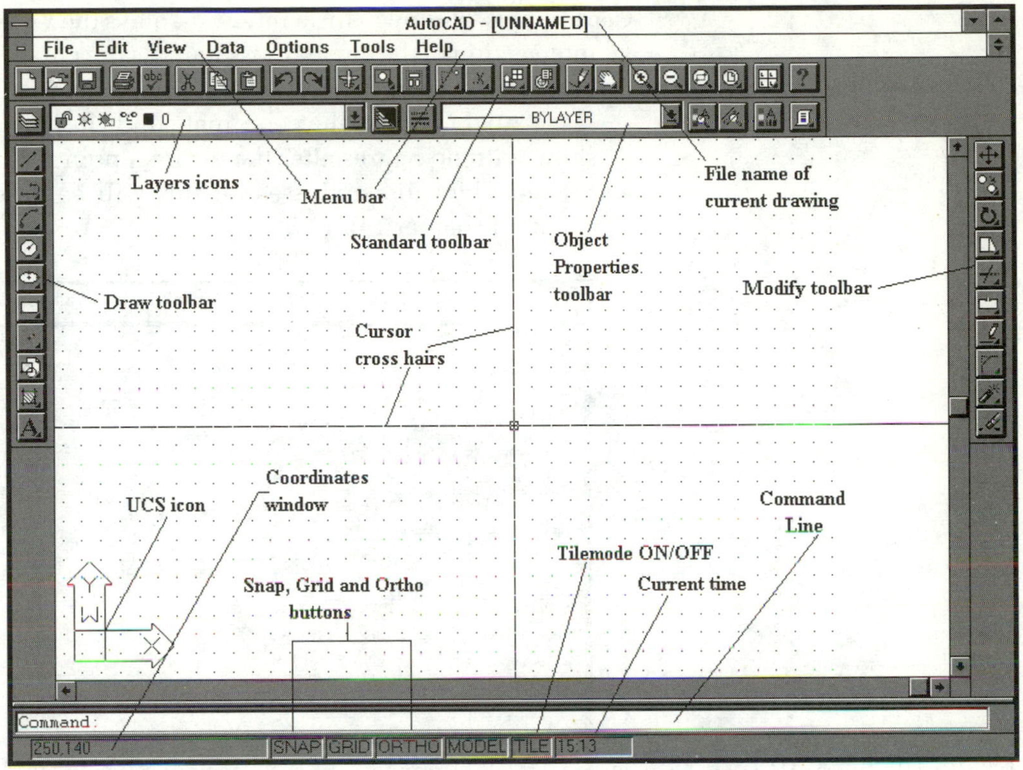

Fig. 1.3 The AutoCAD Release 13 for Windows graphics window

Toolbars: Groups of icons representing tools or commands. Four toolbars are shown in the graphics window of Fig. 1.3. On the left-hand side of the window the **Draw** toolbar and on the right-hand side, the **Modify** toolbar. That at the top is the **Standard** toolbar. Another toolbar, already mentioned – the **Object Properties** – is positioned below the **Standard** toolbar at the top of the graphics window.

Command line: In Release 13 the command line is contained in an AutoCAD text window. That shown in Fig. 1.3 has been reduced in size so that only one line of text is showing. However, the Command Line window can be **dragged** upwards and the window changes to a Text window, with the name Command Line in its name bar. It can be enlarged to the size of a full AutoCAD Text window.

Snap, Grid, and Ortho buttons: Shown along the bottom of the graphics window. A *double-click* on any of these buttons toggles Snap, Grid or Ortho respectively on or off.

Tilemode and Model Space buttons: These toggle the Model and Paper Space screens. These will be described later (Chapter 15).

Cursor cross-hairs: Two types of cursor, both positioned under the control of the digitiser (in this book a mouse) will be seen in Release 13 – an arrow cursor and two crossing lines with a small **pick box** at the intersection of the hair lines.

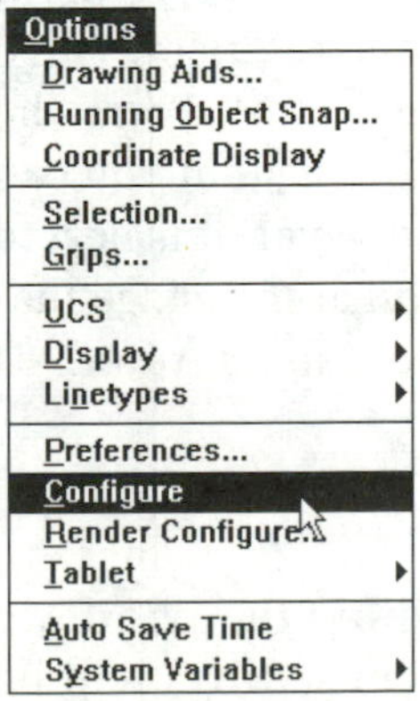

Fig. 1.4 The **Options** pull-down menu

Coordinates window: This window displays the x,y coordinates of the intersection of the cursor cross hairs as the cursor hairs are moved under movement of the digitiser. Coordinates are described later (page 29). In Fig. 1.3 the coordinate units have been configured to show with no figures after the decimal point.

UCS icon: The value and uses for this will be described in a later chapter (Chapter 14).

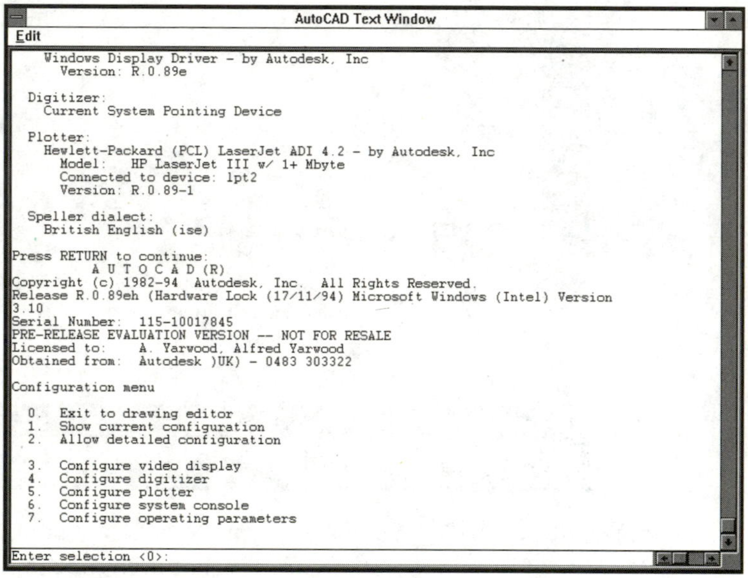

Fig. 1.5 The **AutoCAD Text Window** showing configuiration details

Configuring AutoCAD R13

It is assumed that the reader is starting up AutoCAD R13 after it has been configured for digitiser (mouse); video (monitor screen) and printer. To see the configuration for the computer in use, *left-click* on **Configure** in the **Options** pull-down menu (see Fig. 1.4). An AutoCAD Text window appears with details of the digitiser, video and printer already configured for your R13 (Fig. 1.5). Press the **Return** key of the keyboard and a list appears showing that you can re-configure the three items again if you wish. However, it is best to leave them alone for the time being. You may find at this stage that you cannot re-configure until you have learned more about AutoCAD R13.

Configuration in relation to Windows

Because Release 13 for Windows is operating within the Windows environment, some of the AutoCAD configuration settings will be the same as those which have been set under the control of the

Fig. 1.6 The **Main** window in the Windows **Program Manager**

Fig. 1.7 The Windows **Control Panel**

Control Panel of Windows. Some of the screen colours and the printer/plotter will be the same as those set for other applications working within Windows on the same computer. To see the colour settings, *double-click* on the **Control Panel** icon in the **Main** window (Fig. 1.6). When the **Control Panel** window appears, *double-click* on the **Color** icon (Fig. 1.7). The **Color** dialogue box appears (Fig. 1.8) in which the colours for the various parts of windows within Windows can be set. Go back to the **Main** window and *double-click* on the **Windows Setup** icon, followed by a *left-click* on **Options** in the menu bar of the window. The **Change System Settings** dialogue box appears (Fig. 1.9) from which settings for the display screen, the keyboard and mouse can be set.

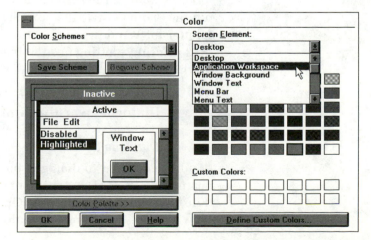

Fig. 1.8 The **Color** window with its dialogue boxes

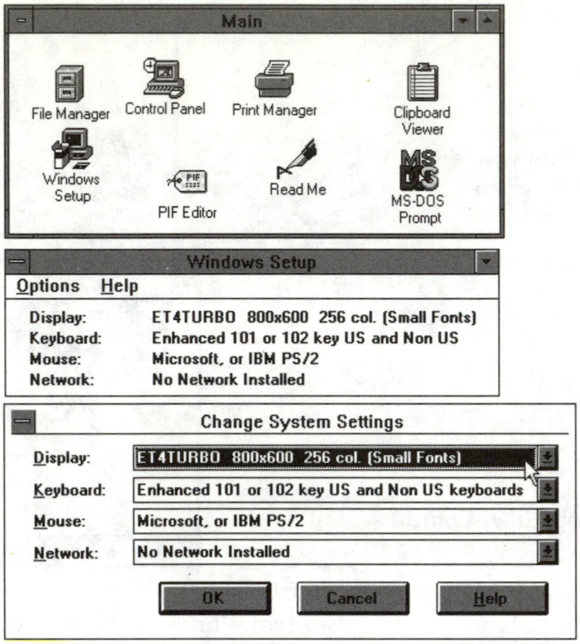

Fig. 1.9 The **Windows Setup** window and its dialogue boxes

The AutoCAD digitiser device

Throughout this book, a mouse is used as a digitiser or selection device. Other forms of digitiser can be used in conjunction with AutoCAD R13, but in this book the only digitiser referred to will be the mouse used with other Windows applications.

In particular several forms of digitising tablet can be used with AutoCAD R13, but these will not be referred to in this book.

Configuring the printer or plotter

Finally to set the printer or plotter for a Windows application, *double-click* on the **Printers** icon in the **Control Panel**. This brings up the **Printers** dialogue box (Fig. 1.10), from which the printer or plotter for Windows applications) can be set. However, AutoCAD R13 printing/plotting need not be done with the printer/plotter set in this way.

Dialogue, warning and message boxes

Dialogue boxes

We have referred to dialogue boxes above. They are an important feature in AutoCAD. A typical one is shown in Fig. 1.11 – The **Select File** box, which appears when **Open...** is selected from the **File** pull-down menu. It is from this dialogue box that files are selected for

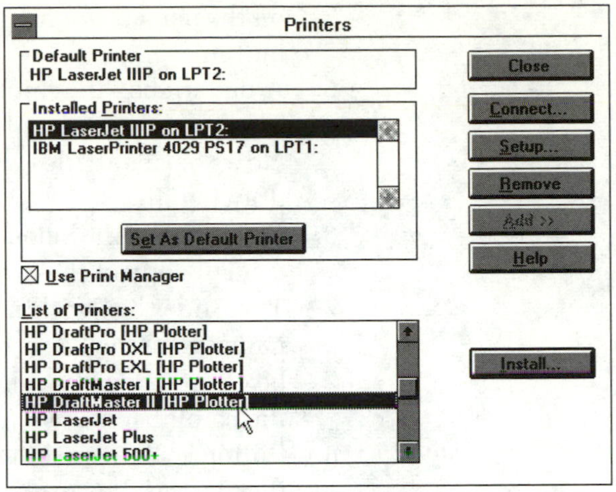

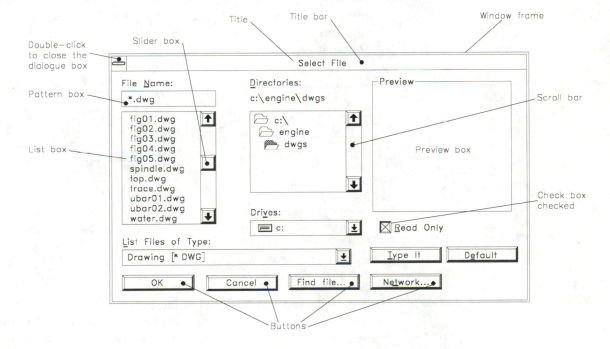

Fig. 1.10 The Windows
Printers dialogue boxes

opening into the AutoCAD graphics window. The parts of a dialogue
box are as follows:

1. The window frame outline.
2. The title of the dialogue box within the title bar of the box.

Fig. 1.11 A typical AutoCAD
dialogue box – the **Select File**
dialogue box

3. The button at the top left of some dialogue boxes by which the box
can be closed. A *double-click* on the button closes the dialogue
box.
4. List boxes in which lists of the files from which one can choose to
open. Either a *double-click* on a selected filename, or a *left-click*

on the name, which highlights, followed by a *left-click* on the **OK** button

5. A pattern box in which the name of the type of file is displayed. The * in front of the filename extension is known as a **wildcard** – *.dwg means all files with the extension .dwg. These are AutoCAD drawing files.

6. In the case of the **Select File** dialogue box, a **Preview** box in which a small copy of the drawing about to be opened is displayed;

7. The Slider box within a Scroll bar. If the List box contains more names than can be accommodated within the area in the dialogue box, further names can be seen by either moving the Slider box in the scroll bar or by *left-clicks* on the up and down arrows.

8. Buttons. Of those shown in Fig. 1.11 a *left-click* on **OK** will cause the dialogue box to close and the selected drawing to appear. *Left-click* on **Cancel** closes the dialogue box without any other action taking place. *Left-click* on **Type It** and the filename will need to be *entered* from the keyboard. *Left-click* on **Find File...** and the **Find File** dialogue box appears.

9. Check boxes. A cross appearing in a box shows it is checked and the feature will be in operation. A *left-click* on a checked box unchecks it, the cross disappears and the feature becomes inoperative.

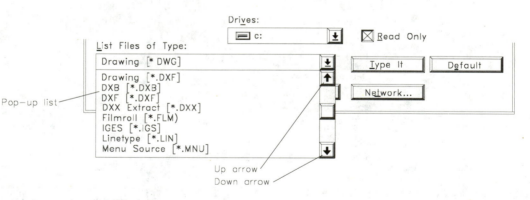

Fig. 1.12 The **List Files of Type** pop-up list

10. A Pop-up list. A left-click on the name in the box of the Pop-up brings down a List box containing options from which one can make a choice. Fig. 1.12 shows the **Files of Type** pop-up list. In the **Select File** dialogue box, there is usually only one type of file available – those with the extension ***.dwg**.The **Drives** box will provide another Pop-up list showing the disk drives available on the computer in use. Up and down arrows allow the operator to 'scroll' the list within the list box up or down.

Warning boxes

A number of warning boxes giving the operator a choice of actions appear on occasion. Fig. 1.13 is a typical example. A new file has been selected for opening with a drawing in the graphics window. Before the new drawing can be opened, the operator is asked whether the drawing on screen is to be saved or not, or whether the new file is not to be opened – *left-click* on the **Cancel** button.

Fig. 1.13 A typical warning box.

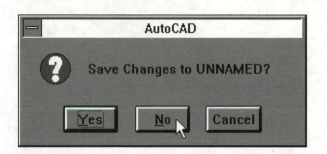

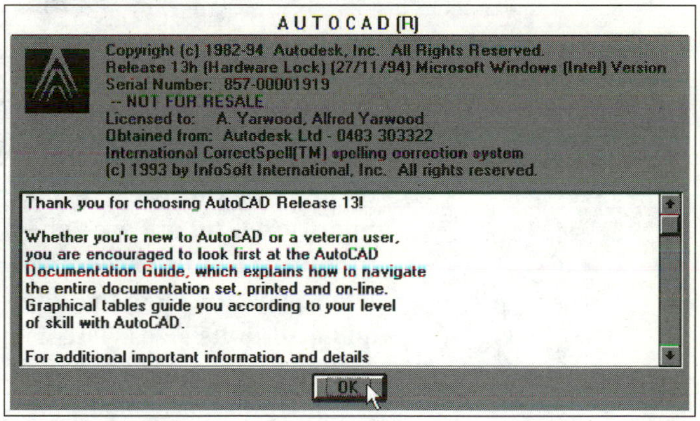

Fig. 1.14 A message box. This one is the AutoCAD message box

Message boxes

Fig. 1.14 shows a typical message box. This one appears when **About AutoCAD...** is selected from the **Help** pull-down menu.

Calling dialogue boxes

There are two ways in which dialogue boxes can be called to the screen – by selection from a pull-down menu or by entering a dialogue box command at the command line from the keyboard.

Selection from a pull-down menu

If a name in a pull-down menu is followed by three full stops (...), when that name is selected (*left-click* on the name), the dialogue box associated with the name appears on screen. For example a *left-click* on **Drawing Aids...** in the **Options** pull-down menu (Fig. 1.15)

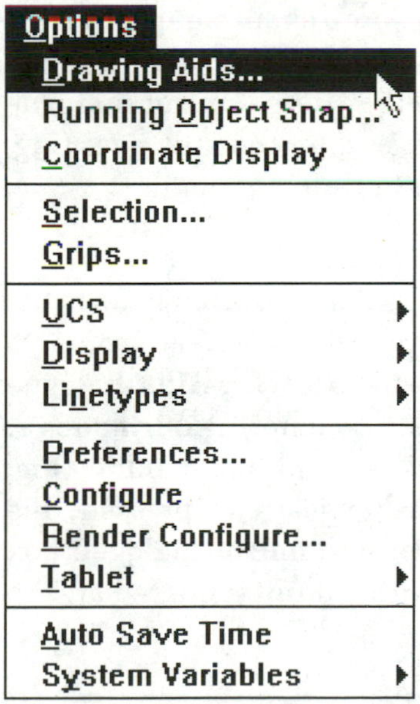

Fig. 1.15 Selection of **Drawing Aids...** from the **Options** pull-down menu

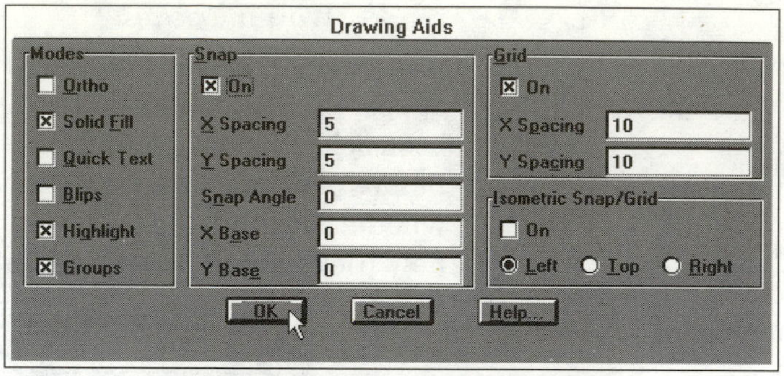

Fig. 1.16 The **Drawing Aids** dialogue box

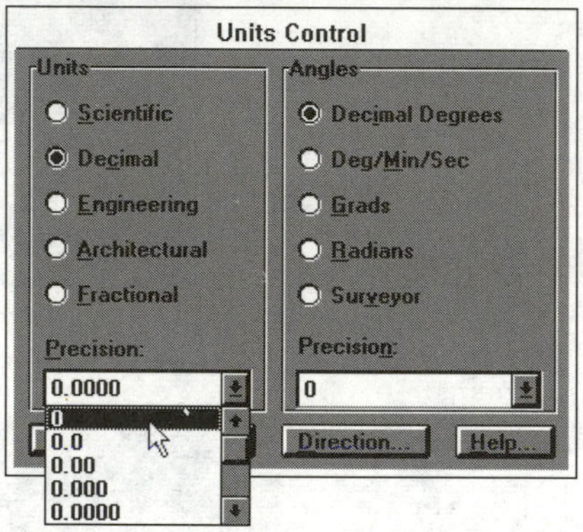

Fig. 1.17 The **Units Control** dialogue box

causes the **Drawing Aids** dialogue box to appear (Fig. 1.16). In this dialogue box **Blips** have been turned off – check box with no cross; **Snap** and **Grid** are on – check box with crosses; **Snap** has been set to 5 units; **Grid** has been set to 10 units. More about **Snap** and **Grid** later (page 30). Note that there are no decimal figures after the snap and grid units sizes. This is because in the **Units Control** dialogue box, units have been set to show no figures after the unit sizes (Fig. 1.17). **Units...** is selected from the **Data** pull-down menu.

Entering a command at the keyboard

Many of the dialogue boxes in AutoCAD R13 can be brought on to the screen by entering dd calls from the keyboard. There are some 25 such calls available in R13. For example the **Drawing Aids** dialogue box could have been brought on to screen by entering **ddrmodes** at the keyboard. The letters appear in the command line window (Fig. 1.18) and when the **Enter** key of the keyboard is pressed, the dialogue box appears on screen. The **Units Control** dialogue box could have been brought on screen with **ddunits** entered in the command line from the keyboard.

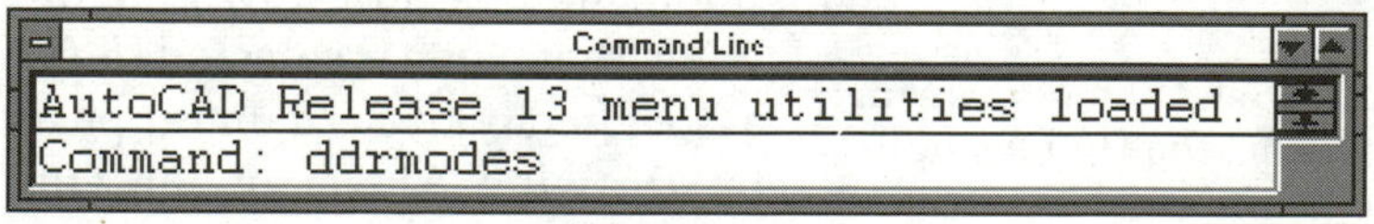

Fig. 1.18 Calling a dialogue box with a dd call

Note: Some dialogue boxes contain their own secondary dialogue boxes. As an example, if the **Preferences** dialogue box is on screen, a *left-click* on the **Fonts...** button brings up the **Font** dialogue box. Similarly secondary dialogue boxes can be brought on screen in the **Preferences** dialogue box from the buttons marked **Color...** and **Environment...**. An example is given in Fig. 1.19.

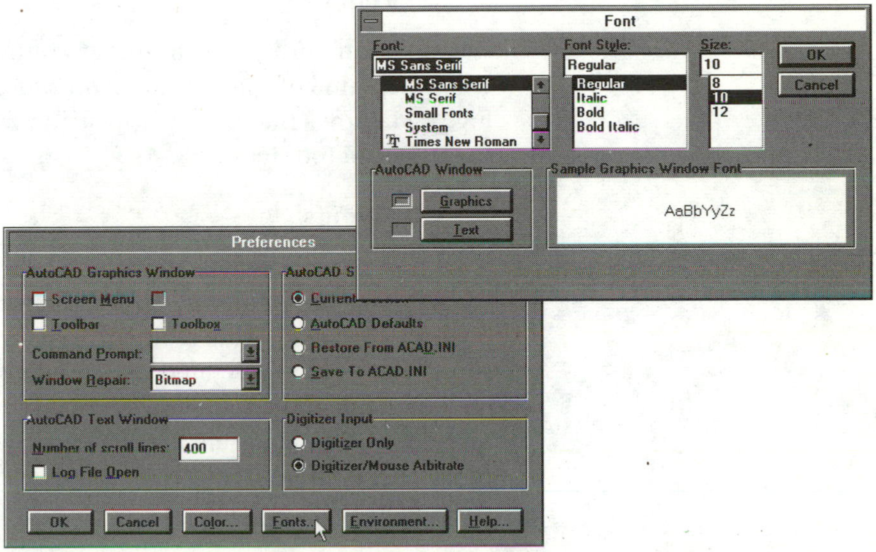

Fig. 1.19 The **Font** dialogue box from the **Fonts...** button in the **Preferences** dialogue box

Toolbars, tools and tool tips

Drawing in AutoCAD R13 is carried out with the aid of tools (or commands). For example, lines are drawn with the aid of the tool **Line**, circles are drawn with the aid of the tool **Circle**. Tools (commands) are represented by icons, each tool or command having its own unique icon. The icons for tools are held in toolbars, for example the group of icons for tools used for drawing are held in a toolbar named **Draw**. Icons for tools for modifying details in drawings are held in the toolbar **Modify**. There are a number of toolbars in

Fig. 1.20 The command line prompts seen when the toolbar **Dimensioning** is called from the **Tools** pull-down menu

AutoCAD R13, each with its own distinctive name. Toolbars can be called from the **Tools** pull-down menu. When they are called from the menu they can be placed in a variety of positions on the screen – Left, Right, Top, Bottom or Floating. Fig. 1.20 shows the command line when the **Dimensioning** toolbar is brought on screen from the **Tools** pull-down menu.

Tool tips

When the cursor is moved, under control of the mouse, over a tool icon, the name of the tool the icon represents appears in a **tool tip**. Fig. 1.21 shows the tool tip appearing when the cursor is placed on the **Polyline** tool icon.

Flyouts

Hold down the left mouse button while the cursor is positioned on the **Polyline** tool icon and a further group of icons associated with polylines appears – this group of icons is known as a **Flyout**. Fig 1.22 shows the flyout associated with the **Polyline** tool icons in the **Draw** toolbar. Each of the tool icons in the flyout has its own tool tip. Note that when a tool is selected from a flyout, the selected tool icon replaces the original icon in the toolbar. Fig. 1.22 shows this change when **Multiline** is selected.

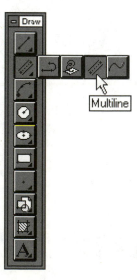

Fig. 1.21 The **Draw** toolbar with the tool tip for the **Polyline** icon showing

Fig. 1.22 The Flyouts associated with the **Polyline** tool icon

Entering commands at the command line

Instead of calling tools or commands from icons in toolbars or from pull-down menus an operator can enter the tool or command name at the command line from the keyboard. Some tools or commands can be entered as abbreviations (see page 70). For example a polyline can be drawn by either a left-click on the **Line** tool icon in the **Draw** toolbar or by entering **line** or **l** (abbreviation for line) at the keyboard. The following **prompts** appear at the command line:

> **Command:** *enter* line *Return*
> **From point:** *left-click* anywhere on the screen
> **To point:** *left-click* at another point on the screen

A line appears.

Note: The above method of showing commands entered at the command line from the keyboard will be used throughout this book. What shows at the command line will be in **bold** type. The action necessary at the prompt (*enter*, *left-click*, etc.) is shown in *italic* type. The word *Return* means that either the **Return** or **Enter** key of the keyboard must be pressed or that a *right-click* is necessary. The speedier method of working is usually to *right-click*.

Questions

1. What is meant in this book by the terms: *left-click*, *right-click* and *double-click*?
2. What is a **pick box** in AutoCAD?
3. How does one start up AutoCAD R13 for Windows?
4. Can you identify and name the parts of the AutoCAD R13 graphics window?
5. What do three fullstops (...) after a name in a pull-down menu signify?
6. What is an AutoCAD Text window?
7. Some AutoCAD R13 for Windows configuration settings must be made from the Windows **Program Manager**. Can you name some of these settings?
8. Which digitising device is used in the descriptions of the construction of drawings in this book?
9. What is meant by the term **dialogue box**?
10. What is a **message box**?
11. What is a **toolbar**?
12. What is a **flyout**?
13. What is a **tool tip**?

14. When a toolbar is placed to the right, the left or the top of the AutoCAD R13 graphics window, does the name of the toolbar show?

15. In which positions can a toolbar be placed in the AutoCAD graphics window?

CHAPTER 2

AutoCAD R13 for DOS

Introduction

The AutoCAD R13 graphics editor for DOS looks completely different from the AutoCAD R13 for Window graphics window as can be see with reference to Fig. 2.1. The DOS standard graphics editor as supplied with the software contains a menu bar with the names of a number of pull-down menus along the top of the graphics editor, an on-screen menu to the right and a command line at the bottom. There are no toolbars with their associated icons, tool tips and flyouts.

Layer, Ortho and Snap

If the arrow cursor is moved away from the menu bar under the movement of the mouse, the menu bar changes to indicate five details:

1. The current layer colour showing in a box top left of the screen.
2. The name of the current layer.
3. If Ortho is on, the word **Ortho** shows.
4. If Snap is on, the word **Snap** shows.
5. The current position of the cursor in terms of the x,y, coordinates.

These details are illustrated in Fig. 2.2.

Starting AutoCAD R13 for DOS

It will be remembered that the Windows version is started by a *double-click* on the **AutoCAD R13** icon in the Windows **Program Manager**. There is no such start up icon for the DOS version. To start-up the DOS version, it is usual to enter the name of a **batch** file from the keyboard. This batch file, which is probably named **acadr13.bat**, is automatically added to the hard disk when AutoCAD is installed in a computer. This **batch file** contains settings pointing to the directories containing the files which allow AutoCAD to run. When

Fig. 2.1 The AutoCAD R13
graphics editor for DOS

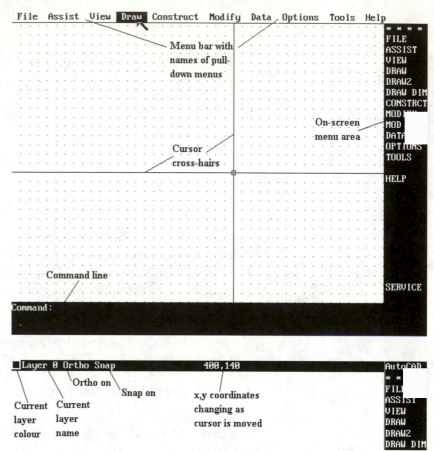

Fig. 2.2 The top line of the
AutoCAD R13 DOS graphics
editor when the arrow cursor
is not placed in the menu bar

a computer working with MS-DOS is switched on, the opening
screen may show a number of messages finishing with what is
known as the **C:\>** prompt. The screen may however only come up
with the **C:\>** prompt. It depends upon how the computer has been
configured. To start up AutoCAD R13 for DOS from the **C:\>** prompt:

> **C:\>** *enter* acadr13 *Return*

and after a few seconds the AutoCAD R13 graphics editor appears on
screen as shown in Fig. 2.1.

In some circumstances, such as if you are using the computer at
a college or a training centre, other methods of starting up AutoCAD
R13 may be in use. For example if in a college situation, when the
computer is switched on, a list of options may appear on screen,
among which the method of start-up for R13 may be included. The
batch file **acadr13.bat** may also be given a different name. Personally
I always shorten my batch files as far as possible and my R13 DOS
start-up batch file is named just **a.bat**.

AutoCAD R13 for DOS pull-down menus

The pull-down menus cover a different set of commands from those for the Windows versions. Whereas commands were shown in the Windows versions as tool and command icons in toolbars, in the DOS version they appear in either pull-down menus or in menus in the on-screen menu area. Examples of the pull-down menus selected by a *left-click* on the names in the menu bar are shown in Fig. 2.3 and Fig. 2.4.

It will be noted that some of the menus contain sub-menus – those commands followed by an arrow pointing outwards. It will also be noted from Fig. 2.3 and Fig. 2.4 that selecting some of the commands will bring up a dialogue box in the same way as in the Windows version. Figures 2.5 and 2 6 show examples of dialogue boxes called by *left-clicks* on names in the pull-down menus which are followed by three full stops (...). These dialogue boxes are similar to those in the Windows version. Dd calls for bringing up dialogue boxes can be made in exactly the same way as in the Windows version – by entering the call at the command line from the keyboard.

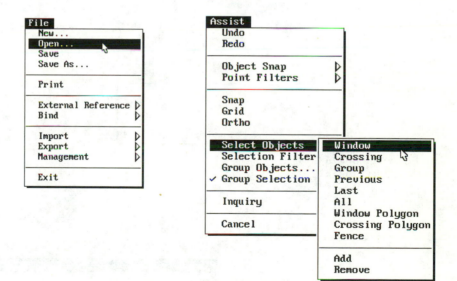

Fig. 2.3 Some of the pull-down menus of the AutoCAD R13 for DOS

AutoCAD R13 for DOS on-screen menus

Commands can also be called, if wished, from the command names in the on-screen menus and in their associated sub-menus. Note that the pull-down menu names in the menu bar are repeated in the on-screen menu which is showing when R13 is first started up and the cursor is moved into the area of the menu bar. As an example of how to use the on-screen menus, a *left-click* on **DRAW** causes the menu

Draw	Modify	View	
Line	Properties...	Redraw View	
Construction Line		Redraw All	
Ray	Move		
Sketch	Rotate	**Zoom**	**In**
	Align	Pan	Out
Polyline			
3D Polyline	Stretch	Named Views...	Window
Multiline	Scale	3D Viewpoint Prese	All
	Lengthen	3D Viewpoint	Previous
Spline	Point	3D Dynamic View	Scale
Arc ▷			Dynamic
Circle ▷	Trim	✓ Tiled Model Space	Center
Ellipse ▷	Extend	Floating Model Spa	Left
	Break ▷	Paper Space	Limits
Rectangle			Extents
Polygon	Edit Polyline	Tiled Viewports	Vmax
2D Solid	Edit Multiline...	Floating Viewports	
	Edit Spline	Preset UCS...	
Point ▷	Edit Text...	Named UCS...	
Insert ▷	Edit Hatch...	Set UCS ▷	
	Attribute ▷		
Surfaces ▷	Explode		
Solids ▷			
	Erase		
Hatch...	Oops!		
PostScript Fill			

Options
Drawing Aids...
Running Object Snap...
Coordinate Display
Selection...
Grips...
UCS ▷
Display ▷

Construct	
Copy	
Offset	
Mirror	
Array	**Rectangular**
	Polar
Chamfer	
Fillet	
Region	
Bounding Polyline...	
Block	
Attribute...	
3D Array ▷	
3D Mirror	
3D Rotate	

Fig. 2.4 Some more of the pull-down menus of the AutoCAD R13 for DOS

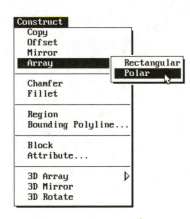

Fig. 2.5 The **Drawing Aids** dialogue box in which settings such as those for **Snap** and **Grid** are set

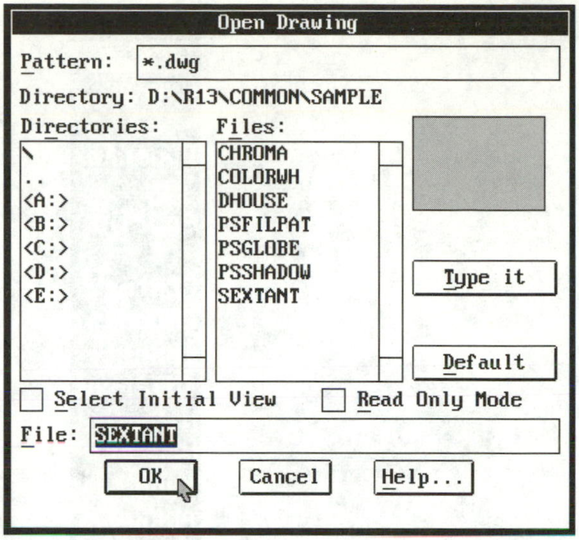

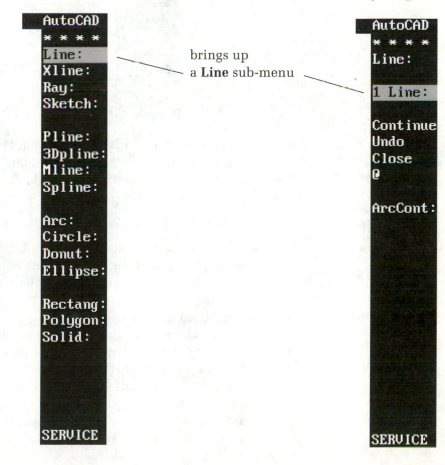

Fig. 2.6 The **Open Drawing** dialogue box from the **File** pull-down menu

to be replaced by a **DRAW** sub-menu (Fig. 2.7). As a command name is selected, so it highlights – it becomes surrounded by a lighter

brings up a **Line** sub-menu

Fig. 2.7 The **DRAW** sub-menu and the **Line** sub menu

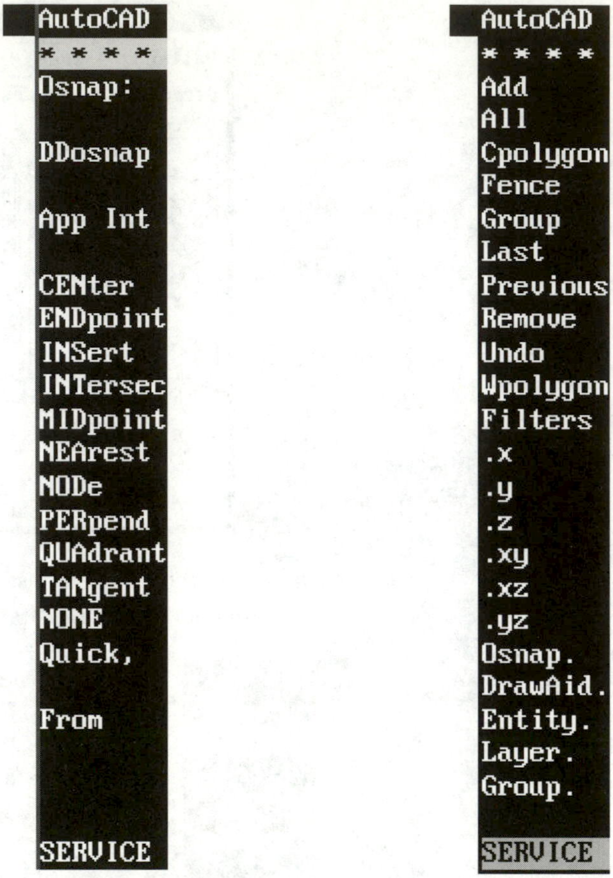

```
┌──────────────┐      ┌──────────────┐
│ AutoCAD      │      │ AutoCAD      │
│ * * * *      │      │ * * * *      │
│ Osnap:       │      │ Add          │
│              │      │ All          │
│ DDosnap      │      │ Cpolygon     │
│              │      │ Fence        │
│ App Int      │      │ Group        │
│              │      │ Last         │
│ CENter       │      │ Previous     │
│ ENDpoint     │      │ Remove       │
│ INSert       │      │ Undo         │
│ INTersec     │      │ Wpolygon     │
│ MIDpoint     │      │ Filters      │
│ NEArest      │      │ .x           │
│ NODe         │      │ .y           │
│ PERpend      │      │ .z           │
│ QUAdrant     │      │ .xy          │
│ TANgent      │      │ .xz          │
│ NONE         │      │ .yz          │
│ Quick,       │      │ Osnap.       │
│              │      │ DrawAid.     │
│ From         │      │ Entity.      │
│              │      │ Layer.       │
│              │      │ Group.       │
│              │      │              │
│ SERVICE      │      │ SERVICE      │
└──────────────┘      └──────────────┘
```

Fig. 2.8 The **Osnaps** menu appearing with a *left-click* on ****, and the **Services** menu activated by a *left-click* on **SERVICES**

coloured rectangle to show that it has been selected. In the example shown in Fig. 2.7, a *left-click* on **Line:** in the sub-menu brings up another sub-menu. A further *left-click* on **Line:** in the second sub-menu causes a prompt to appear at the command line:

Command: _line From point:

Note that a colon (:) after a command name means that it is an active command (or tool) and the prompts which appear at the command line show that actions can then be taken in the graphics editor drawing area – for example when **Line:** is selected the operator can commence drawing lines.

One of the on-screen menus is activated by a *left-click* on the four stars (****) at the top of the on-screen menu area. This *left-click* brings up the **Osnaps** menu (Fig. 2.8), from which osnaps can be selected as required. Osnaps are one of the AutoCAD methods of assisting in obtaining accuracy when constructing drawings. Their use will be described in a later chapter (see page 52). Osnaps are also available in the Windows version.

Another of the on-screen menus is activated by a *left-click* on the word **SERVICE** at the bottom of the on-screen menu area (Fig. 2.8). The items in this menu are used with many of the commands available in AutoCAD. They 'service' the commands with which they are used. These service items will be described in later pages.

Entering commands at the command line

As in the Windows version commands can be entered at the Command line from the keyboard. Some commands can be entered by their abbreviations. Command abbreviations are set in the file *acad.pgp* which will be described later (page 70).

Thus to draw a line:

Command: *enter* line *Return*
From point: *pick* a point in the drawing area
To point: *pick* a point in the drawing area

and a line is drawn.

To draw a circle:

Command: *enter* c *Return*
CIRCLE 3P/2P/TTR/<Center point>: *pick*
Diameter/<Radius>: *pick*
Command:

and a circle is drawn.

Windows and DOS drawings compared

If drawings constructed in the Windows version are compared with those drawn in the DOS version it will be found that exactly the same effects can be obtained in either. The difference is in the methods used for constructing drawings. In Windows, most operators will find themselves selecting tools and commands from the icons in the toolbars, with some being called by entering names or abbreviations at the command line. In the DOS version some commands will be selected from pull-down menus, some from on-screen menus and some by entering command names or their abbreviations at the command line.

It should be noted here that if a graphics tablet and an AutoCAD tablet overlay are used in conjunction with a digitising puck, then when using the DOS version most commands will be selected from the AutoCAD tablet overlay. Even when using a tablet overlay, most operators find they will adopt working practices which involve more than one method of calling commands. For example an operator may call most commands from the tablet overlay, a few from entering abbreviations at the command line and occasionally by selection from a pull-down menu or an on-screen menu.

Questions

1. Can you list 10 differences between the AutoCAD R13 DOS graphics editor and the AutoCAD R13 Windows graphics window?
2. The on-screen menu area usually appears in the DOS graphics editor when AutoCAD R13 is started up. Can an on-screen menu be used with the R13 Windows version?
3. Can you name three methods of calling commands when using AutoCAD R13 for DOS?
4. When a small outward facing arrow appears next to a command name in an R13 DOS pull-down menu what does it indicate?
5. What is meant by **highlighting**?
6. There are two methods of calling dialogue boxes on to the AutoCAD screen. What are they?
7. When a colon (:) follows a command name in an on-screen menu, what does it mean?
8. In Windows you would probably be selecting tools from a toolbar when constructing a drawing in the R13 Windows version. What method of selecting tools would you probably use in the DOS version?
9. How is the DOS version of AutoCAD R13 started up?
10. Can you use toolbars in the DOS R13 version?

CHAPTER 3

Using AutoCAD R13 for Windows

Introduction

The remaining chapters of this book deal with the Windows version of AutoCAD R13. Using this version demands that three software packages are loaded into the computer and that the computer has a minimum specification.

Software

1. AutoCAD R13 Windows version.
2. MS-DOS Version 5.0 or higher.
3. Windows 3.1 or higher – running in enhanced mode.

Hardware

1. PC fitted with an Intel 80386, 80486 or Pentium CPU.
2. If 80386 or 80486 of the SX series, then an 80387 co-processor must be fitted.
3. A minimum of 16 Mbytes memory (RAM).
4. Hard disk, with at least 37 Mbytes of free space to allow AutoCAD R13 files to load.
5. A Windows permanent swap space of 40 Mbytes minimum.
6. VGA or, preferably, higher display monitor and video card.
7. A mouse, although it is possible to use a digitising tablet with a puck.

Fig. 3.1 shows a typical setup for running AutoCAD R13 Windows version. The computer shown has a 'tower' type case, but the more common desk top type case is just as suitable. The VDU shown has a 14 inch (35 cm) screen, but if costs allow, it is preferable to work with any CAD package on a larger screen – 17 inch (43 cm) or larger, the larger the better. Fig. 3.1 shows a suitable setup for the hardware to run AutoCAD R13.

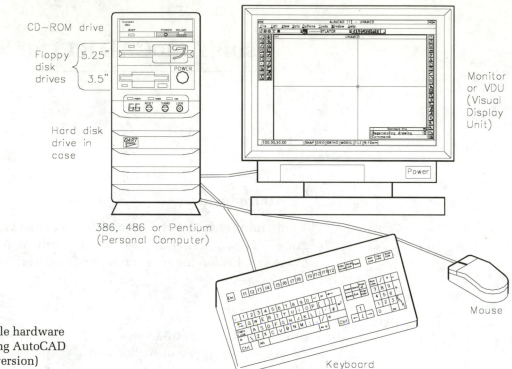

CD—ROM drive

Floppy 5.25"
disk
drives 3.5"

Hard disk
drive in
case

386, 486 or Pentium
(Personal Computer)

Monitor
or VDU
(Visual
Display
Unit)

Power

Mouse

Keyboard

Fig. 3.1 A suitable hardware
set-up for running AutoCAD
R13 (Windows version)

Why use computer-aided design software?

There are many advantages in using a computer-aided design (CAD) software package for constructing technical drawings. Among these advantages are:

1. Any technical drawing which can be produced 'by hand' can be created in a CAD package.
2. Drawing with the aid of CAD is much quicker than working 'by hand'. A skilled operator can produce drawings as much as 10 times as fast as when working 'by hand'.
3. There is less tedium when working with CAD. Features such as text which can be rather tedious when entered freehand can be added to a drawing with the minimum of effort.
4. Drawings can be inserted into other drawing, without having to redraw them.
5. Parts of drawings can be copied, moved, mirrored, arrayed etc. without the need to redraw. In fact a basic rule when drawing with CAD is:

   Never draw the same detail twice

6. Adding dimensions to a drawing is very fast and, when using associative dimensioning, reduces the possibility of dimensioning error.

7. Drawings created in CAD can be saved as files on a disk system, considerably reducing the amount of space required for the storage of drawings.
8. Drawings can be printed or plotted to any scale from the same drawing, reducing the need to make a separate drawing for each scale.

There are some disadvantages when comparing hand drawing with CAD drawing, the most serious being the initial expense in the setting up of the necessary equipment, particularly in a large design office. There is also the disadvantage that CAD is sometimes unsuitable for the making of design sketches, many of which may need to be drawn freehand. A further disadvantage lies in the need to fully train an operator new to CAD draughting.

The graphical interface of Windows

Windows is a graphical user interface (GUI) which incorporates windows, icons, a mouse, pull-down menus and dialogue boxes. The term 'WIMP' (**W**indows, **I**cons, **M**ouse, **P**ull-down menus) is sometime used with reference to the GUI of many modern software applications.

The AutoCAD R13 Windows version involves a full GUI:

1. The AutoCAD graphics editor is itself in a window; the Command Line is within a window.
2. Tools are represented by icons.
3. The digitising device will usually be the mouse used for Windows, although other digitisers can be used.
4. A number of pull-down menus containing commands are incorporated; dialogue boxes are available for setting parameters.

Windows

Windows in the sense used here have the following features, illustrated in Fig. 3.2:

1. A border surrounds the window.
2. The window displays a title in the title bar.
3. The window can be removed from the screen by a *double-click* in the button at the top left corner of the window.
4. The window can be made to fill the screen by a *left-click* on the upward pointing arrow in the button at the top right of the window. The arrow in the button is replaced by two arrows when the window is enlarged. A *left-click* on the two-arrow button and the window reverts to its original size.
5. The window can be reduced to its icon by a *left-click* on the downward facing arrow in the button at the top right of the window.

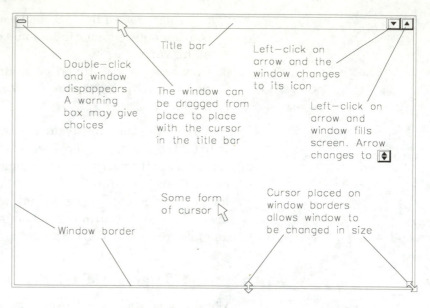

Fig. 3.2 The features of a window

6. Some form of cursor will be in the window. This cursor can be moved under control of the mouse. The arrow takes different forms depending upon the application in use.

7. The window can be re-sized by moving the cursor, under mouse control, on to a border and then **dragging** the border to re-size the window. An example of the re-sizing of a window by **dragging** the cursor placed over a corner of the window border is shown in Fig. 3.3.

8. The entire window and its contents can be moved from place to place in the screen by placing the cursor within the title bar and dragging with mouse movement. Fig. 3.4 shows the Command line window moved within the AutoCAD R13 window.

The Preferences dialogue box

The AutoCAD R13 graphics window can have its colours, the fonts showing in parts of the R13 window and the directories from which

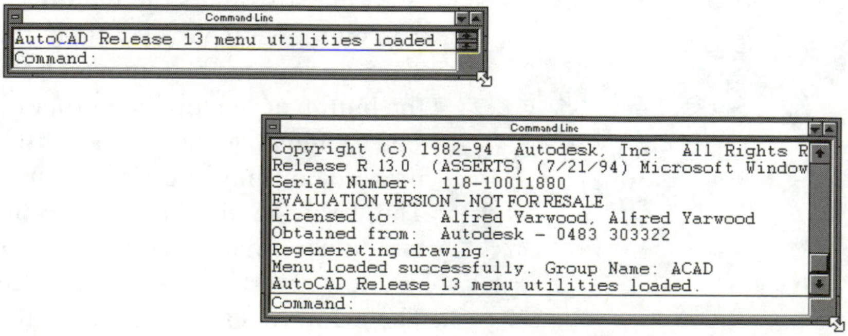

Fig. 3.3 Re-sizing a window

Fig. 3.4 *Dragging* a window
from place to place

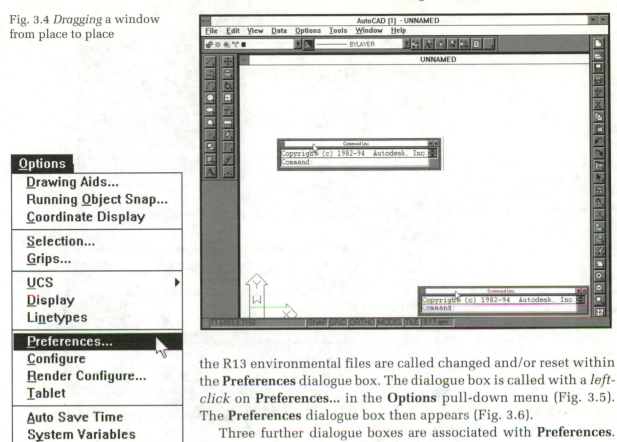

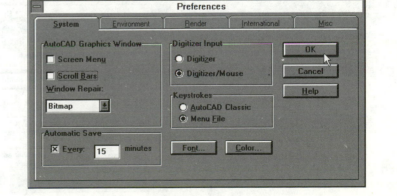

Options

Drawing Aids...
Running Object Snap...
Coordinate Display

Selection...
Grips...

UCS   ►
Display
Linetypes

Preferences...
Configure
Render Configure...
Tablet

Auto Save Time
System Variables

Fig. 3.5 Selecting **Preferences...**
from the **Options** pull-down
menu

the R13 environmental files are called changed and/or reset within
the **Preferences** dialogue box. The dialogue box is called with a *left-
click* on **Preferences...** in the **Options** pull-down menu (Fig. 3.5).
The **Preferences** dialogue box then appears (Fig. 3.6).

Three further dialogue boxes are associated with **Preferences**.
These are:

1. **AutoCAD Windows Colors** in which colours of the graphics
   window can be set or changed – Fig. 3.7.
2. **Font** in which the font for the text appearing in the graphics
   window can be set or changed – Fig. 3.8.

Fig. 3.6 The **Preferences**
dialogue box

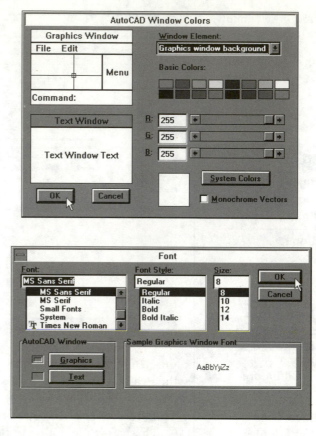

Fig. 3.7 The **AutoCAD Window Colors** dialogue box called from the **Preferences** dialogue box

Fig. 3.8 The **Font** dialogue box, called from the **Preferences** dialogue box

3. **Environment** in which the directories holding the R13 files can be set or changed – Fig. 3.9.

Usually there is no need to make any changes to the **Preferences** settings and it is probably inadvisable to experiment with the environmental settings, but experimenting with the colour and font settings can do no harm.

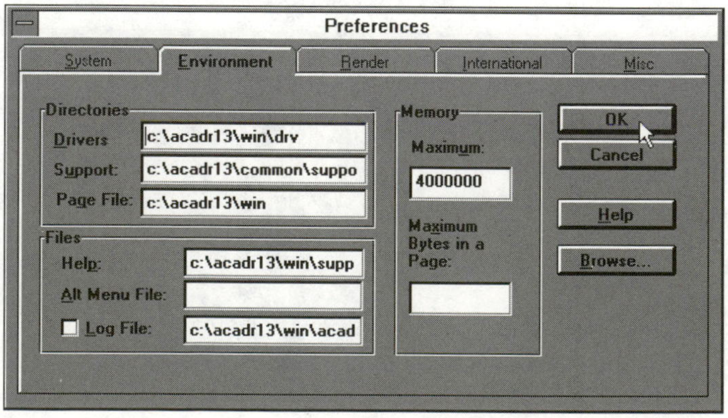

Fig. 3.9 The **Environment** dialogue box called from the **Preferences** dialogue box

The AutoCAD coordinate system

All constructions in AutoCAD are carried out in either a two-dimensional (2D) or in a three-dimensional (3D) coordinate system. 2D coordinates are given in terms of X and Y, the X units indicating the number of units horizontally and the Y units indicating the number of units vertically. Any point on the screen can then be referred to in terms of x,y. A point x,y = (100,100) is 100 units horizontally and 100 units vertically from an origin point where x,y = (0,0). 3D coordinates include a third direction, which is vertical to the 2D plane in which the x,y coordinates points lie. More about the third coordinate (z) when 3D drawing is described. Fig. 3.10 shows a number of points with their x,y coordinate numbers in an AutoCAD R13 graphics window.

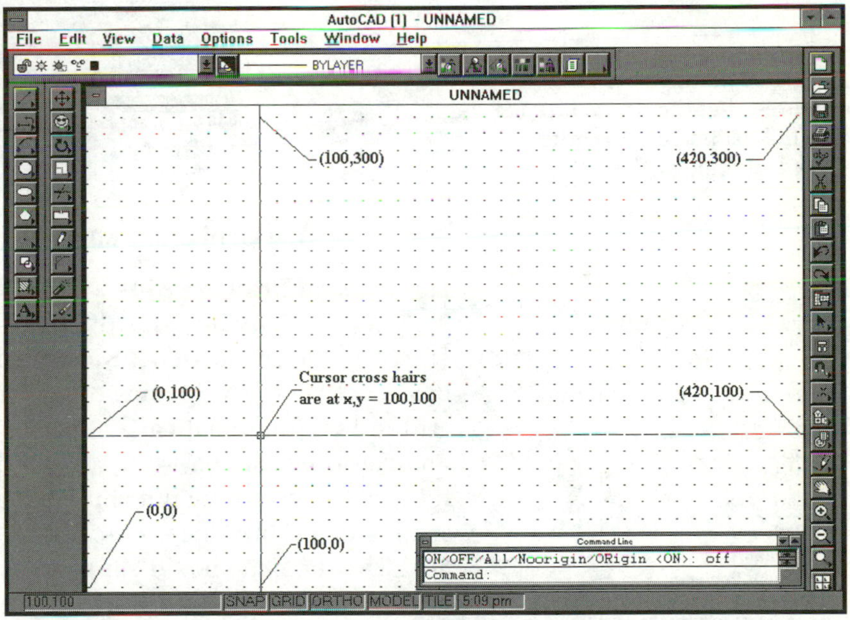

Fig. 3.10 2D x,y coordinate points in an AutoCAD R13 graphics window

Setting up a metric A3 AutoCAD R13 window

Most of the drawings for exercises throughout this book are designed to be worked in a graphics window suitable for plotting or printing full size on an A3 sheet. To take the first steps in setting up this A3 sheet screen, follow the procedure described below for the settings of **Units**, **Snap**, **Grid**, **Blips** and **Limits**. Further details about setting up a file which can be loaded with all the settings needed for a metric A3 screen will be given in later pages.

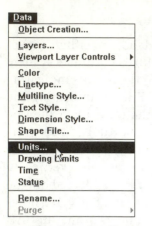

Fig. 3.11 Selecting **Units...**
from the **Data** pulldown menu

Fig 3.12 Setting **Units** to 0
figures after the decimal point
in the list box of the **Units**
Control dialogue box

Setting Units

Left-click on **Units...** in the **Data** pull-down menu (Fig. 3.11). The
Units Control dialogue box appears. *Left-click* in the **Precision** box
and again on **0.0** in the list box which then drops down (Fig. 3.12),
followed by yet another *left-click* on the **OK** button of the dialogue
box. The coordinate numbers in the coordinates box of the R13
graphics window will now show coordinates without figures after
the decimal point.

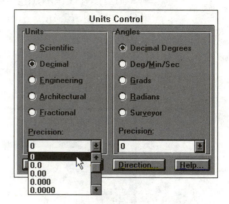

Setting Grid and Snap

Left-click on **Drawing Aids...** in the **Options** pull-down menu (Fig.
3.13). In the **Drawing Aids** dialogue box which appears (Fig. 3.14),
enter 5 in the box next to **X Spacing** in the **Snap** area of the dialogue
box and 10 in the **X Spacing** of the **Grid** area. The **Y Spacing** of both
grid and snap automatically adjust to the **X Spacing**. Then check that
Snap and **Grid** are on – crosses should appear in their check boxes.
If the check boxes are not showing crosses, *left-click* in them to set
snap and grid on. Then *left-click* on the **OK** button of the dialogue
box. The dialogue box disappears and grid dots spaced at 10 unit
intervals vertically and horizontally can be seen in the graphics
window.

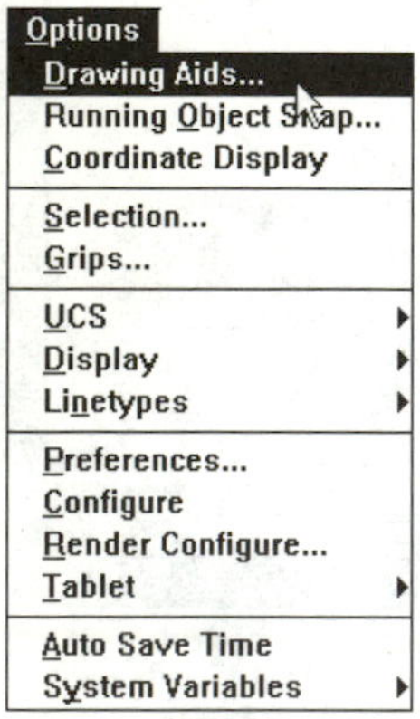

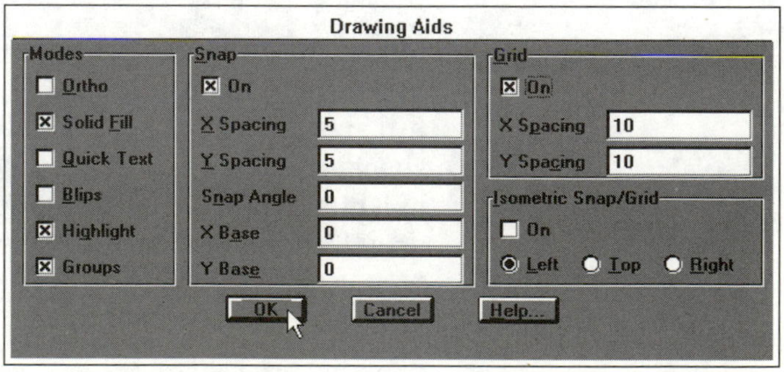

Fig. 3.13 Selecting **Drawing
Aids...** from the **Options** pull-
down menu

Fig. 3.14 The **Drawing Aids**
dialogue box showing the
Grid and **Snap** settings

Personally I prefer **Blips** to be off. Blips are tiny crosses which appear at points selected on the screen when constructing drawings. Some operators prefer **Blips** to be set on, finding them useful when working at an AutoCAD work station. It is up to the user. However, it will be seen in Fig. 3.14 that **Blips** have been set off – no cross in its check box.

Setting the screen limits

A metric A3 sheet is 420 mm by 297 mm. To accommodate these sizes in terms of coordinate units, the **Limits** of the window will be set to:

At the bottom left-hand corner *x,y* = (0,0).
At the top right-hand corner *x,y* = (420,297).

To set these limits, either *left-click* on **Drawing Limits** in the **Data** pull-down menu (see Fig. 3.11) or, *enter* the word **limits** at the Command Line. There is no dialogue box associated with limits, so no matter which of these two methods you use, the figures must be entered at the Command Line. Fig. 3.15 shows what appears in the Command Line window, no matter which method is employed.

To achieve these settings, *enter* the following at the Command Line:

Command: *enter* limits *Return*
ON/OFF/<Lower left corner> <0,0>: *Return*
Upper right corner <12,9>: *enter* 420,297 *Return*
Command: *enter* z (for Zoom) *Return*
All/Center/Dynamic/Extents/Left/Previous/Vmax/Window/ <Scale(X/XP)>: *enter* a (for All) *Return*
Regenerating drawing.
Command:

Why use **Zoom**? Because the graphics window, which was set to limits of 12,9, will not be reset to 420,297 until the graphics window is zoomed to its limits by **Zoom All**.

For the time being the R13 graphics window has been set up as the equivalent to a metric A3 sheet in which each coordinate unit can be regarded as equal to 1 millimetre. Remember however that

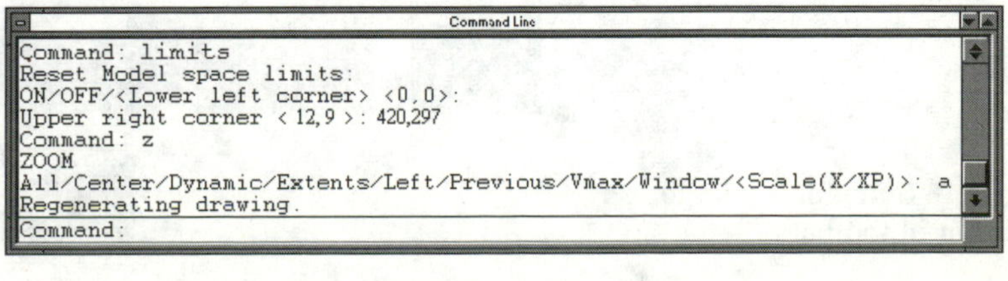

```
Command Line
Command: limits
Reset Model space limits:
ON/OFF/<Lower left corner> <0,0>:
Upper right corner < 12,9 > : 420,297
Command: z
ZOOM
All/Center/Dynamic/Extents/Left/Previous/Vmax/Window/<Scale(X/XP)>: a
Regenerating drawing.
Command:
```

Fig. 3.15 The Command Line when settings **Limits**

this is only correct if the drawing in the graphics window is printed or plotted full size. Further features are to be added to this A3 sheet setup. These will be described later.

Toolbars

Toolbars are icons representing tools (or commands) which appear on screen in groups. Each tool in R13 has its own icon in a toolbar. A *left-click* on a tool icon brings that tool into action, giving rise to prompts associated with the tool appearing in the Command Line window. There are many toolbars, each containing a group of associated tools. Fig. 3.16 shows some toolbars in an R13 window, but this does not show all the toolbars available. If you wish to see all the toolbars:

> **Command:** *enter* toolbar *Return*
> **Toolbar name (or all):** *enter* all *Return*
> **Show/Hide:** *enter* s (for Show) *Return*
> **Command:**

and all the toolbars appear. Be careful **NOT** to use the **Hide** prompt, because this will remove all toolbars, including those at the sides and along the top of the R13 window. To remove an unwanted toolbar *left-click* on the tiny button at the top left corner of the toolbar.

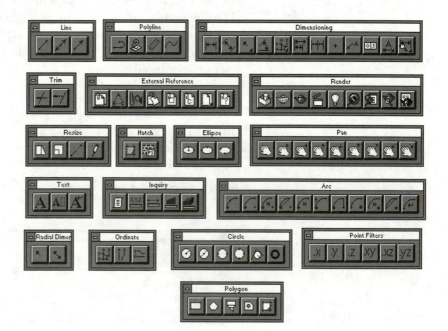

Fig. 3.16 Some of the large number of toolbars

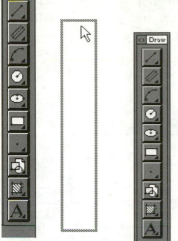

Fig. 3.17 Dragging a toolbar

Fig. 3.18 The toolbar placed
on the left of the screeen –
loses its title

Fig. 3.19 A three-row toolbar
floating in the graphics
window

Notes

1. Toolbars can be **dragged** around the screen under mouse control. Position the cursor into the title bar, or in an area surrounding the icon buttons, hold down the left-hand mouse button and move the mouse. The toolbar moves in sympathy with the mouse movement.
2. Each toolbar includes a title in its title bar. The title disappears when the toolbar is dragged to the left, right or top of the R13 graphics window (Fig. 3.18).
3. Toolbars can be left to **float** anywhere in the R13 window. When floating, the toolbar title shows in its title bar. A tiny button will also appear in the left-hand end of the title bar. A *left-click* on this button causes the toolbar to disappear.
4. *Left-click* on a tool icon in a toolbar and prompts associated with the tool represented by the chosen icon will appear in the Command Line window. When a response is made to the prompt, other prompts will automatically appear.
5. Left-click on any toolbar name in the sub-menu which appears when **Toolbars** in the **Tools** pull-down menu is selected. The Command Line will show:

Command: ACAD.TB_DIMENSIONING *Return*
Show/Hide/Left/Right/Top/Bottom/Float: *enter* F (for Float) *Return*
Position <0,0>: *enter* 50,50 *Return*
Rows <1>: *enter* 3 *Return*
Command:

and the dimensioning toolbar will appear in a 3-row form – Fig. 3.16.

Tool tips and flyouts

Move the mouse until the cursor is on any tool icon. As the cursor moves on to an icon, it changes to an arrow cursor and a **Tool tip** appears showing the name of the tool represented by the icon – Fig. 3.19. All the icons in R13 show tool tips.

Move the cursor on to any tool icon which shows a small arrow in its button and hold down the left-hand button of the mouse. A

Flyout appears showing more icons of tools associated with the chosen tool icon. Fig. 3.20 shows the flyout associated with the **Polyline** tool with the tool tip for **Multiline** showing.

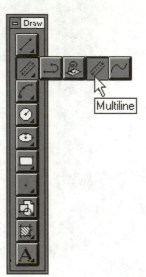

Fig. 3.20 The tool tip for the **Line** icon and the flyout from the **Polyline** icon and the **Multiline** tool tip

Prompts

When a tool has been selected and is being used, **prompts** appear in the Command Line window telling the operator what action(s) should be taken to make use of the tool. Prompts may take the following form:

1. Be just be a single statement such as **Next point:**.
2. Contain a number of alternatives, each of which will commence with a single capital letter or with two capital letters. To use an alternative, *enter* the capital letter(s) and further prompts will appear.
3. Part of a prompt line will be contained in brackets (< >); the prompt in the brackets is the current prompt.
4. When finished with using a tool for any purpose, press the **Enter** key and the Command Line reverts to **Command:** ready for the next command. Pressing **Enter** without selecting another tool repeats the prompts sequence of the tool in use.

Practice drawing using Line, Polyline, Circle and Arc

Line

Left-click on the **Line** tool icon or *enter* **l** (for **Line**) at the Command Line. The Command Line shows:

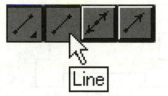

Fig. 3.21 The **Line** tool icon and its **Tool tip**

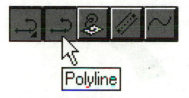

Fig. 3.22 The **Polyline** tool icon and its **Tool tip**

Command: _line From point: *pick* any point on screen
To point: *pick* another point
To point: *pick* another point
To point: *pick* another point
To point: *pick* another point
To point: *enter* c (for Close) *Return*
Command:

Examples of lines are shown in Fig. 3.22.

Polyline

Example 1

Left-click on the **Polyline** tool or *enter* **pl** (for **Pline**) at the Command Line. The Command Line shows:

Command:_pline From point: *pick* any point on screen
Arc/Close/Halfwidth/Length/Undo/Width/<Endpoint of line>: *pick* another point
Arc/Close/Halfwidth/Length/Undo/Width/<Endpoint of line>: *pick* another point
Arc/Close/Halfwidth/Length/Undo/Width/<Endpoint of line>: *pick* another point
Arc/Close/Halfwidth/Length/Undo/Width/<Endpoint of line>: *Return*
Command:

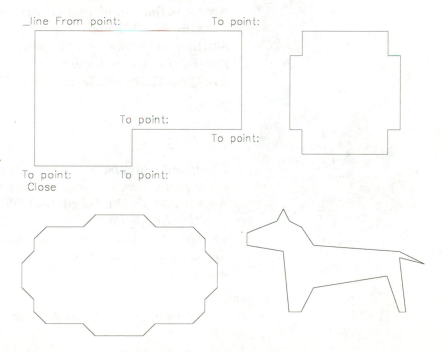

Fig. 3.23 Examples of drawing with **Line**

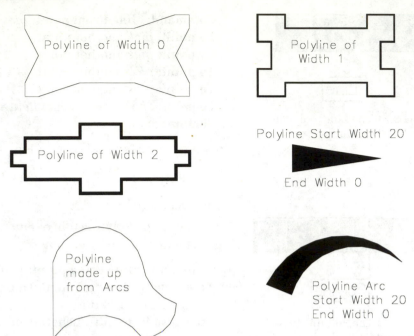

Fig. 3.24 Example of drawings
with **Polyline**

Example 2

Command_polyline
From point: *pick* any point on screen
Arc/Close/Halfwidth/Length/Undo/Width/<Endpoint of line>: *enter*
   w (for Width) *Return*
Starting width <0>: *enter* 2 *Return*
Ending Width <2>: *Return* (accept the 2)
Arc/Close/Halfwidth/Length/Undo/Width/<Endpoint of line>:

and so on.

Example 3

Command_polyline
From point: *pick* any point on screen
Arc/Close/Halfwidth/Length/Undo/Width/<Endpoint of line>: *enter*
   a (for Arc) *Return*
<Endpoint of arc>: *enter* s (for Second)
Second point: *pick* a point
End point: *pick* a point

and so on.
   Examples of polylines in drawings are shown in Fig. 3.24.

Fig. 3.25 The **Multiline** tool
and its **Tool tip**

Multiline

The **Multiline** tool icon is on the flyout of the **Polyline** tool. *Left-click* on the **Multiline** tool icon or *enter* **Mline** (for **Multiline**) at the Command Line. The Command Line shows:

Command:_mline
Justification = Top, Scale = 10.00, Style = STANDARD
Justification/Scale/STyle/<From point>: *pick* any point on screen
To point: *pick* another point
Close/Undo/To point: *pick* another point
Close/Undo/To point: *pick* another point
Close/Undo/To point: *enter* c (for Close) *return*
Command:

Examples of mulitlines are shown in Fig. 3.26

Fig. 3.26 Examples of drawings
with **Multiline**

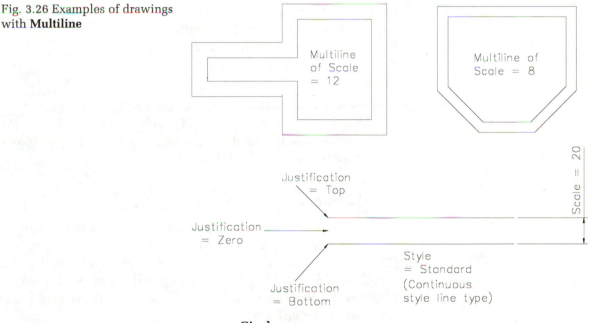

Circle

Left-click on the **Circle** tool icon or *enter* c (for **Circle**) at the Command Line. The Command Line shows:

Command: _circle
3P/2P/TTR/<Center point>: *pick* any point on screen
Diameter/<Radius>: *pick* another point
Command:

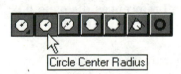

Fig. 3.27 One of the tool tips
on the **Circle** flyout from the
Draw toolbar

Examples of circles are shown in Fig. 3.27.

Arc

There are a number of **Arc** tool icons in the **Arc** flyout. Fig. 3.28 shows all of them with their **Tool tips**.

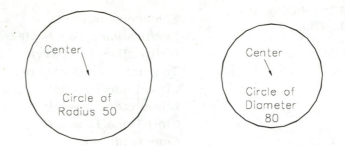

Fig. 3.28 Examples of drawings with **Circle**

Left-click on the **3 Points** icon or enter **a** (for **Arc**) at the Command Line. The Command Line shows:

Command: _arc
Center/<Start point>: *pick* any point on screen
Center/End/<Second point>: *pick* another point
End point: *pick* another point
Command:

Each of the **Arc** tools shows some of the possibilities of changing the selected tool by entering the letter(s) of a different prompt. Examples of arcs drawn after selecting different arc tools or entering different prompt initials are shown in Fig. 3.30.

Questions

1. Why is it best to use the largest monitor screen which can be afforded when working with AutoCAD?
2. Can you list five advantages of using CAD software for the construction of technical drawings against drawing 'by hand'?
3. What is the purpose of the button displayed at the top left-hand corner of a window?
4. What happens with a *left-click* on the arrow at the top right-hand of a window?
5. What settings can be changed in the **Preferences** dialogue box when working in AutoCAD R13?
6. What is meant by the term **dragging**?
7. Can you explain the AutoCAD 2D coordinate system?
8. How are the coordinate limits for an AutoCAD R13 graphics window set?
9. What is a **tool tip**?

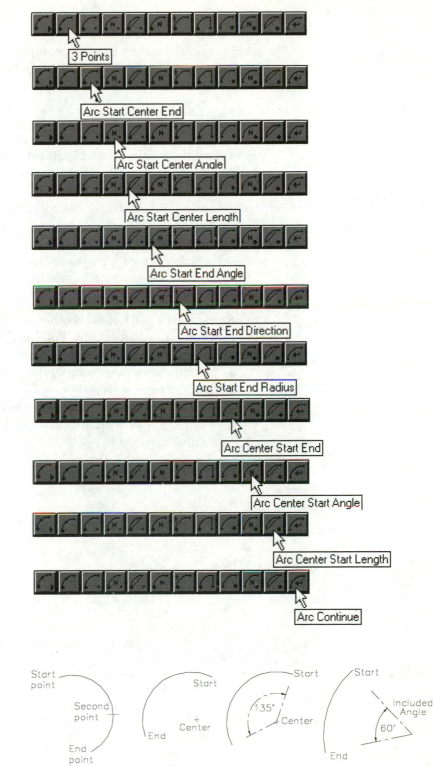

Fig. 3.29 All the **Arc** tools in the **Arc** flyout

Fig. 3.30 Examples of drawings with **Arc**

10. What is a **Flyout**?
11. What is a **floating** toolbar?
12. What is meant by **current prompt**?
13. How can you tell from a list of prompts which is **current**?

Exercises

For the purpose of the exercises given below, set up the AutoCAD R13 graphics window with **Limits** set to 420,297, **Grid** set to 10 units and **Snap** set to 5 units. As the cursor hairs are moved around the screen under the action of the mouse movement, the Coords window at the bottom left of the screen will show the position of the cursor in 2D *x,y* coordinate units as the cursor snaps from point to point at 5 unit intervals. Where dimensions are shown in the exercise drawings, the figures are in coordinate units of length and you can work out the necessary *x,y* coordinate positions by using simple arithmetic.

1. Start-up R13 and without bothering what you draw, practise with the following tools: **Line**, **Polyline**, **Multiline**, **Circle** and **Arc**. While practising in this way, try as many of the prompt suggestions as possible from those seen in the Command Line window when each of the tools is in action.
2. By moving the cursor under mouse control, copy the drawings given in Fig. 3.31 with the aid of the **Line** tool.
3. Copy the drawings in Fig. 3.32 with the aid of the **Polyline** tool.

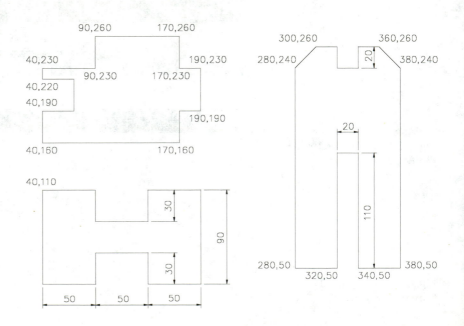

Fig. 3.31 Exercise 2

4. Copy the drawings in Fig. 3.33 with the aid of the **Multiline** tool.
5. Copy the drawings shown in Fig. 3.34 using the **Polyline** and **Circle** tools.
6. Working with the aid of the **Line**, **Circle** and **Arc** tools, copy the drawing given in Fig. 3.35.

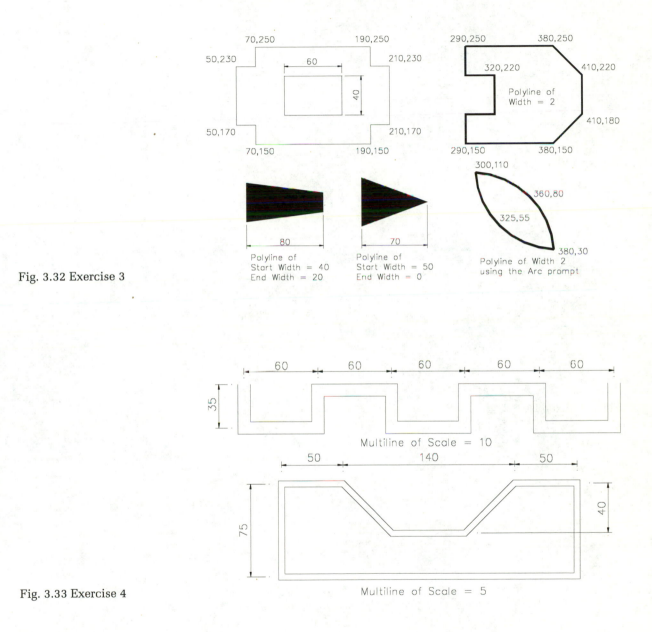

Fig. 3.32 Exercise 3

Fig. 3.33 Exercise 4

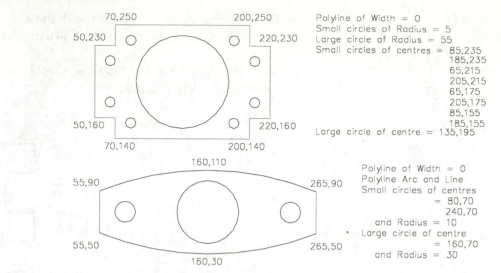

Polyline of Width = 0
Small circles of Radius = 5
Large circle of Radius = 55
Small circles of centres = 85,235
                         185,235
                         65,215
                         205,215
                         65,175
                         205,175
                         85,155
                         185,155
Large circle of centre = 135,195

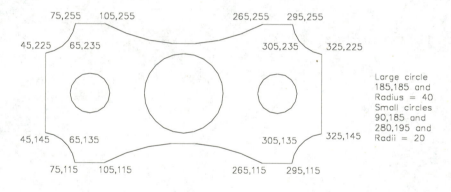

Polyline of Width = 0
Polyline Arc and Line
Small circles of centres
            = 80,70
              240,70
and Radius = 10
Large circle of centre
            = 160,70
and Radius = 30

Fig. 3.34 Exercise 5

Large circle
185,185 and
Radius = 40
Small circles
90,185 and
280,195 and
Radii = 20

Fig. 3.35 Exercise 6

Accurate construction of drawings

Introduction

In order to achieve accurate drawings with AutoCAD, full use is made of two systems:

1. In two-dimensional drawing (2D) the coordinate system employing x,y axes and in three-dimensional drawing (3D) the coordinate system employing x,y and z axes.
2. Object Snaps (**Osnaps**), by which points in an existing drawing can be accurately joined to other points.

These two methods will be demonstrated in this chapter in examples of drawings using the tools **Line**, **Polyline** (Pline) and **Circle**.

Using absolute coordinates

Set up the AutoCAD R13 graphics screen for drawing as if working on an A3 sheet, in which working to full size (scale 1:1), each coordinate unit can be regarded as being equal to 1 mm. This was described in the last chapter.

Example 1 – Line tool

Left-click on the **Line** tool icon or *enter* **L**, followed by pressing the *Return* key (Fig. 4.1) and the prompt **_line From point:** appears in the Command Line window. With the **Line** tool construct Fig. 4.2 as follows:

Command: _line
From point: *enter* 50,50 *Return*
To point: *enter* 250,50 *Return*
To point: *enter* 250,100 *Return*
To point: *enter* 300,100 *Return*
To point: *enter* 300,200 *Return*
To point: *enter* 250,200 *Return*
To point: *enter* 250,250 *Return*

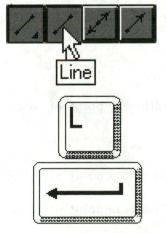

Fig. 4.1 *Left-click* on the **Line** tool icon or *enter* **L** followed by pressing **Return**

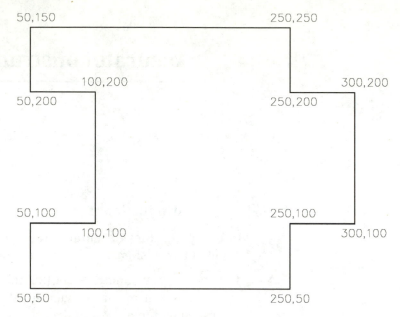

50,150   250,250

100,200   300,200
50,200   250,200

50,100   250,100
100,100   300,100

50,50   250,50

Fig. 4.2 Example 1

To point: *enter* 50,150 *Return*
To point: *enter* 50,200 *Return*
To point: *enter* 100,200 *Return*
To point: *enter* 100,100 *Return*
To point: *enter* 50,100 *Return*
To point: *enter* c (for Close) *Return*
Command:

Example 2 – Polyline tool

Left-click on the **Polyline** tool icon or *enter* **PL**, followed by pressing the **Return** key (Fig. 4.3) and the prompt **Command_pline From point:** appears in the Command Line window. With the **Polyline** tool construct Fig. 4.4 as follows:

Command: _pline
From point: *enter* 60,240 *Return*
Arc/Close/Halfwidth/Length/Undo/Width/<Endpoint of line>:
    enter w (for Width) *Return*
Starting width <0>: *enter* 1 *Return*
Ending width <1>: *Return*
Arc/Close/Halfwidth/Length/Undo/Width/<Endpoint of line>:
    enter 210,240 *Return*
Arc/Close/Halfwidth/Length/Undo/Width/<Endpoint of line>:
    enter 230,220 *Return*
Arc/Close/Halfwidth/Length/Undo/Width/<Endpoint of line>:
    enter 280,220 *Return*

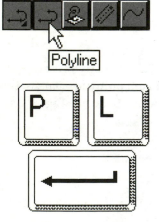

Fig. 4.3 *Left-click* on the **Polyline** tool icon or *enter* **PL** followed by pressing **Return**

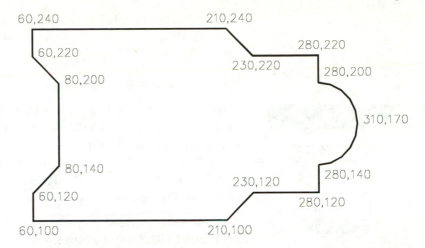

Fig. 4.4 Example 2

Arc/Close/Halfwidth/Length/Undo/Width/<Endpoint of line>:
    enter 280,200 *Return*

Arc/Close/Halfwidth/Length/Undo/Width/<Endpoint of line>:
    enter a (for Arc) *Return*

Angle/CEnter/CLose/Direction/Halfwidth/Line/Radius/
Second pt/Undo/Width/<Endpoint of arc>: *enter* s (for Second
pt) *Return*

Second point: *enter* 310,170 *Return*

Endpoint: *enter* 280,140 *Return*

<Endpoint of arc>: *enter* l (for Line) *Return*

Arc/Close/Halfwidth/Length/Undo/Width/<Endpoint of line>:
    enter 280,120 *Return*

Arc/Close/Halfwidth/Length/Undo/Width/<Endpoint of line>:
    enter 230,120 *Return*

Arc/Close/Halfwidth/Length/Undo/Width/<Endpoint of line>:
    enter 210,100 *Return*

Arc/Close/Halfwidth/Length/Undo/Width/<Endpoint of line>:
    enter 60,100 *Return*

Arc/Close/Halfwidth/Length/Undo/Width/<Endpoint of line>:
    enter 60,120 *Return*

Arc/Close/Halfwidth/Length/Undo/Width/<Endpoint of line>:
    enter 80,140 *Return*

Arc/Close/Halfwidth/Length/Undo/Width/<Endpoint of line>:
    enter 80,200 *Return*

Arc/Close/Halfwidth/Length/Undo/Width/<Endpoint of line>:
    enter 60,220 *Return*

Arc/Close/Halfwidth/Length/Undo/Width/<Endpoint of line>:
    enter c (for Close) *Return*

Command:

Note: This second example may appear to be very long and the
reader may feel that the drawing will be rather difficult, but when

working with the **Polyline** tool, the prompts appear in the Command Line window automatically and the construction of Fig. 4.4 is much easier than may at first appear from the given sequence.

Example 3 – Circle tool

With the **Line** tool or the **Polyline** tool (set to Width 0) construct the outline as shown in Fig 4.6, following a sequence similar to those for the first and second examples. To add the circles as shown in Fig. 4.7, either *left-click* on the **Circle Center Radius** tool icon, or *enter* **C**, followed by pressing the **Return** key (Fig. 4.5). Construct the circles of Fig. 4.7 as follows:

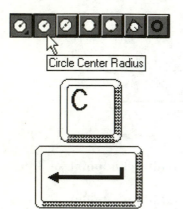

Fig. 4.5 *Left-click* on the **Circle** tool icon or *enter* **C**, followed by pressing **Return**

Command:_circle
3P/2P/TTR/<Center point>: *enter* 110,220 *Return*
Diameter/<Radius>: *enter* 10 *Return*
Command: *Return* (revert to Circle command prompts)
3P/2P/TTR/<Center point>: *enter* 270,220 *Return*
Diameter/<Radius>: *enter* 10 *Return*
Command: *Return* (revert to Circle command prompts)
3P/2P/TTR/<Center point>: *enter* 270,100 *Return*
Diameter/<Radius>: *enter* 10 *Return*
Command: *Return* (revert to Circle command prompts)
3P/2P/TTR/<Center point>: *enter* 110,100 *Return*
Diameter/<Radius>: *enter* 10 *Return*
Command: *Return* (revert to Circle command prompts)
3P/2P/TTR/<Center point>: *enter* 190,160 *Return*
Diameter/<Radius>: *enter* 60 *Return*
Command:

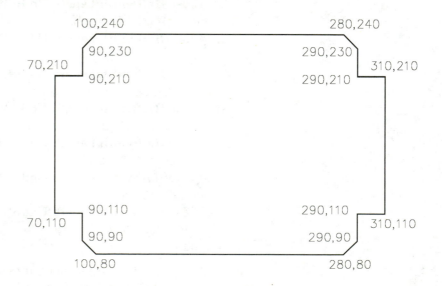

Fig. 4.6 The outline of Example 3

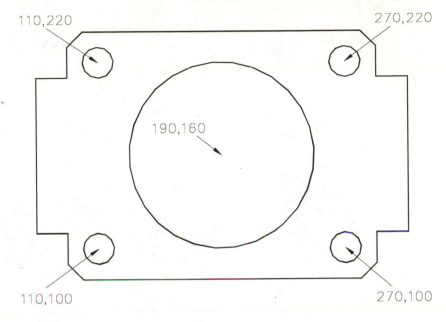

Fig. 4.7 Example 3

Example 4 – Circle tool

Left-click on the **Circle** tool icon or *enter* **C**, followed by pressing the **Return** key. Construct the circles of Fig. 4.8 as follows:

Command:_circle
3P/2P/TTR/<Center point>: *enter* 3P (3 Point) *Return*
First point: *enter* 70,240 *Return*
Second point: *enter* 120,260 *Return*
Third point: *enter* 140,170 *Return*
Command: *Return* (revert to Circle command prompts)
3P/2P/TTR/<Center point>: *enter* 2P (2 Point) *Return*
First point: *enter* 220,240 *Return*
Second point: *enter* 330,200 *Return*
Command: *Return* (revert to Circle command prompts)
3P/2P/TTR/<Center point>: *enter* 100,90 *Return*
Diameter/<Radius>: *enter* 50 *Return*
Command: *Return* (revert to Circle command prompts)
3P/2P/TTR/<Center point>: *enter* 240,90 *Return*
Diameter/<Radius>: *enter* 20 *Return*
Command: *Return* (revert to Circle command prompts)
3P/2P/TTR/<Center point>: *enter* ttr (TTR) *Return*
Enter Tangent spec: *pick* first circle
Enter second Tangent spec: *pick* second circle
Radius <20>: *enter* 40 *Return*
Command:

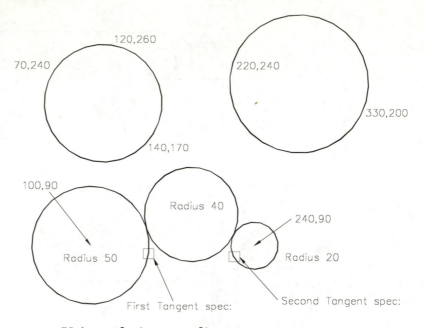

120,260

70,240

220,240

330,200

140,170

100,90

Radius 40

240,90

Radius 50

Radius 20

First Tangent spec:

Second Tangent spec:

Fig. 4.8 Example 4

Using relative coordinates

When coordinates of positions in the R13 graphics window are entered **relative** to each other the symbol @ must be placed in front of the coordinates.

Example 5 – Line tool

Left-click on the **Line** tool icon or *enter* **L**, followed by pressing the **Return** key (Fig. 4.1) and the prompt **_line From point:** appears in the Command Line window. With the **Line** tool construct Fig. 4.9 as follows:

Command: _line
From point: *enter* 70,250 *Return*
To point: *enter* @230,0 *Return*
To point: *enter* @0,–30 *Return*
To point: *enter* @30,–30 *Return*
To point: *enter* @0,–80 *Return*
To point: *enter* @–30,–30 *Return*
To point: *enter* @0,–30 *Return*
To point: *enter* @–50,0 *Return*
To point: *enter* @0,30 *Return*
To point: *enter* @–130,0 *Return*
To point: *enter* @0,–30 *Return*
To point: *enter* @–50,0 *Return*
To point: *enter* @0,30 *Return*

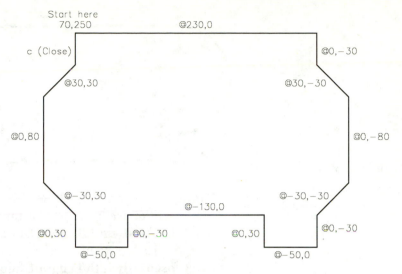

Fig. 4.9 Example 5

To point: *enter* @–30,30 *Return*
To point: *enter* @0,80 *Return*
To point: *enter* @30,30 *Return*
To point: *enter* c (Close) *Return*
Command:

Notes

@ must precede any relative coordinate unit numbers.
Positive *x* coordinate units are horizontally to the right.
Positive *y* coordinate units are vertically upwards.
Negative *x* coordinate units are horizontally to the left.
Negative *y* coordinate units are vertically downwards.

Example 6 – Polyline tool

Command: _pline
From point: *enter* 70,240 *Return*
Arc/Close/Halfwidth/Length/Undo/Width/<Endpoint of line>:
    enter w (for Width) *Return*
Starting width <0>: *enter* 2 *Return*
Ending width <2>: *Return*
Arc/Close/Halfwidth/Length/Undo/Width/<Endpoint of line>:
    enter @210,0 *Return*
Arc/Close/Halfwidth/Length/Undo/Width/<Endpoint of line>:
    enter a (Arc) *Return*
Angle/CEnter/CLose/Direction/Halfwidth/Line/Radius/
    Second pt/Undo/Width/<Endpoint of arc>: *enter* s (for Second
    pt) *Return*
Second point: *enter* @40,–40 *Return*

70,240   @210,0

@40,40   @40,−40

@−40,40   @−40,−40

@0,20   @0,−20
                    @−210,0

Fig. 4.10 Example 6

Endpoint: *enter* @−40,−40 *Return*
<Endpoint of arc>: *enter* l (for Line) *Return*
Arc/Close/Halfwidth/Length/Undo/Width/<Endpoint of line>:
    enter @0,−20 *Return*
Arc/Close/Halfwidth/Length/Undo/Width/<Endpoint of line>:
    enter @−210,0 *Return*
Arc/Close/Halfwidth/Length/Undo/Width/<Endpoint of line>:
    enter @0,20 *Return*
Arc/Close/Halfwidth/Length/Undo/Width/<Endpoint of line>:
    enter a (Arc) *Return*
**Angle/CEnter/CLose/Direction/Halfwidth/Line/Radius/
    Second pt/Undo/Width/<Endpoint of arc>:** *enter* s (for Second
    pt) *Return*
Second point: *enter* @−40,40 *Return*
Endpoint: *enter* @40,40 *Return*
**Angle/CEnter/CLose/Direction/Halfwidth/Line/Radius/
    Second pt/Undo/Width/<Endpoint of arc>:** *Return*
Command:

Other tools in the Draw toolbar

Example 7 – Ellipse tool

Left-click on the **Ellipse** tool icon or *enter* **ellipse** followed by
pressing **Return**. With the **Ellipse** tool construct the three ellipses
shown in Fig. 4.12 as follows:

Command: _ellipse
Arc/Center/<Axis endpoint 1>: _c
Center of ellipse: *enter* 110,200 *Return*
Axis endpoint: *enter* 180,200 *Return*
<Other axis distance>/Rotation: *enter* 110,175 *Return*
Command: *Return* (revert to Ellipse command prompts)
Arc/Center/<Axis endpoint 1>: Enter 40,90 *Return*
Axis endpoint 2: *enter* 200,90 *Return*

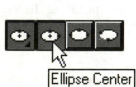

Ellipse Center

Fig. 4.11 *Left-click* on the
Ellipse tool icon or *enter*
ellipse followed by pressing
Return

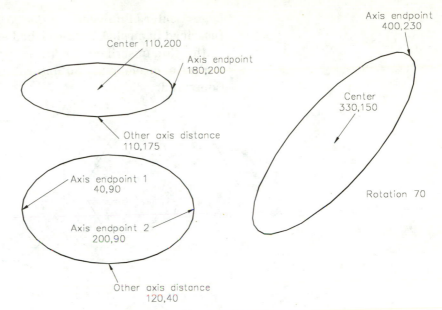

Fig. 4.12 Example 7

<Other axis distance>/Rotation: *enter* 120,40 *Return*
Command: *Return* (revert to Ellipse command prompts)
Arc/Center/<Axis endpoint 1>: _c
Center of ellipse: *enter* 330,350 *Return*
Axis endpoint: *enter* 400,230 *Return*
<Other axis distance>/Rotation: *enter* r (for Rotation) *Return*
Rotation around major axis: *enter* 70 *Return*
Command:

Example 8 – Polygon tool

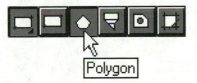

Fig. 4.13 *Left-click* on the **Polygon** tool icon or *enter* **polygon** followed by pressing **Return**

Left-click on the **Polygon** tool icon or *enter* **polygon**, followed by pressing **Return**. With the **Polygon** tool construct the polygons shown in Fig. 4.14 as follows:

Command: _polygon
Number of sides <4>: *enter* 6 *Return*
Edge<Center of polygon>: *enter* 80,210 *Return*
Inscribed in circle/Circumscribed about circle (I/C) <I>:
Radius of circle: *enter* 60 *Return*
Command: (revert to Polygon command prompts)
Number of sides <6>: *enter* 8 *Return*
Edge<Center of polygon>: *enter* e *Return*
First endpoint of edge: *enter* 200,150 *Return*
Second endpoint of edge: *enter* @50,0 *Return*
Command: (revert to Polygon command prompts)
Number of sides <8>: *enter* 5 *Return*

Edge<Center of polygon>: *enter* 95,70 *Return*
Inscribed in circle/Circumscribed about circle (I/C) <I>: *enter c*
    (for Circumscribed) *Return*
Radius of circle: *enter* 50 *Return*
Command:

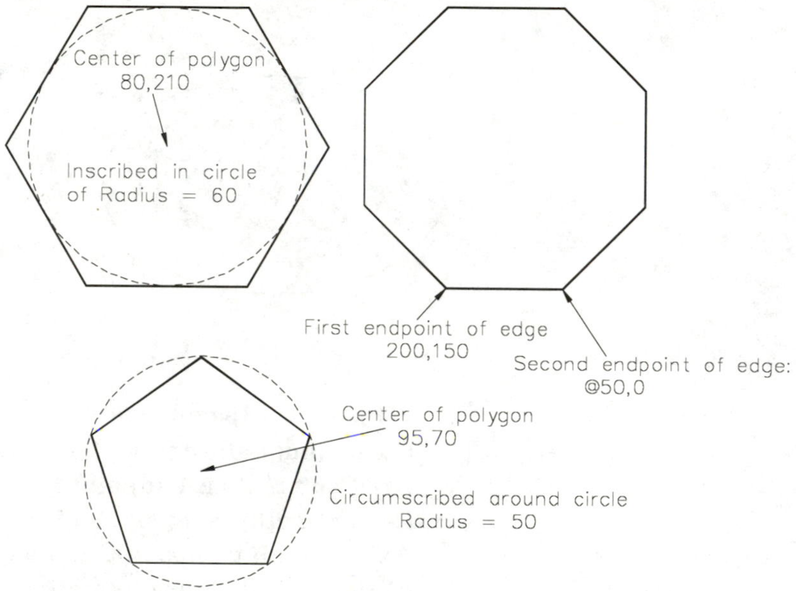

Fig. 4.14 Example 8

Notes

1. In Fig. 4.14 the broken line circles represent the Inscribed and Circumscribed circles to the polygons. These circles do not appear when the **Polygon** tool is being used.
2. Remember that the prompt in brackets (i.e. shown between < and >) is the current prompt in all Command Line prompts.

Object Snap

When an Object Snap (**Osnap**) is in operation, positioning of the next point selected can be made with precision. When any Osnap is in operation, a pick box appears at the intersection of the cursor cross lines. As the mouse is moved, so the pick box moves in sympathy. If the pick box of an Osnap is positioned on part of an object (entity) on screen, the next point picked will snap on to the part of that object to which the Osnap refers. Osnaps are available for the following points on any object (entity) in the graphics window:

Endpoint: Snaps to the nearest endpoint of the entity.
Midpoint: Snaps to the nearest central point of the entity.

Intersection: Snaps to any intersection of entities covered by the pick box.

Center: Snaps to the centre of any arc or circle covered by the pick box.

Quadrant: Snaps to the nearest quadrant of any arc or circle covered by the pick box.

Perpendicular: Snaps to the point on an entity to form a perpendicular from another point.

Tangent: Snaps to a point on an arc or circle which will form a tangent from another point.

Node: Snaps to a point formed by the tool **Point**.

Nearest: Snaps to a point on an entity nearest to the part covered by the pick box.

There are a few other Osnaps which will be referred to later when describing the construction of 3D models.

Fig. 4.15 shows examples of the use of Osnaps.

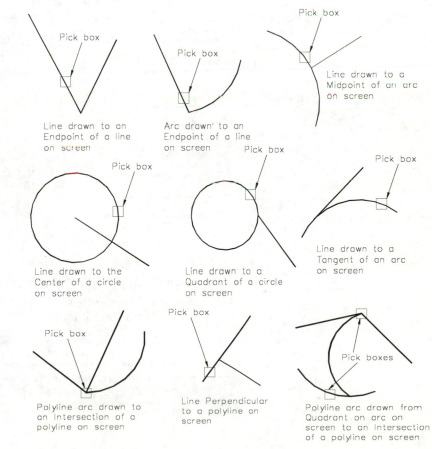

Fig. 4.15 Examples of the use of the Osnaps **Endpoint**, **Midpoint**, **Center**, **Quadrant**, **Tangent**, **Intersection**, and **Perpendicular**

Fig. 4.16 The **Shift** key of the keyboard

From
Endpoint
Midpoint
Intersection
Apparent Intersection
Center
Quadrant
Perpendicular
Tangent
Node
Insertion
Nearest
Quick,
None
.X
.Y
.Z
.XZ
.YZ
.XY

Fig. 4.17 The **Osnap** and **Filters** menu appearing when **Shift** and the right mouse button are pressed.

Fig. 4.18 The **Options** pull-down menu and the **Running Object Snap** dialogue box.

Setting Osnaps

There are several methods by which an **Osnap** or several **Osnaps** can be set.

Using Shift and the right-hand mouse button

When an **Osnap** is required, press the **Shift** key of the keyboard (Fig. 4.16) and the right hand mouse button. The **Osnaps** and **Filters** menu appears at the cursor position – Fig. 4.17. A selection can be made by a *left-click* on the required **Osnap** in the menu.

Using the Running Object Snap dialogue box

Left-click on **Running Object Snap...** in the **Options** pull-down menu. The dialogue box appears. *Left-clicks* in any of the **Osnap** boxes will set the required **Osnap**. The dialogue box also contains a slider with the aid of which the size of the Osnap pick box can be set. When an Osnap is set in the dialogue box, it remains in action until it is set off – no cross in its check box.

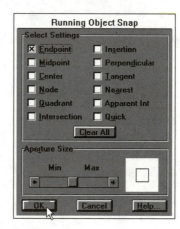

Using the Object Snap toolbar

When the **Object Snap** toolbar is on screen, an **Osnap** can be selected by a *left-click* on the appropriate icon. Fig. 4.19 shows the **Endpoint** Osnap selected from the toolbar.

Fig. 4.19 The **Object Snaps** toolbar with **Endpoint** selected

Using the Command Line

Enter **osnap** at the Command Line followed by an abbreviation for the required Osnap. For example to set the **Midpoint** Osnap:

> **Command:** *enter* osnap *Return*
> **Object snap modes:** *enter* mid *Return*
> **Command:**

and the **Midpoint** Osnap will be set until:

> **Command:** *enter* osnap *Return*
> **Object snap modes:** *enter* off *Return*
> **Command:**

Using the on-screen menu

Left-click on **Preferences...** in the **Options** pull-down menu and in the **Preferences** dialogue box which then appears (Fig. 4.20), check the box against the name **Screen Menu**, followed by a *left-click* on the **OK** button of the dialogue box. A screen menu appears on the right-hand side of the R13 graphics window headed by the word **AutoCAD** with four stars below the name (Fig. 4.21). A *left-click* on the four stars and the on-screen menu changes to display the names of all the Osnaps, from which a choice can be made.

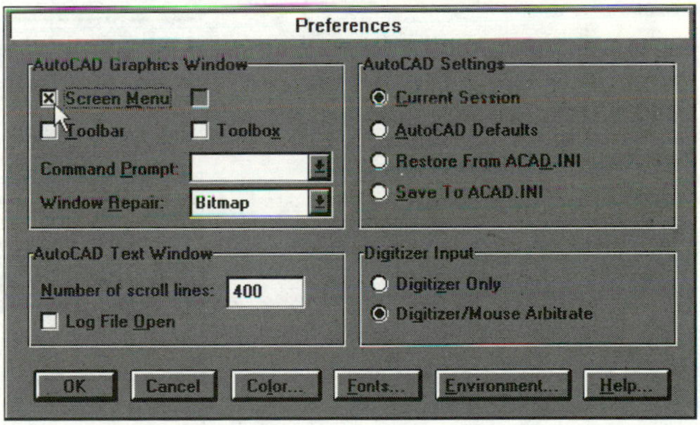

Fig. 4.20 The **Preferences** dialogue box showing the **Screen Menu** box checked

Note: It can be seen from the above that **Osnaps** can be set in a variety of ways. Perhaps this variety will impress upon the reader the importance of using Osnaps to ensure accurate drawing practices.

Fig. 4.21 The four stars in the on-screen menu

Help

There are several methods of accessing Help when required:

1. Pressing the **F1** key of the keyboard invokes a Help window relating to the tool in use. Fig. 4.22 shows the Help window for the **Line** tool.

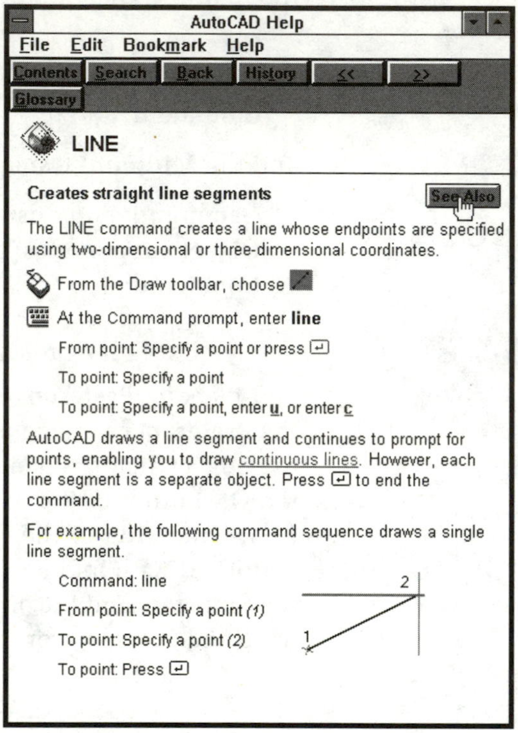

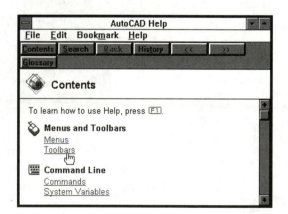

Fig. 4.22 The **LINE** Help window which appears when the **F1** key is pressed while the **Line** tool is in use

2. Press **F1** when no tool is in use and the Help window illustrated in Fig. 4.23 appears.

Fig. 4.23 The **AutoCAD Help** window which appears with a press of **F1** when no tool is in use

Position the cursor over any item showing in green , followed by a *left-click* and a Help window for the item will appear. A *left-click* on any of the buttons at the top of the window and the window changes to show the **Contents**, a **Search** list, to go **Back** to a previous Help window, etc. according to which button is selected.

3. A variety of Help windows can be selected from the list which appears in the pull-down window appearing with a *left-click* on **Help** in the menu bar. The **Help** pull-down menu is shown in Fig. 4.24.

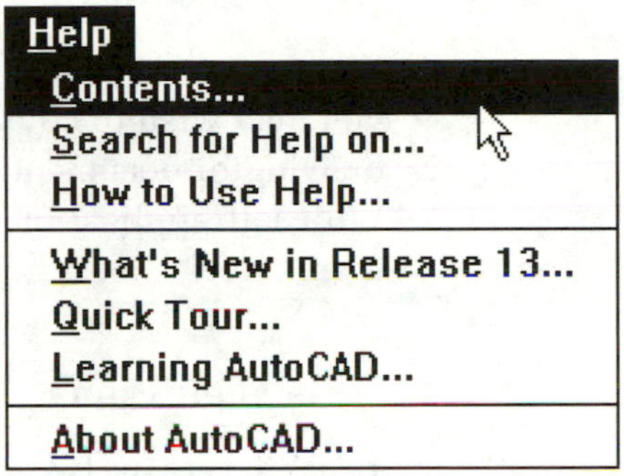

```
Help
  Contents...
  Search for Help on...        ⟋
  How to Use Help...

  What's New in Release 13...
  Quick Tour...
  Learning AutoCAD...

  About AutoCAD...
```

Fig. 4.24 The **Help** pull-down menu

Keyboard short-cuts

Function keys

Along the top edge of a computer keyboard are a line of keys labelled **F1** to **F12**. Older keyboards may only have 10 function keys. Pressing the function keys provide short-cut methods of making settings or changing the screen as follows

F1   A **Help** window appears for the tool currently in use.

F2   Toggles between the R13 graphics window and an AutoCAD Text window.

F4   If a graphics tablet is connected to the computer pressing **F4** toggles between the tablet being on and off.

F5   Toggles between the three Isoplanes. See page 132.

F6   Toggles **Coords** on/off. When off, movement of the cursor is not reflected by changes in the coordinate position of the cursor in the Coords window.

F7   Toggles **Grid** on/off. When off no grid points show.

F8   Toggles **Ortho** on/off.

F9   Toggles **Snap** on/off.

Key combinations

Pressing the **Ctrl** and another key will produce the following effects:

Ctrl/B   Toggles **Snap** on/off.

Ctrl/D   Toggles **Coords** on/off.

Ctrl/E		Swithces between the three **Isoplanes**. See page 132.
Ctrl/G		Toggles **Grid** on/off.
Ctrl/I	**Help**.	
Ctrl/O		Toggles **Ortho** on/off.
Ctrl/T		Toggles **Tablet** control on/off (if fitted).
Esc		Cancels the operation currently in action.

The Alt/Tab short-cut

When working in Windows using several applications – for example you may wish to construct a drawing in AutoCAD and transfer the drawing to a document being produced in a word processing application. With both applications working pressing **Alt/Tab** will switch between them; more about this in Chapter 11.

Questions

1. What are the two methods of calling the **Line** tool? Or the **Polyline** tool?
2. What is meant by constructing using the **absolute coordinate** method?
3. What is meant by constructing using the **relative coordinate** method?
4. What is the abbreviation for calling the **Circle** tool instead of selecting its icon from the **Draw** toolbar?
5. What is an **Object Snap**?
6. What is the purpose of an **Osnap**?
7. What is a **pick box**?
8. How many methods are there of setting **Osnaps**?
9. How is a **Help** window called on to the screen when using any tool?
10. What happens in AutoCAD when the **Esc** key is pressed?

Note: Snap, **Grid** and **Ortho** can also be set by *left-clicks* in the appropriate window showing along the bottom edge of the R13 graphics window – Fig. 4.25.

Fig. 4.25 The windows showing along the bottom edge of the R13 graphics window

Exercises

1. With the aid of the **Line** tool and using the **absolute coordinates** method, copy the drawing given in Fig. 4.26.

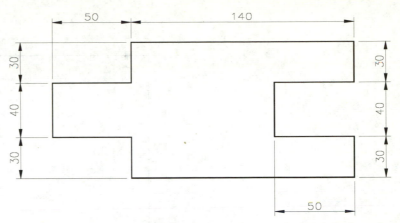

Fig. 4.26 Exercise 1

2.   With the aid of the **Line** tool and using the **relative coordinates** method, copy the drawing given in Fig. 4.27.

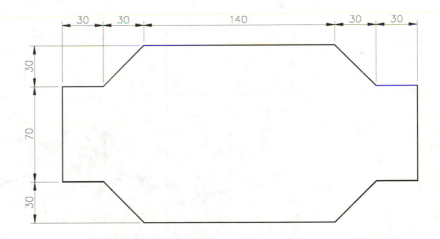

Fig. 4.27 Exercise 2

3.   Using a combination of **absolute** and **relative coordinate** methods, construct the drawing given in Fig. 4.28. Use **Circle**, **Ellipse** and either **Line** or **Polyline** tools.

4.   Using a combination of **absolute** and **relative coordinates** and suitable **Osnaps** construct the drawing given in Fig. 4.29. Use **Circle**, and either **Line** or **Polyline** tools.

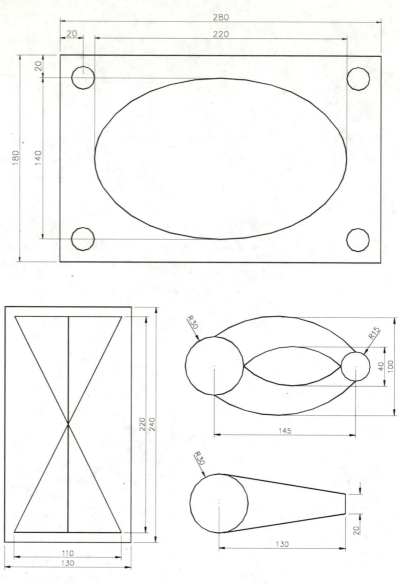

Fig. 4.28 Exercise 3

Fig. 4.29 Exercise 4

5. Using either **coordinate** method and suitable **Osnaps**, construct the drawing given in Fig. 4.30. Use **Circle**, and either **Line** or **Polyline** tools.

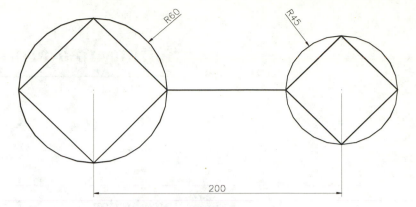

Fig. 4.30 Exercise 5

6. Using a combination of **coordinates** methods and a variety of **Osnaps** copy the given drawing Fig. 4.31.

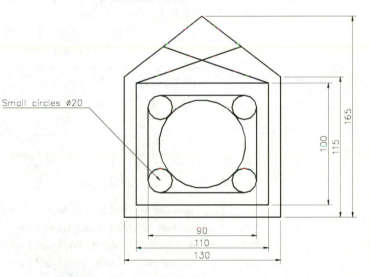

Fig. 4.31 Exercise 6

7. Call the main AutoCAD R13 **Help** window on to the screen and practise using the buttons marked **Contents**, **Search**, **Back**, **History**, **<<**, **>>** and **Glossary**. Practise a number of *left-clicks* on the items coloured green in the various windows which appear. Try to make yourself thoroughly familiar with the **Help** facility, which is very complex in Release 13.

8. Practise using the various key short-cuts given on page 57. The use of these can not only save time, but makes for easier and more efficient drawing methods. For example, the use of the **Snap** short-cut can be of great benefit to an operator.

CHAPTER 5

Setting up a prototype drawing file

Introduction

AutoCAD R13 software includes two prototype drawing files **acad.dwg** and **acadiso.dwg** held in the **acadr13\common\support** directory. Usually the prototype acadiso.dwg is suitable for drawing as if on an A3 sheet of drawing paper, with each coordinate unit representing 1 millimetre. The reader may however wish to set up his/her own prototype drawing file with parameters set for personal preferences rather than to accept the existing prototype files. Reference was made in Chapter 3 to setting **Units**, **Snap**, **Grid**, **Blips** and **Limits** for an AutoCAD R13 graphics window suitable for drawing as on an A3 drawing sheet. Further steps to be taken to set up a prototype drawing file will now be considered.

Warning

If other operators are to use the computer at which you are working, please do not save your own prototype file to either the name **acad.dwg** or **acadiso.dwg**, but rather save it to a different filename. Other operators may not wish to work to the same prototype parameters as are suggested in this book, preferring to accept the standard prototype settings or settings of their own choice.

It may be that the **Limits** of the acad prototype files are not suitable, particularly if you wish to work to an A4 or an A2 sheet settings.

Starting a new drawing

Left-click on **File** in the menu bar, followed by another *left-click* on **New...** in the **File** pull-down menu. The **Create New Drawing** dialogue box appears on screen (Fig. 5.1). A *left-click* on the button labelled **Prototype...** brings another dialogue box listing names of possible prototype files. Fig. 5.1 shows that the prototype drawing which would appear with a *left-click* on the **OK** button of the dialogue box would be the acadiso.dwg. This could be changed, either by selecting from the dialogue box which appears when the **Preferences...** button is selected, or by *entering* the name of your own prototype drawing file in the box next to the **Prototype...** button.

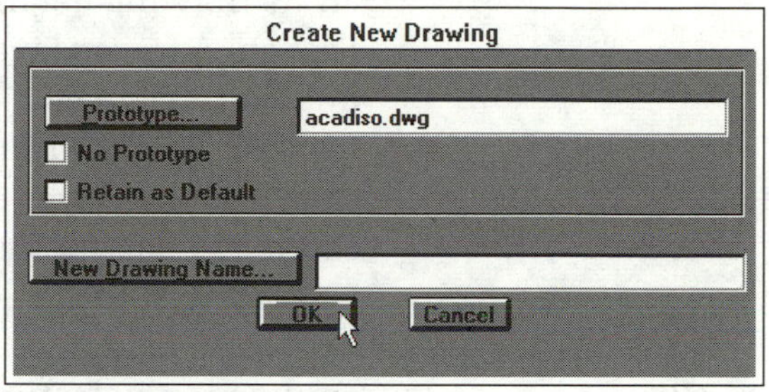

Fig. 5.1 The **Create New Drawing** dialogue box

Layers

Layers are an important feature of any CAD software system. AutoCAD R13 allows an unlimited number of layers to be set. *Left-click* on **Layers...** in the **Data** pull-down menu (Fig. 5.2), noting the statement bottom left of the graphics window (Fig. 5.3). The **Layer Control** dialogue box appears (Fig. 5.4). Each layer can be given its own name, its own colour and its own linetype. Each layer can be set to be on, off, frozen, thawed or locked. These features are set with the aid of the various buttons seen in The **Layer Control** dialogue box and they have the following effects:

Layer name: The name given to the layer by the operator. Each name must be distinct from all others and it is best if the name has some meaning to the operator.

Fig. 5.2 **Layers...** in the **Data** pull-down menu

Fig. 5.3 The statement appearing bottom left of the graphics window when **Layers...** is selected

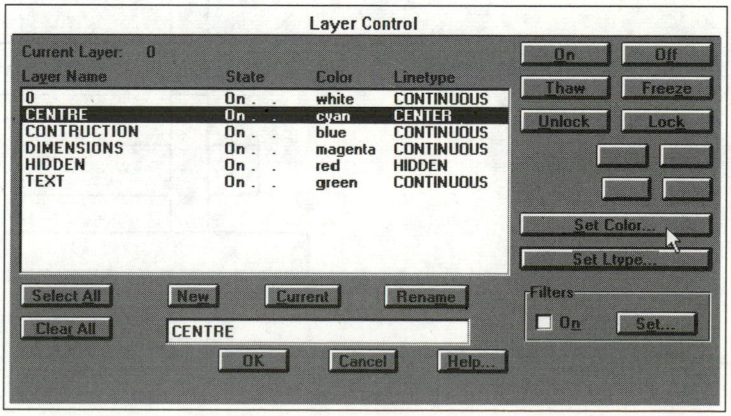

Fig. 5.4 The **Layer Control** dialogue box

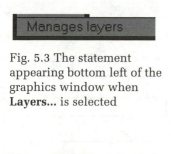

Layer State:

On Any details drawn on the layer can be seen. Drawing details can be modified as wished – e.g. they can be erased, moved, copied, etc.

Off The layer is hidden and any drawing details on the layer cannot be seen. A layer which is off can be turned on again, when all its drawing details will reappear.

Frozen A frozen layer is turned off and cannot be turned back on until it is **Thawed**.

Locked A locked layer can be drawn on, but what has been drawn on the layer cannot be modified in any way – e.g. parts cannot be erased, moved, copied, etc.

Unlocked A locked layer can be unlocked.

Colour: Any colour available within the AutoCAD system can be applied to the features drawn on a layer.

Linetype: Any of the available linetypes in AutoCAD R13 can be applied to a layer.

Current: Any layer can be selected as the current layer on which constructions can take place. To set a layer as current, *left-click* on its name, which highlights, then *left-click* on the button marked **Current**. A message top right of the dialogue box informs the operator of the current layer.

Layers are similar to tracings in hand drawing work, in that details of drawings on those layers which are on can be seen in position

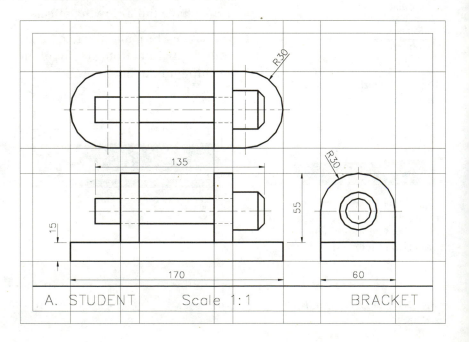

Fig. 5.5 An orthographic
projection drawn on layers

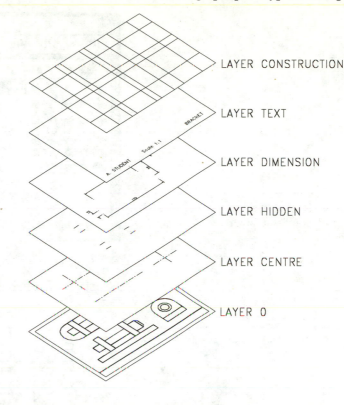

LAYER CONSTRUCTION

LAYER TEXT

LAYER DIMENSION

LAYER HIDDEN

LAYER CENTRE

LAYER 0

Fig. 5.6 A diagrammatic representation of the layers used in constructing Fig. 5.5

relative to drawing features on all other layers as if each separate feature was drawn on its own sheet of tracing paper. As an example, the drawing Fig. 5.5 shows a simple bracket in three third angle orthographic views, complete with centre lines, hidden detail, text and dimensions as well as construction lines. Fig. 5.6 shows, in a diagrammatic form, the relationship between the various layers, each of which holds its own drawing feature.

When a number of layers have been set in the **Layer Control** dialogue box, a *left-click* on the **Layer control** button (Fig. 5.7) causes a to window appear showing the state of all layers in icon form. The meanings of the icons are shown in Fig. 5.8.

A suggested Prototype drawing file

The prototype drawing used to produce the orthographic projection of Fig. 5.5 was created as follows:

1. First set **Units**, **Snap**, **Grid**, **Blips** and **Limits** as stated on pages 30 to 32.
2. *Left-click* on **Linetype...** in the **Data** pull-down menu (Fig. 5.2). *Left-click* on the linetypes you wish to use, or *left-click* on the **Load**

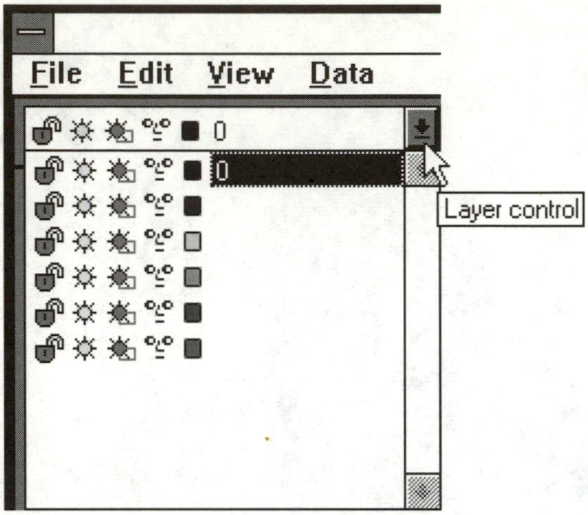

Fig. 5.7 The Menu appearing with a *left-click* on the **Layer control** button

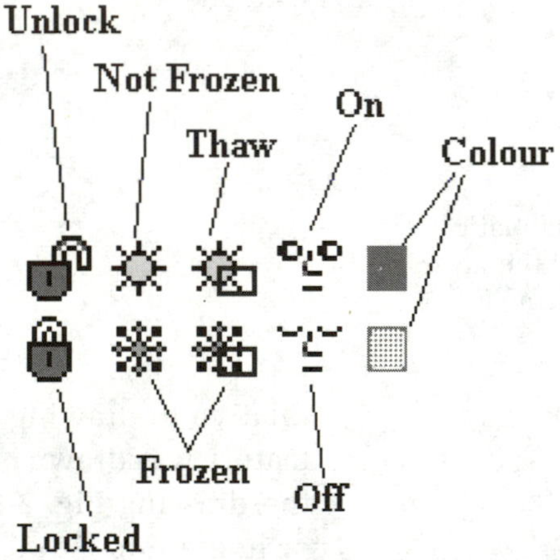

Fig. 5.8 The meanings of the icons showing in the window which appears with a *left-click* on the **Layer control** button

button and the **Load or Reload Linetypes** dialogue box appears. Either *left-click* on the required linetypes – **CENTER** and **HIDDEN** or, as shown in Fig. 5.9, *left-click* on the **Select All** button to load all linetypes.

3. *Left-click* on **Layers...** in the **Data** pull-down menu and make **New** layers **CENTRE**, **CONSTRUCTION**, **DIMENSIONS**, **HIDDEN** and **TEXT** as shown in Fig. 5.4 on page 63. This is carried out by *entering* the name in the box at the bottom of the screen, followed by a *left-click* on the **New** button. The name entered then appears in the layer name list.

4. Allocate each layer a colour as suggested in Fig. 5.4. First *left-click* on the layer name, and the name highlights. Then *left-click* on the **Set Color** button of the **Layer Control** dialogue box. The **Select Color** dialogue box appears (Fig. 5.10). Either *enter* the required colour name in the **Color:** box, or *left-click* on one of the colours in the **Full Color Palette**. The colour name or its number appears against the layer name.

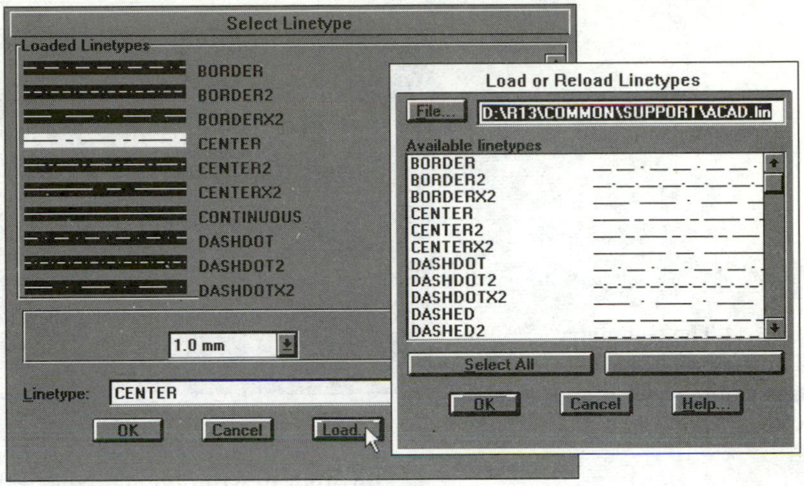

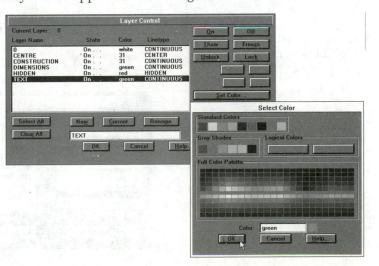

Fig. 5.9 The **Select Linetype** dialogue box

5. *Left-click* on a layer name. Then *left-click* on the **Set Linetype** button. The required linetype can then be selected from the **Select Linetype** dialogue box. The layer names, colours and linetypes have now been set.

6. *Left-click* on **Dimension Style...** in the **Data** pull-down menu (Fig. 5.2). The **Dimension Style** dialogue box appears (Fig. 5.11). Various features for your dimension style can be set in the three dialogue boxes appearing when the buttons **Geometry...**, **Format** and **Annotation...** are selected. Fig. 5.11 shows the settings for the colour of the dimension lines, the spacing between the dimension line and the dimension itself, the length of the extension of the extension line beyond the dimension line, the type of arrow and its length and whether the dimension should have a centre mark or not. Fig. 5.12 shows the **Geometry** for the resulting dimensions as they would appear in a drawing.

Fig. 5.10 The **Select Color** dialogue box which appears with a *left-click* on the **Color** button

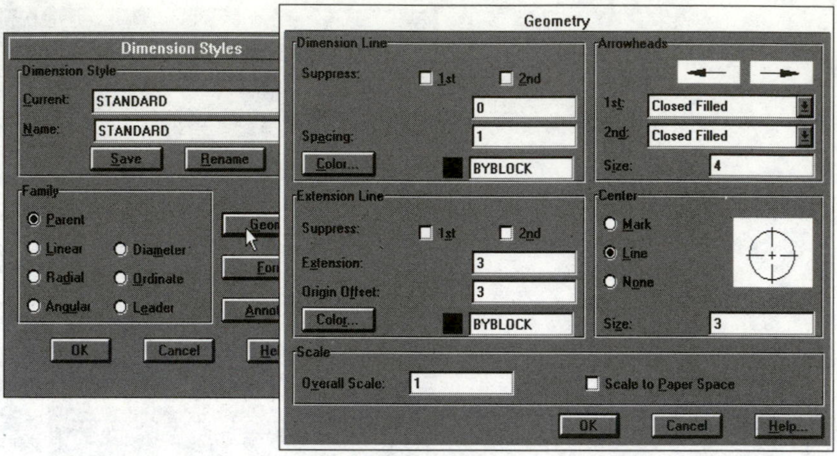

Fig. 5.11 The **Geometry** dialogue box from the **Dimension Styles** dialogue box

The other two dialogue boxes of the **Dimension Style** dialogue box are used to set **Format** and **Annotation**. More about these settings in Chapter 10.

7. *Left-click* on **Text Style...** in the **Data** pull-down menu (Fig. 5.2). The Command Line will show:

Command: _style Text style name (or ?) <STANDARD> *Return* **Existing style.**

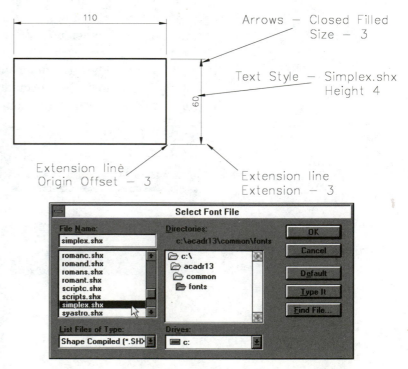

Fig. 5.12 The **Gemoetry** settings for dimensions in out prototype drawing

Fig. 5.13 The **Select Font Style** dialogue box

and the **Select Font Style** dialogue box appears. *Double-click* on the name **simplex.shx** in the list box, or *left-click* on **simplex.shx**, followed by another on the **OK** button. The Command Line shows:

Height <0>: *enter* 6 *return*
Width factor <1>: *Return*
Obliquing angle <0>: *Return*
Backwards <N> *Return*
Upside down <N> *Return*
Vertical <N> *Return*
SIMPLEX is now the current text style.
Command:

and the text style for our prototype drawing file is Simplex set to a height of 6 units.

8. *Left-click* on **Save As... in** the **File** pull-down menu (Fig. 5.14) In the **Save Drawing As** dialogue box, make sure the directory to save to is **acad\support** and in the **File Name** box of the dialogue box *enter* a suitable file name for your prototype drawing file. I have chosen **ay** (my initials). The file will be saved to the filename **acad\support\ay.dwg**, to be selected as a prototype file when required.

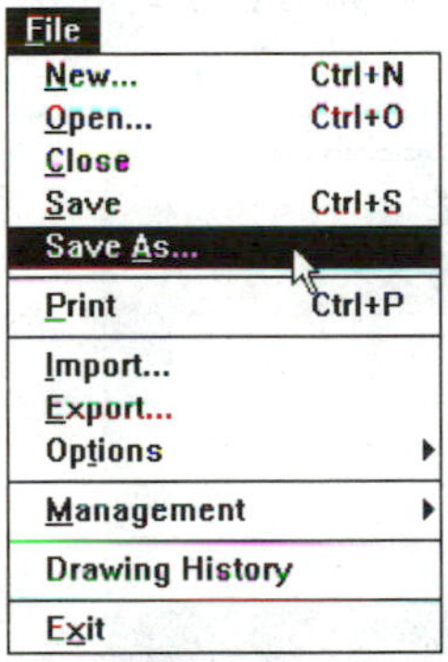

Fig. 5.14 **Save As...** in the **File** pull-down menu

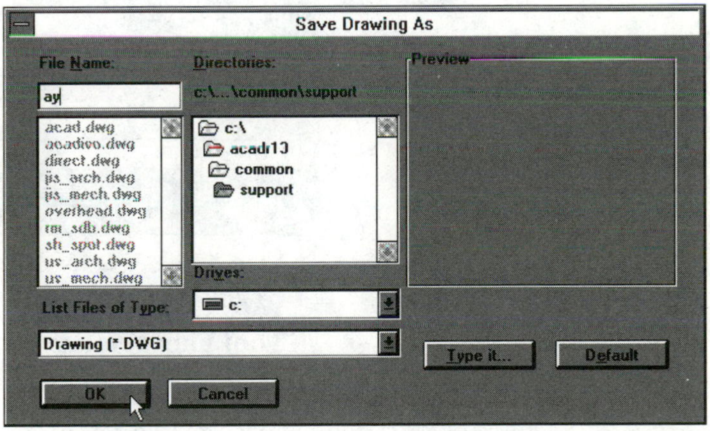

Fig. 5.15 The **Save Drawing As** dialogue box

Notes

1. The prototype file described above and saved as **acad\support\ay.dwg** has parameters as follows:

Limits: 420,297
Snap: set to 5 and on
Grid: set to 10 and on
Units: showing with no figures after the decimal point

Layers: 0, Centre, Construction, Dimensions, Hidden and Text, each of a different colour and with appropriate linetypes
Dimensions: style set
Text: style Simplex of height 6 units.

2. When starting a new drawing you now have the choice of either the acad prototype drawings (acad.dwg and acadiso.dwg) or your own. *Left-click* on **New...** in the **File** pull-down menu (Fig. 5.14) and in the **Create New Drawing** dialogue box (Fig. 5.1), first *left-click* on the **Prototype...** button, which changes the dialogue box to the **Prototype Drawing File** dialogue box (Fig. 5.16), then *double-click* on the name of your prototype drawing file name in the list box of the new dialogue box. Your prototype drawing file will then load. Or *enter* the name of your prototype drawing file in the **File Name** box of the dialogue box, followed by a *left-click* on the **OK** button of the dialogue box.

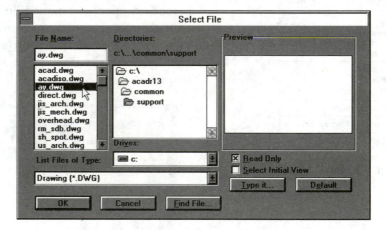

Fig. 5.16 The **Prototype Drawing File** dialogue box from which a prototype drawing file can be selected

Tool abbreviations

Tools for drawing can either be called by selection of a tool icon from a toolbar or the name of the tool can be *entered* at the Command Line. To call some tools an abbreviation of the tool name can be *entered* in place of the full name. The abbreviations are set in the file **acad\support\acad.pgp**, which can be easily amended to include further tool name abbreviations if wished. Some operators may wish to construct drawings by calling tools by *entering* abbreviations, rather than by either entering the tool name or selecting a tool icon. Some may wish to work with some abbreviations and some tool icons.

Changing the acad.pgp file

To change or add to the **acad.pgp** file, switch to the MS-DOS prompt **C:\>** and at the prompt:

> **C:\>** *enter* edit r13\acad\support\acad.pgp *Return*

The DOS editor appears showing the contents of the file, part of which is given below.

> **; Sample aliases for AutoCAD Commands**
> **; These examples reflect the most frequently used commands.**
> **; Each alias uses a small amount of memory, so don't go**
> **; overboard on systems with tight memory.**
>
> **A,   *ARC**
> **C,   *CIRCLE**
> **CP,   *COPY**
> **DV,   *DVIEW**
> **E,   *ERASE**
> **L,   *LINE**
> **LA,   *LAYER**
> **LT,   *LINETYPE**
> **M,   *MOVE**
> **MS,   *MSPACE**
> **P,   *PAN**
> **PS,   *PSPACE**
> **PL,   *PLINE**
> **R,   *REDRAW**
> **T,   *MTEXT**
> **Z,   *ZOOM**

You can add abbreviations to the file in the same form as those already included: for example

> **MI,   *MIRROR** for an abbreviation for the **Mirror** tool

and save the file to its correct filename. Next time you use AutoCAD R13, the tool name abbreviations you have added can be used in place of the full tool name.

Questions

1. What is meant by the term **prototype drawing** in AutoCAD R13?
2. In which directory would you expect to find the file for the AutoCAD prototype drawing?
3. Why is it unwise to save your own prototype drawing file to the name acad.dwg?

4. What is meant by the term **Layer** in CAD drawing?
5. Can you draw on a **locked** layer?
6. What is the purpose of locking a layer?
7. How can a **Frozen** layer be brought back into use?
8. In which AutoCAD file can tool abbreviations be added?
9. In which AutoCAD directory would you expect to find the file to which tool abbreviations can be added?
10. To what **Limits** would you set a screen if drawing as if on an A4 sheet of drawing paper? As if on an A2 sheet of drawing paper?

CHAPTER 6

The 2D Modify tools

Introduction

The **Modify** tools are for editing or modifying objects (entities) or
groups of objects already drawn in the AutoCAD graphics window.
The **Modify** tools have a common selection set which can be seen in
icon form in the **Select Objects** toolbar (Fig. 6.1). When using the
Modify tools the **Select Objects** toolbar can be called to screen to
allow its features to be selected as required.

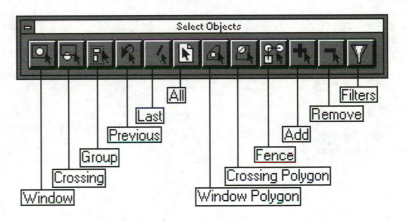

Fig. 6.1 The tools in the **Select
Objects** toolbar

Note: All **floating** toolbars can be placed in the graphics window in
vertical, horizontal or in a box form. Fig. 6.1 shows the **Select
Objects** toolbar placed in a horizontal position and Fig. 6.2 shows
two other forms for this toolbar. A toolbar can be easily and quickly
changed in shape by positioning the cursor over the frame of the
toolbar window, pressing the left-hand mouse button and **dragging**.
As the mouse is moved, so the toolbar changes shape. Fig. 6.2 also
shows this action applied to the **Modify** toolbar as it floats.

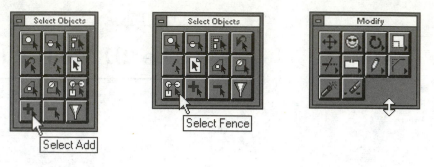

Fig. 6.2 Various shapes of floating toolbars

Fig. 6.3 The names of the tools icons in the **Modify** toolbar

The Modify toolbar

Fig. 6.3 shows the **Modify** toolbar with the names of the tools as selected in the toolbar. I prefer to have the **Modify** toolbar always in either the left-hand or the right-hand column of the AutoCAD R13 graphics window because the tools in this toolbar are in frequent use when working in AutoCAD R13, whereas Fig. 6.3 shows the toolbar floating, complete with its name in its title bar. Some operators may prefer to have the toolbar floating.

Fig. 6.4 shows the names of the tools in the **Flyouts** of the tool icons. Note that there are no flyouts for **Move**, **Explode** and **Erase**. The 3D tools which will be found in the flyouts of **Copy** and **Rotate** are not shown in Fig. 6.4. These will be referred to later in Chapter 14.

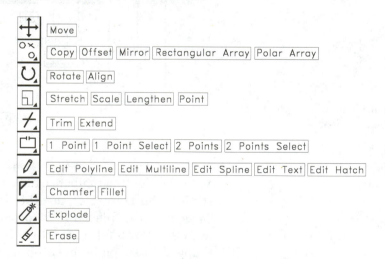

Fig. 6.4 The names of the 2D tools found in the flyouts from the tools in the **Modify** toolbar

Using the Modify and Select Objects tools

Example 1 – Move tool

Taking the tool **Move** as an example, Fig. 6.5 shows the results of moving an outline composed of lines and arcs. First *left-click* on the

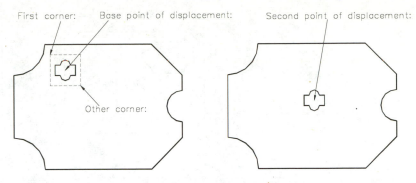

First corner: Base point of displacement: Second point of displacement:

Other corner:

Fig. 6.5 Example 1 – using
Move

Fig. 6.6 The **Move** tool icon
from the **Modify** toolbar

Move tool icon in the **Modify** toolbar, then *left-click* on the **Select Window** icon in the **Select Objects** toolbar. The Command Line prompts will be:

> **Command:** _move
> **Select objects:** _w
> **First corner:** *pick*
> **Other corner:** *pick* **4 found.**
> **Select objects:** Return
> **Base point of displacement:** *pick*
> **Second point of displacement:** *pick*
> **Command:**

The same result would have been achieved by selecting the **Move** tool, *entering* **w** (for Window) and pressing **Return** on the keyboard in response to the first **Select objects:** prompt. Also, because the acad.pgp file contains the abbreviation **M** for **Move**, *entering* **m** instead of selecting the **Move** tool icon would have started the action of the move tool.

Example 2 – Copy tool

Upper drawings of Fig. 6.8. *Left-click* on the **Copy** tool icon in the **Modify** toolbar, followed by a *left-click* on **Select Window** icon in the **Select Objects** toolbar.

> **Command:** _copy
> **Select objects:** _w
> **First corner:** *pick*

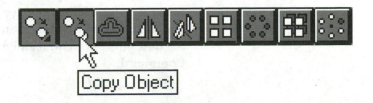

Fig. 6.7 **Copy Object** from the
Copy flyout in the **Modify**
toolbar

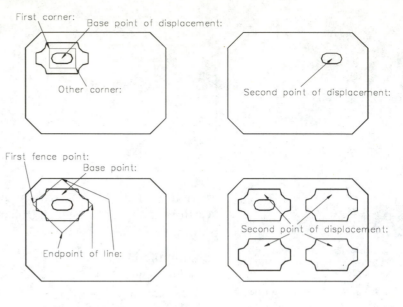

Fig. 6.8 Second and third examples – using **Copy**

Other corner: *pick*
<First point of displacement>/Multiple: *pick*
Second point of displacement: *pick*
Command:

Example 3 – Multiple Copy tool

Lower drawings of Fig. 6.8. *Left-click* on the **Copy** tool icon in the **Modify** toolbar, followed by a *left-click* on **Select Fence** icon in the **Select Objects** toolbar.

Command: _copy
Select objects: _f
First fence point: *pick*
Undo/<Endpoint of line>: *pick*
Undo/<Endpoint of line>: *pick*
Undo/<Endpoint of line>: *pick*
Undo/<Endpoint of line>: *Return*
<First point of displacement>/Multiple: *enter*m (Multiple) *Return*
Base point: pick point as shown
Second point of displacement: *pick*
Second point of displacement: *pick*
Second point of displacement: *pick*
Second point of displacement: *pick*
Second point of displacement: *Return*
Command:

Notes

1. Note the use of a fence in selecting objects. The fence must cross each of the objects being chosen.
2. The abbreviation **cp** for **Copy** is in the **acad.pgp** file. Thus instead of selecting the **Copy** tool icon, *entering* **cp** at the Command Line will start up the command prompts.
3. Instead of selecting the **Select Fence** icon *entering* **f** at the **Select objects:** prompt will start up the Fence prompts.

Example 4 – Rotate tool

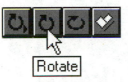

Fig. 6.9 The **Rotate** tool icon from the **Modify** toolbar

Fig. 6.10. *Left-click* on the **Rotate** tool icon in the **Modify** toolbar, followed by a *left-click* on **Crossing Window** icon in the **Select Objects** toolbar. Note that rotation takes place in a counter clockwise (ccw) direction. So the 6 positions of the hour handle of the clock will be **Rotation angle** 0, 300, 240, 180, 120 and 60 to give the 12:00, 2:00, 4:00, 6:00, 8:00 and 10:00 o'clock positions.

> **Command:** _rotate
> **Select objects:** _c
> **First corner:** *pick*
> **Other corner:** *pick* **1 found**
> **Select objects:** *Return*
> **Base point of displacement:** *pick*
> **<Rotation angle>/Reference:** *enter* 300 *Return*
> **Command:**

First corner: Other corner:

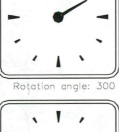

Base point of displacement: Rotation angle: 300   Rotation angle: 240

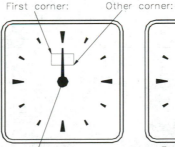
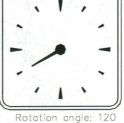

Fig. 6.10 Example 4 – using **Rotate**

Rotation angle: 180   Rotation angle: 120   Rotation angle: 60

This gives the 2:00 o'clock position. Repeat for 240, 180, 120 and 60 to give the other rotation positions.

Example 5 – Stretch tool

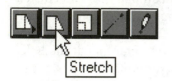

Fig. 6.11 The **Stretch** tool icon from the **Modify** toolbar

Fig. 6.12. *Left-click* on the **Stretch** tool icon in the **Stretch** flyout of the **Modify** toolbar, followed by a *left-click* on the **Select Crossing Window** in the **Select Objects** toolbar.

Command: _stretch
Select objects: _c
First corner: *pick*
Other corner: *pick*
Base point of displacement: *pick*
Second point of displacement: *pick*
Command:

Notes

1. When using **Stretch** the **Select objects:** prompt must be answered by using the **Select Crossing Window** or by *entering* **c** (crossing).
2. Note the effect of using **Stretch** on arcs as seen in the lower drawing of Fig. 6.12.

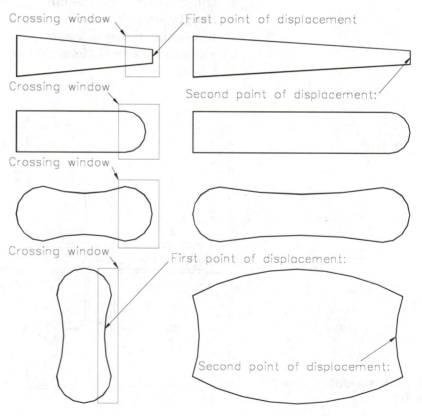

Fig. 6.12 Example 5 – using **Stretch**

3. **Stretch** can be used for moving features within a drawing. Two examples are given in Fig. 6.13. In the upper drawings a door symbol has been moved to a new position. In the lower drawings, a battery symbol has been moved to a new position.

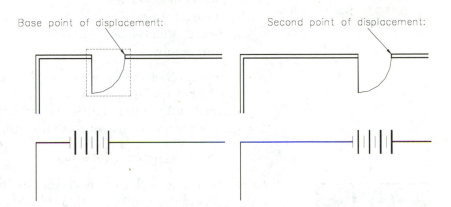

Fig. 6.13 Moving features within a drawing with the **Stretch** tool

Example 6 – Scale tool

Fig. 6.14. *Left-click* on the **Scale** tool icon in the **Resize** flyout of the **Modify** toolbar (Fig. 6.15), followed by a *left-click* on **p** in the **Select Objects** toolbar.

Command: _scale
Select objects: _cp
First polygon point: *pick*
Undo/<Endpoint of line: *pick*
Undo/<Endpoint of line: *pick*

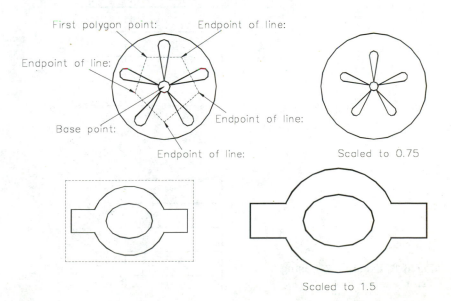

Fig. 6.14 Example 6 – using **Scale**

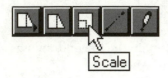

Fig. 6.15 The **Scale** tool icon
from the **Modify** toolbar

Undo/<Endpoint of line: *pick*
Undo/<Endpoint of line: *pick*
Undo/<Endpoint of line: *pick*
Undo/<Endpoint of line: *Return* **6 found**
Select objects: *Return*
Base point: *pick*
Scale <Reference>: *enter .75 Return*
Command:

Note: Fig. 6.14 shows two examples of scaling with the **Scale** tool. The upper drawings show the use of a crossing polygon to scale entities within other entities which are not to be scaled. The lower drawing show the use of a window to select all the drawing.

Example 7 – Trim tool

Fig. 6.17. *Left-click* on the **Trim** tool icon in the **Trim** flyout of the **Modify** toolbar, followed by a *left-click* on **Select Fence** in the **Select Objects** toolbar at the prompt **Select object to trim/Undo:**

Command _trim
Select cutting edge(s)...
Select objects: *pick*
Select objects: *Return* **1 found**
Select object to trim/Undo: _f
First fence point: *pick*

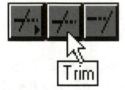

Fig. 6.16 The **Trim** tool icon in
the **Modify** toolbar

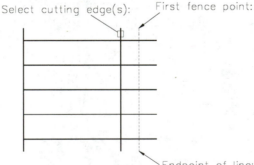

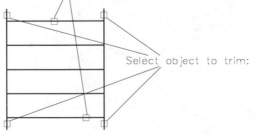

Fig. 6.17 Example 7 – using
Trim

Undo/<Endpoint of line>: *pick*
Undo/<Endpoint of line>: *Return*
Command:

Note: The lower drawings of Fig. 6.17 show the use of **Trim** to trim single projecting lines.

Example 8 – Extend tool

Fig. 6.19. *Left-click* on the **Extend** tool icon in the **Trim** flyout of the **Modify** toolbar. Three examples are given in Fig. 6.19:

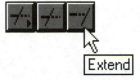

Fig. 6.18 The **Extend** tool icon in the **Modify** toolbar tool

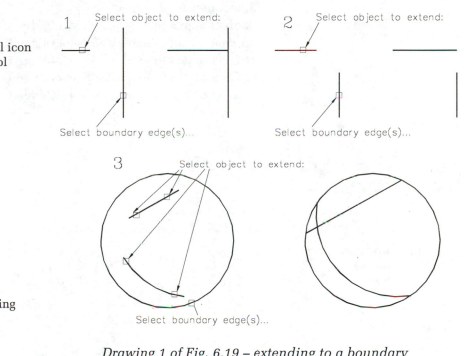

Fig. 6.19 Example 8 – using **Extend**

Drawing 1 of Fig. 6.19 – extending to a boundary

Command: _extend
Select boundary edge(s)...
Select objects: *pick* **1 found**
Select objects: *Return*
<Select object to extend>/Project/Edge/Undo: *pick*
Command:

Drawing 2 of Fig. 6.19 – extending to presumed boundary

Command: _extend
Select boundary edge(s)...
Select objects: *pick* **1 found**
Select objects: *Return*

<Select object to extend>/Project/Edge/Undo: *enter* e (Edge) *Return*
Extend/No extend/<Extend>: *Return*
<Select object to extend>: *pick*
Command:

> *Drawing 3 of Fig. 6.19 – extending arcs and lines to circles*

Command: _extend
Select boundary edge(s)...
Select objects: *pick* **1 found**
Select objects: *Return*
<Select object to extend>/Project/Edge/Undo: *pick*
<Select object to extend>/Project/Edge/Undo: *pick*
<Select object to extend>/Project/Edge/Undo: *pick*
<Select object to extend>/Project/Edge/Undo: *pick*
<Select object to extend>/Project/Edge/Undo: *Return*
Command:

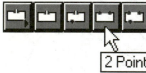

Fig. 6.20 The **Break** tool icon in the **Modify** toolbar

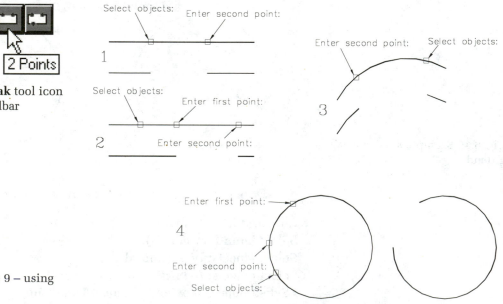

Fig. 6.21 Example 9 – using **Break**

Example 9 – Break tool

Fig. 6.20. *Left-click* on the **2 Points** icon in the **Break** flyout of the **Modify** toolbar. Four examples are given in Fig. 6.21.

Drawing 1 of Fig. 6.21 – selecting two break points

Command: _break
Select objects: *pick*
Enter second point (or F for first point): *pick*
Command:

Drawing 2 of Fig. 6.21 – using the f (First) option

Command: _break
Select objects: *pick*
Enter second point (or F for first point): *enter* f (for First) *Return*
Enter first point: *pick*
Enter second point: *pick*
Command:

Drawing 3 of Fig. 6.21 – breaking an arc

This example follows the same prompts sequence as for Drawing 1. However, it must be noted that the breaking must use a counter clockwise direction (ccw).

Drawing 4 of Fig. 6.21 – breaking a circle

This example follows the same prompts sequence as for Drawings 2. However, note that the break must use a ccw direction.

Example 10 – Chamfer tool

Fig. 6.22. *Left-click* on the **Chamfer** tool icon in the **Feature** flyout of the **Modify** toolbar. First set the required **Distances**.

Command: _chamfer
Polyline /Distances/<Select first line>:
Enter first chamfer distance: *enter* 15 *Return*
Enter second chamfer distance<15>: *Return*
Command: *Return*

Drawing 1 of Fig. 6.23

Then select lines to be chamfered.

Polyline/Distances/<Select first line>: *pick*
Select second line: *pick*
Command:

Drawing 2 of Fig. 6.23

If **Distances** are both entered as nil (0), lines which do not meet at a corner will meet. Note this does not apply to polylines.

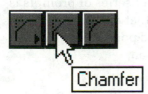

Fig. 6.22 The **Chamfer** tool icon from the **Modify** toolbar

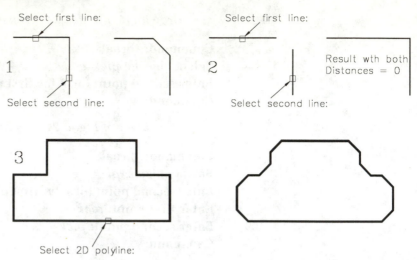

Fig. 6.23 Example 10 – using
Chamfer

Drawings of Fig 6.23

If a p (for Polyline) is entered in response to the **Polyline/Distances/<Select first line>** prompt, each corner of a closed polyline will be chamfered.

Example 11 – Fillet tool

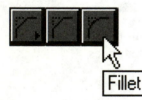

Fig. 6.24 The **Fillet** tool icon
from the **Modify** toolbar

Fig. 6.24. *Left-click on* the **Fillet** tool icon in the **Feature** flyout of the **Modify** toolbar. The structure of the **Fillet** tool series of prompts is similar to that for the **Chamfer** tool, except that only one distance (the **Radius** of the fillet) needs to be set. Closed polylines are filleted at each corner if the **Polyline** prompt is chosen.

Command: _fillet
Polyline/Radius/<Select first object>: *enter* r (Radius) *Return*
Enter fillet radius: *enter* 15 *Return*
Command: *Return*
Polyline/Radius/<Select first object>: *pick*
Select second object: *pick*
Command:

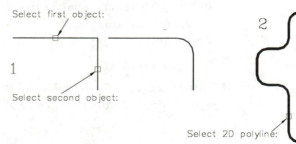

Fig. 6.25 Example 11 – using
Fillet

Example 12 – Erase tool

Fig. 6.26 The **Erase** tool icon from the **Modify** toolbar

Fig. 6.26. *Left-click on* the **Erase** tool icon in the **Modify** toolbar (there is no flyout for **Erase**). Fig. 6.27 shows two examples of using the tool, the first by the erasing of single objects, the second using the **Select Crossing** tool from the **Select Objects** toolbar, or *entering* **c** (for Crossing) at the command line in response to the **Select objects:** prompt.

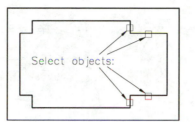
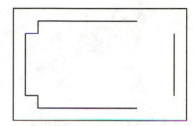
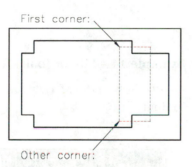
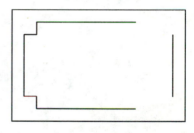

Fig. 6.27 Example 12 – using **Erase**

Example 13 – Offest tool

Fig. 6.28. *Left-click* on the **Offset** tool icon in the **Copy** flyout of the **Modify** toolbar.

> **Command: _offset**
> **Offset distance or Through/<Through>:** *enter* 6 *Return*
> **Select object to offset:** *pick*
> **Side to offset:** *pick*
> **Command:**

Fig. 6.28 The **Offset** tool icon from the **Modify** toolbar

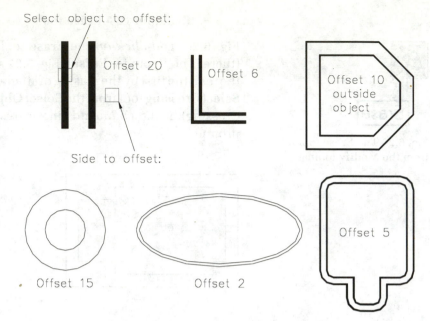

Fig. 6.29 Example 13 – using
Offset

Example 14 – Mirror tool

Fig. 6.30. *Left-click* on the **Mirror** tool icon in the **Copy** flyout of the
Modify toolbar.

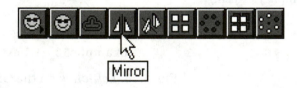

Fig. 6.30 The **Mirror** tool icon
from the **Modify** toolbar

Command: _mirror
Select objects: _w
First corner: *pick*
Other corner: *pick*
Select objects: *Return* **2 found**
First point on mirror line: *pick*
Second point: *pick*
Delete old objects <N>: *Return* (accept No)
Command:

Fig. 6.31 shows three examples of outlines which have been acted
upon by the **Mirror** tool. In the right-hand example, the original
outline was mirrored in both horizontal and vertical directions.

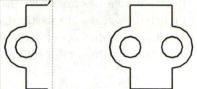

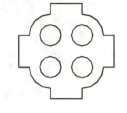
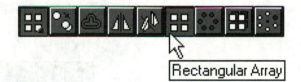

Fig. 6.31 Example 14 – using
Mirror

Example 15 – Rectangular Array tool

Fig. 6.32. *Left-click* on the **Rectangular Array** tool icon in the **Copy**
flyout of the **Modify** toolbar.

Command: _array

Fig. 6.32 The **Rectangular
Array** tool icon from the
Modify toolbar

Select objects: _w
First corner: *pick*
Other corner: *pick*
Select objects: *Return* **4 found**
Rectangular or polar array (R/P) <R>: _r
Number of rows (----) <1>: *enter* **5** *Return*
Number of columns (| | |) <1>: *enter* **6** *Return*
Unit cell or distance between rows (----): *enter* **–40** *Return*
Distance between columns (| | |): *enter* **40** *Return*
Command:

Notes

Positive *x* values are horizontally to the right.
Positive *y* values are vertically upwards.
Negative *x* values are horizontally to the left.
Negative *y* values are vertically downwards.

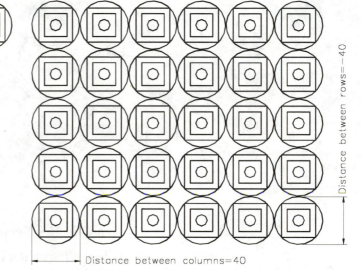

Fig. 6.33 Example 15 – using
Rectangular Array

Example 16 – Polar Array tool

Fig. 6.34. *Left-click* on the **Polar Array** tool icon in the **Copy** flyout
of the **Modify** toolbar.

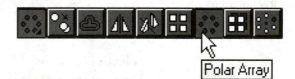

Fig. 6.34 The **Polar Array** tool
icon from the **Modify** toolbar

Command: _polar array
Select objects: _all
Select objects: *Return*
Rectangular or polar array (R/P) <R>: _p
Center of array: *pick*
Number of items:
Angle to fill (+ve=ccw, −ve=cw) <360>:
Rotate objects as they are copied? <Y>:
Command:

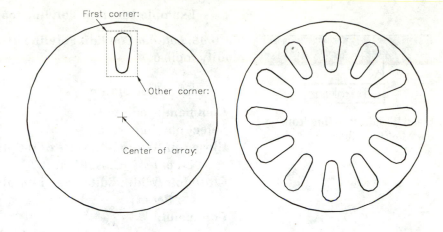

Fig. 6.35 Example 16 – using
Polar Array

Fig. 6.36 The **Align** tool icon
from the **Modify** toolbar

Example 17 – Align tool

Fig. 6.36. *Left-click* on the **Align** tool icon in the **Rotate** flyout of the
Modify toolbar.

Command: _align
Select objects:
Select objects: *Return*
1st source point:
1st destination point:
2nd source point:
2nd destination point:
3rd source point: *Return*
<2d> or 3d transformation: *Return* (accept 2d)
Command:

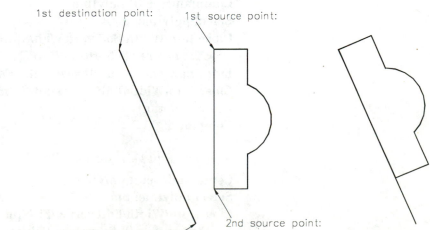

Fig. 6.37 Example 17 – using
Align

Fig. 6.38 **Edit Polyline** from
the **Modify** tollbar

Example 18 – Edit Polyline tool

Fig. 6.38. *Left-click* on **Edit Polyline** in the **Special Edit** flyout of the **Modify** toolbar.

The Close option

Command: _edit polyline
Select polyline: *pick*
**Close/Join/Width/Edit vertex/Fit/Spline/Decurve/Ltype gen/eXit/
    <X>:** *enter* c (Close) *Return*
**Close/Join/Width/Edit vertex/Fit/Spline/Decurve/Ltype gen/eXit/
    <X>:** *Return*
Command:

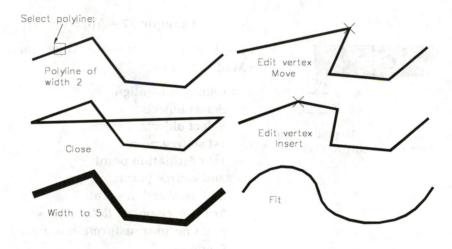

Fig. 6.39 Example 18 – using
Edit Polyline

The Width option

Command: _edit polyline
Select polyline: *pick*
**Close/Join/Width/Edit vertex/Fit/Spline/Decurve/Ltype gen/eXit/
    <X>:** *enter* w (Width) *Return*
Enter new width for all segments: *Enter* 5 *Return*
**Close/Join/Width/Edit vertex/Fit/Spline/Decurve/Ltype gen/eXit/
    <X>:** *Return*
Command:

The Edit vertex option

Command: _edit polyline
Select polyline: *pick*
**Close/Join/Width/Edit vertex/Fit/Spline/Decurve/Ltype gen/eXit/
    <X>:** *enter* e (Edit vertex) *Return*

**Next/Previous/Break/Insert/Move/Regen/Straighten/Tangent/Width/
eXit/<N>:** *enter* m (Move) *Return*
Enter new location: *pick*
**Next/Previous/Break/Insert/Move/Regen/Straighten/Tangent/Width/
eXit/<N>:** *enter* i (Insert) *Return*
Enter location of new vertex
**Next/Previous/Break/Insert/Move/Regen/Straighten/Tangent/Width/
eXit/<N>:** *enter* x (eXit) *Return*
**Close/Join/Width/Edit vertex/Fit/Spline/Decurve/Ltype gen/eXit/
<X>:** *Return*
Command:

The Fit option

Command: _edit polyline
Select polyline: *pick*
**Close/Join/Width/Edit vertex/Fit/Spline/Decurve/Ltype gen/eXit/
<X>:** *enter* f (Fit) *Return*
**Close/Join/Width/Edit vertex/Fit/Spline/Decurve/Ltype gen/eXit/
<X>:** *Return*
Command:

Note: A sufficient number of the options available with the **Edit Polyline** options have been given to encourage the reader to experiment with those not given above.

Notes on the Modify tools

1. Remember there is a choice between selecting tools from a toolbar and *entering* the tool name or its abbreviation at the Command Line. If an abbreviation for a **Modify** tool is in the **acad.pgp** file it may be quicker to *enter* that abbreviation rather than to *left-click* on a tool icon. The abbreviations in the **acad.pgp** file for **Modify** tools as found on the R13 disks as purchased are:

   CP, *COPY
   E, *ERASE
   M, *MOVE

2. A few of the least-used **Modify** tools have not been mentioned in this chapter. However, sufficient descriptions of the tools have been given to allow the reader to be able to understand the prompt sequences of any **Modify** tools not mentioned. Some which have not been included here will be described in later chapters, where their use is appropriate to the contents of the chapter.

3. Many of the **Select Objects** tools have been shown in use in this chapter. All of them have an abbreviation which can be entered at the Command Line if wished. It imay be quicker and hence more efficient to *enter* the abbreviation rather than to select the **Select Objects** tool. The abbreviations are:

w   Select Window.
c   Select Crossing Window.
g   Select Group (not included in this chapter).
l   Select Last (not included in this chapter).
all Select All.
wp Select Window Polygon.
cp Select Crossing Polygon.
f   Select Fence.
a   Select Add.
r   Select Remove (not included in this chapter).
fi Select Filters (not included in this chapter).

Questions

1.   What is the purpose of the **Select Objects** tools?
2.   How can a floating toolbar in a single horizontal strip of icons be changed into one with several lines of icons?
3.   What is the purpose of the **Rotate** tool?
4.   How can objects be copied many times over without having to select the **Copy** tool icon for each copy?
5.   When selecting a group of objects for moving how can **Select Fence** be of value?
6.   What are the differences between the two tools **Rectangular** and **Polar Array**?
7.   What happens to an arc when it is stretched along its length by the **Stretch** tool?
8.   How can symbols be moved within a drawings, without having to redraw the drawing?
9.   What is the purpose of the **Trim** tool?
10   What are the differences between the **Trim** and the **Extend** tools?

Exercises

1. Seven stages in constructing the Polar Array for this exercise are given in Fig 6.40. Construct the array.
2. Six stages in constructing the Rectangular Array for this exercise are given in Fig. 6.41. Construct the array.

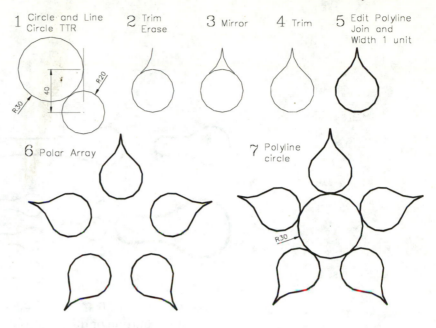

Fig. 6.40 Exercise 1

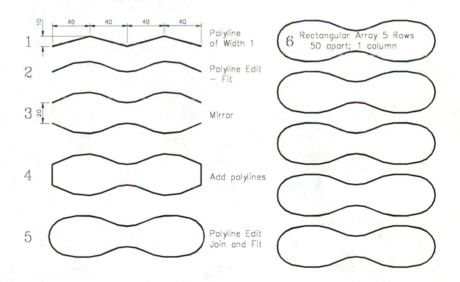

Fig. 6.41 Exercise 2

3. Ten stages of constructions are given in Fig. 6.42. Starting from Stage 1 work through all ten stages. You will have to copy some of the results when working some of the stages.

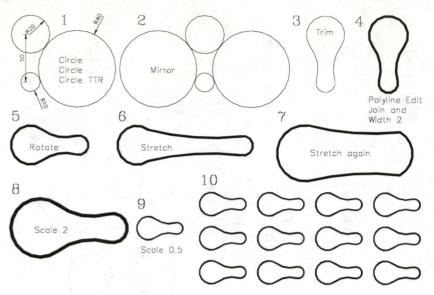

Fig. 6.42 Exercise 3

4. Figures 6.43 and 6.44. Fig. 6.43 shows the constructions upon which the outline of the pivot link of Fig. 6.44 is based. Fig. 6.44 includes a list of the tools used to complete the outlines of the link. Construct the outline of the link to the details given.

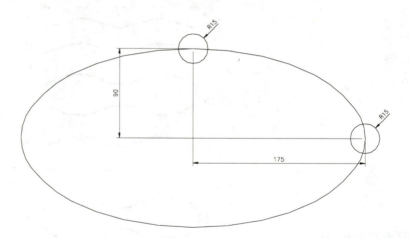

Fig. 6.43 Basic construction for Exercise 4

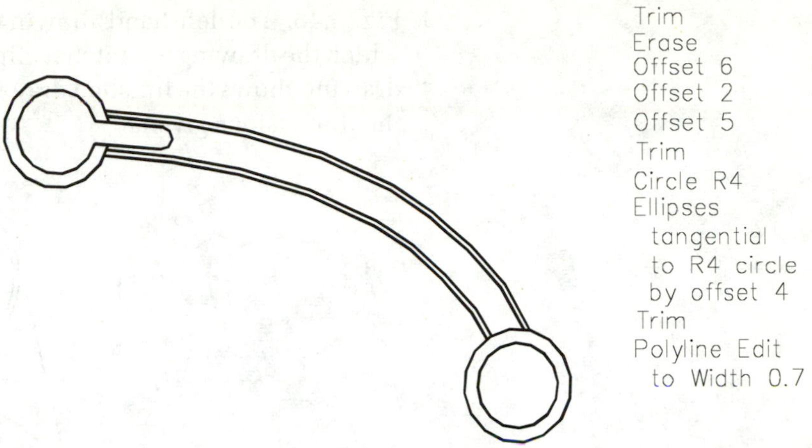

Trim
Erase
Offset 6
Offset 2
Offset 5
Trim
Circle R4
Ellipses
 tangential
 to R4 circle
 by offset 4
Trim
Polyline Edit
 to Width 0.7

Fig. 6.44 Exercise 4

5. The left-hand drawing of Fig. 6.45 shows the construction on which the outline of a clip (the right-hand drawing) is based. The **Modify** tools used to complete the outline are included with Fig. 6.46. Construct the clip to the sizes and modifying methods shown.

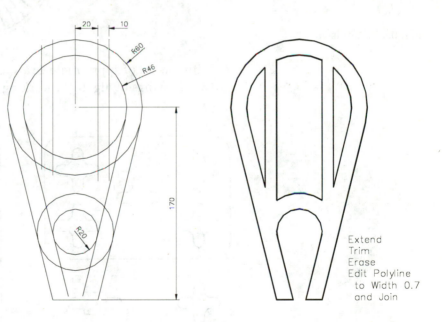

Fig. 6.45 Exercise 5

Extend
Trim
Erase
Edit Polyline
 to Width 0.7
 and Join

6. Fig. 6.46. The left-hand drawing shows the constructions upon which the drawing of a ratchet clip has been drawn. The right-hand drawing shows the finished drawing. Copy the finished drawing to the dimensions given.

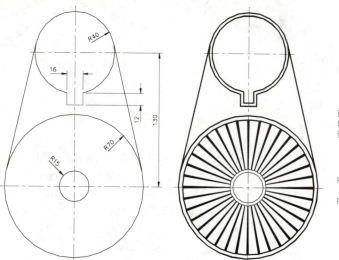

Break
Offset 3
Edit Polyline
    Width 0.7
    Join

Polyline
    Width 2 to 0.5
Polar Array
    36 times

Fig. 6.46 Exercise 6

7. With the aid of appropriate **Draw** and **Modify** tools, construct the two drawings of Fig. 6.47, working to the given dimensions.

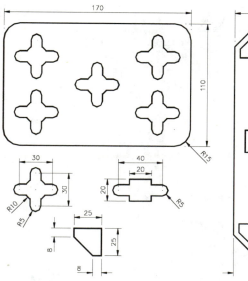

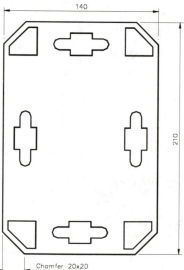

Fig. 6.47 Exercise 7

8. Using the tools **Polygon**, **Copy (Multiple)**, **Edit Polyline** and **Offset** copy the drawing given in Fig. 6.48.

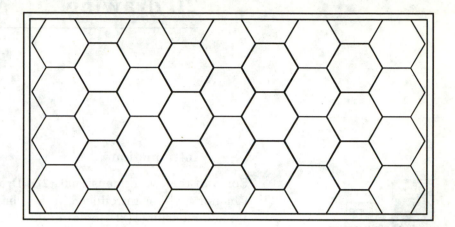

Fig. 6.48 Exercise 8

CHAPTER 7

2D drawing

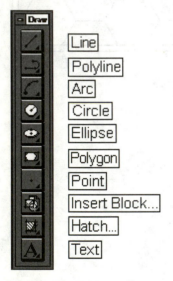

Fig. 7.1 The **Draw** toolbar

Fig. 7.2 The names of the 2D tools found on the flyouts from the tools in the **Draw** toolbar

Introduction

Some of the two-dimensional (2D) **Draw** tools not referred to in Chapter 4 will be introduced in this chapter. There are a number of three-dimensional (3D) tools included in the **Draw** toolbar, but these will be referred to later in the chapters concerned with 3D drawings. Fig. 7.1 shows the names of the flyouts in the **Draw** toolbar. The toolbar shown here is a **floating** one. Personally I prefer the **Draw** toolbar to be permanently in the left-hand column of the R13 graphics window, where its title is not included. Note that there are two dialogue boxes which can be called from the **Draw** toolbar – shown by the three full stops after the tool name – **Hatch...** and **Insert Block...**. Fig. 7.2 shows the names of the 2D tools on the fly-outs of the toolbar.

Line	Construction Line	Ray
Polyline	Multiline	Spline

3P	SCE	SCA	SCL	SEA	SED	SER	CSE	CSA	CSL	Continue

Center	Radius	TTR

Ellipse Center	Ellipse Axis End	Ellipse Arc

Rectangle	Polygon	2D Solid

Point	Divide	Measure

Insert	Insert Block...	Block

Hatch...	Postscript Fill

Text	DText	Single-line Text

3P	3 Point
S	Start
C	Center
E	End
A	Angle
L	Length
D	Direction
R	Radius

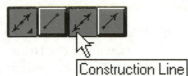

Construction Line

Fig. 7.3 The **Construction Line**
tool icon from the **Draw**
toolbar

Basic drawing tools

The Construction Line tool

To initiate the **Construction Line** prompts, *left-click* on the **Construction Line** tool icon in the **Line** flyout of the **Draw** toolbar (Fig. 7.3), or *enter* **xline** at the Command Line. Construction Lines:

1. Are best placed on the **Construction** layer.
2. Are intended to form construction frameworks of lines upon which drawings can be based.
3. Are lines of infinite length which ignore the **Limits** of the graphics screen, extending in any direction beyond the Limits to infinity in any direction.
4. Can be drawn at any angle.
5. Can be acted upon by the **Modify** tools – such as **Erase**, **Move** etc.
6. Respond to positioning of objects drawn using other tools, with the aid of the **Object Snaps**.
7. Can be either 2D or 3D.

When the tool is called the Command Line shows:

> **Command: _xline**
> **Hor/Ver/Ang/Bisect/Offset/Perp/<From point>:** *enter* h (Hor) *Return*
> **Through point:** *pick* point or *enter* coordinates
> **Through point:** *pick* point or *enter* coordinates
> **Through point:** *Return*
> **Command:**

which draws two horizontal Construction Lines. In a similar manner vertical (**Ver**), lines at an angle (**Ang**), lines bisecting others already on screen (**Bisect**), lines perpendicular (**Perp**) to other lines can be

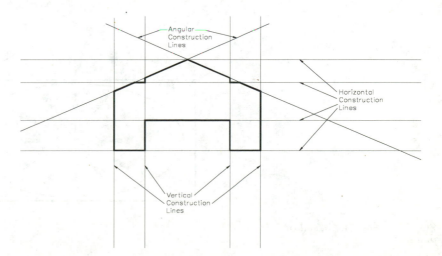

Fig. 7.4 A drawing based on
Construction Lines

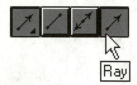

Fig. 7.5 The **Ray** tool icon
from the **Draw** toolbar

drawn. Construction Lines can also be offset with respect to each other with the **Offset** tool. Fig. 7.4 shows a polyline outline drawn with the aid of **Osnaps** in a Construction Line framework.

The Ray tool

Either *left-click* on the **Ray** tool icon in the **Line** flyout of the **Draw** toolbar (Fig. 7.5), or *enter* **ray** at the Command Line. Rays are similar to Construction Lines in that they are intended to be used as lines upon which drawings can be based, are of infinite length and can be drawn at any angle. They can however only be drawn at any angle from a selected point in the graphics window, radiating out from that point. Rays can be drawn in 2D or in 3D. When called the Command Line shows:

> **Command: _ray**
> **From point:** *pick* or *enter* coordinates
> **Through point:** *enter* 15 *Return*
> **Through point:** *enter* 45 *Return*
> **Through point:** *enter* 60 *Return*
> **Through point:** *enter* 75 *Return*
> **Through point:** *enter* 90 *Return*
> **Through point:** *Return*
> **Command:**

This sequence shows some of the **Rays** on which the outline of Fig. 7.6 was based.

The Multiline tool

Left-click on the **Multiline** tool icon in the **Polyline** flyout of the **Draw** toolbar (Fig. 7.7), or *enter* **mline** at the Command Line.

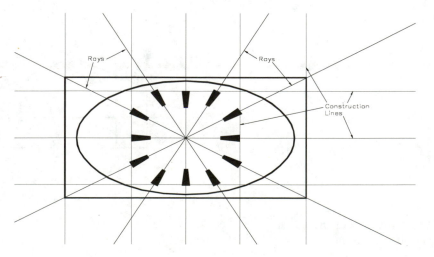

Fig. 7.6 A drawing based on Rays

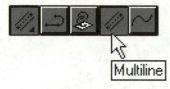

Fig. 7.7 The **Multiline** tool
icon from the **Draw** toolbar

Examples of the use of the tool are shown in Fig. 7.8. The sequence
of prompts and responses for Drawing 1 of Fig. 7.8 were:

Command _mline
Justification = Top, Scale = 5, Style = STANDARD
Justification/Scale/STyle/<From point>: *enter* j (Justification)
  Return
Top/Zero/Bottom <Top>: *enter* z (Zero) *Return*
Justification/Scale/STyle/<From point>: *enter* s (Scale) *Return*
Set multiline scale <5>: *enter* 10 *Return*
Justification/Scale/STyle/<From point>: *enter* st (STyle) *Return*
Multiline style name (or ?): *enter* centre *Return*
Justification/Scale/STyle/<From point>: *pick* (or *enter* coordinates)
Undo/<To point>: *pick* or *enter* coordinates
Close/Undo/<To point>: *pick* or *enter* coordinates
Close/Undo/<To point>: *pick* or *enter* coordinates
Close/Undo/<To point>: *enter* c (Close) *Return*
Command:

Entering a **?** in response to the **Multiline Style (or ?):** prompt brings
up a list of loaded line types.

Fig. 7.8 Examples of
Multilines

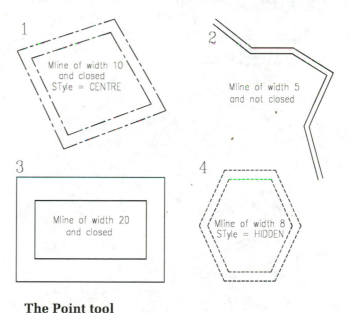

The Point tool

Before selecting the **Point** tool set the **Point** style as follows:

Command: *enter* pdmode *Return*
New value for PDMODE <0>: *enter* 66 *Return*
Command:

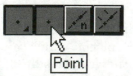

Fig. 7.9 The **Point** tool icon
from the **Draw** toolbar

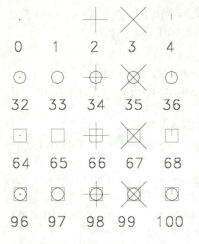

0	1	2	3	4
32	33	34	35	36
64	65	66	67	68
96	97	98	99	100

PDMODE points

Fig. 7.10 The Point shapes as set by PDMODE

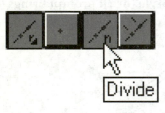

Fig. 7.11 The **Divide** tool icon from the **Draw** toolbar

Fig. 7.12 Examples of the use of the tool **Divide**

Points are then entered as follows:

> **Command:** _point
> **Point:** *pick* or *enter* coordinates
> **Command:**

Fig. 7.10 shows the points reflecting the **pdmodes**.

The Divide tool

This tool (Fig. 7.11) can be associated with the **Point** tool. The tool is used to divide entities into a number of equal parts, each division marked by a Point. It is the **Point** set with **PDMODE** that appears at the dividing points, as shown in Fig. 7.12. The prompts for the tool are:

> **Command:** _divide
> **Select object to divide:** *pick*
> **<Number of segments>/Block:** *enter* 7 *Return*
> **Command:**

Note the prompt **Block**. If a block is within the drawing, it can be used in place of the current **Point**. Blocks will be described in Chapter 12. Fig. 7.14 – showing the use of **Measure** including the use of blocks.

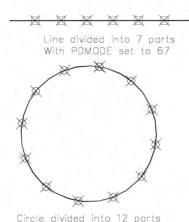

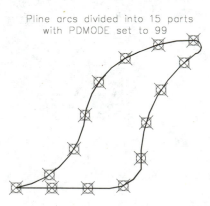

Line divided into 7 parts With PDMODE set to 67

Pline arcs divided into 15 parts with PDMODE set to 99

Circle divided into 12 parts with PDMODE set to 35

The Measure tool

Left-click on the **Measure** tool icon in the **Point** flyout of the **Draw** toolbar. This tool places points at distances along objects which can either be picked or stated as a length. Fig. 7.14 shows the results of using the tool in a variety of circumstances, including the insertion of a block at the measured positions rather than **Points**. The prompts at the Command Line for the tool are:

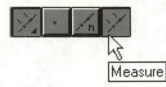

Fig. 7.13 The **Measure** tool from the **Draw** toolbar

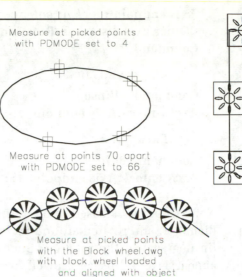

Measure at picked points with PDMODE set to 4

Measure at points 70 apart with PDMODE set to 66

Measure at picked points with the Block wheel.dwg with block wheel loaded and aligned with object

The Block wheel.dwg

Fig. 7.14 Using the **Measure** tool

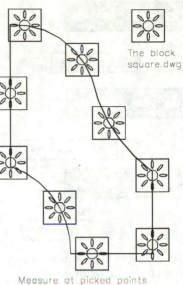

The block square.dwg

Measure at picked points with the block square loaded and not aligned with object

> **Command: _measure**
> **Select objects to measure:** *pick*
> **<Segment length>/Block:** pick or *enter* a length
> **Command:**

For using a block, which must have been already loaded by insertion into the current drawing (Chapter 12):

> **Command: _measure**
> **Select objects to measure:** *pick*
> **<Segment length>/Block:** *enter* b (Block) *Return*
> **Block name to insert:** *enter* wheel *Return*
> **Align block with object <Y>:** *Return*
> **Command:**

The Ellipse tool

Left-click on any one of the **Ellipse** tool icons in the **Ellipse** flyout of the **Draw** toolbar. Fig. 7.16 shows examples of ellipses constructed with each of the tools. The prompts and required responses for the **Ellipse** tool are similar:

Ellipse Center

> **Command: ellipse**
> **Arc/Center/<Axis endpoint 1>:** _c
> **Center of ellipse:** *pick* or *enter* coordinates

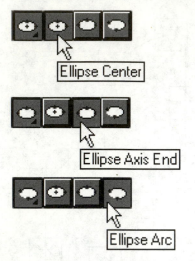

Fig. 7.15 The three **Ellipse** tool icons from the **Draw** toolbar

Axis endpoint: *pick* or *enter* coordinates
<Other axis distance>/Rotation: *pick* or *enter* coordinates
Command:

Ellipse Axis End

Command: ellipse
Arc/Center/<Axis endpoint 1>:

Ellipse Axis Arc

Command: ellipse
Arc/Center/<Axis endpoint 1>: _a

Note: Rotation is based upon a front view of a circle of major axis diameter, and rotated around its horizontal diameter by the figure (in degrees) of the rotation. Such a rotation causes the circle to appear as an ellipse as viewed from the front.

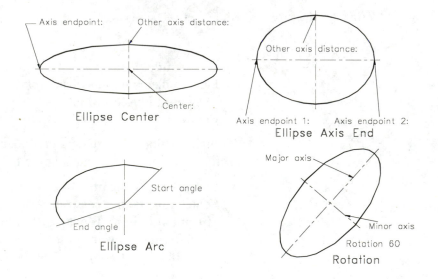

Fig. 7.16 Examples of the use of the tool **Ellipse**

The Rectangle tool

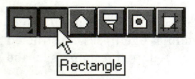

Fig. 7.17 The **Rectangle** tool icon from the **Draw** toolbar

Left-click on the **Rectangle** tool in the **Polygon** flyout of the **Draw** toolbar (Fig. 7.17), or *enter* **rectang** at the Command Line. Fig. 7.18 shows some examples of rectangles constructed with the aid of the tool. The line thickness of the outline of rectangles drawn with the tool are the same as the current **Polyline** width as set when previous polylines have been drawn. If the line width of a **Rectangle** is to be other than that of the current polyline width, then the polyline width must be reset.

Command: _rectang
First corner: *pick* or *enter* coordinates *Return*
Other corner: *pick* or *enter* coordinates *Return*
Command:

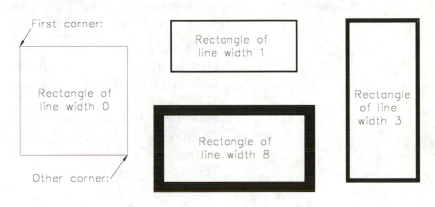

Fig. 7.18 Examples of
rectangles drawn with the tool
Rectangle

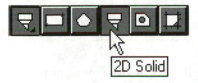

Fig. 7.19 The **2D Solid** tool
icon from the **Draw** toolbar

The 2D Solid tool

Left-click on the **2D Solid** tool icon in the **Polygon** flyout of the **Draw**
toolbar (Fig. 7.19). Fig. 7.20 shows some examples of filled shapes
resulting from the use of the tool. The tool is for constructing 2D
areas which are **filled**. It must be noted that the filling occurs in
triangular areas, so careful choice of the **Third point:** and **Fourth
point:** are necessary to obtain a desired filled outline. Some experi-

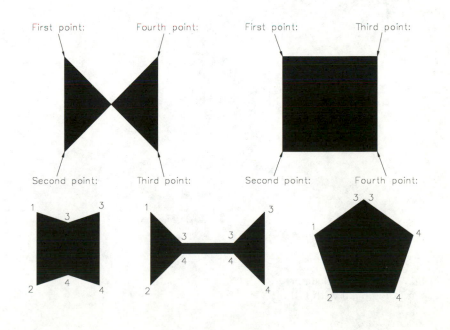

Fig. 7.20 Examples of the use
of the **2D Solid** tool

menting with the tool is advised in order to determine the positioning of the last two points of each set of prompts. The numbers at the corners of the outlines of Fig. 7.20 show the order of *picking* points to obtain the shapes. When a suitable filled shape has been obtained, pressing **Return** concludes the series of prompts. The Command Line sequence of prompts show:

> **Command: _solid**
> **First point:** *pick* or *enter* coordinates *Return*
> **Second point:** *pick* or *enter* coordinates *Return*
> **Third point:** *pick* or *enter* coordinates *Return*
> **Fourth point:** *pick* or *enter* coordinates *Return*
> **Third point:** *pick* or *enter* coordinates *Return*
> **Fourth point:** *pick* or *enter* coordinates *Return*
> **Third point:** *Return*
> **Command:**

Note: The outlines of Fig. 7.20 are **filled** shapes. To change them to outlines only, turn **Fill** off as follows::

> **Command:**
> **ON/OFF<On>:** *enter* off *Return*
> **Command:** *enter* regen *Return*
> **Command:**

The screen regenerates and the filled outlines become empty as shown in Fig. 7.21. The outlines remain filled until the screen is regenerated.

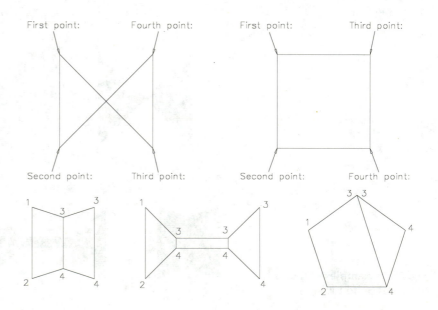

Fig. 7.21 The Filled shapes seen in Fig. 7.20 with **Fill** off

Basic handling tools

Zoom

The **Zoom** tools allow drawing details in the R13 graphics window to be enlarged or reduced in size. Enlarging the detail allows the smallest area of the graphics window to be examined for errors, for modification and for constructing small details. **Zoom** also allows the constructing of the smallest details in very large drawings by working in parts of the drawing limits.

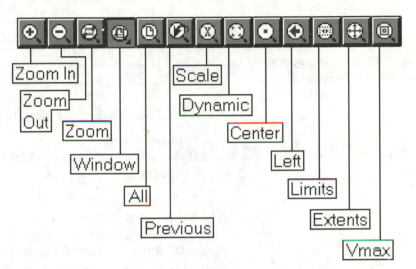

Fig. 7.22 The **Zoom** flyout from the **Standard Toobar**

The icons for **Zoom** are named in Fig. 7.22. In addition to the icons for the **Zoom** prompts, there are two other **Zoom** icons – **Zoom In** and **Zoom Out**. The actions of the prompts of **Zoom** are:

Window: Any part of the graphics window can be placed in a **Zoom** window. Those parts of the drawing within the zoom window will occupy the whole graphics window.

All: The drawing in the graphics window zooms to the limits set by the **Limits** command.

Previous: The drawing reverts to the last zoom.

Scale: The drawing can be scaled up or down (larger or smaller).

Dynamic: A box appears around the whole drawing. This box can be *dynamically* moved or scaled to the required zoom.

Center: The drawing is centred within the graphics window.

Left: The drawing can be zoom to the left-hand window margin

Limits: The drawing zooms to the screen limits.

Extents: The drawing enlarges (or reduces) in size so that its features press right up against the edges of the R13 graphics window.

Vmax: Zooms out as far as possible.

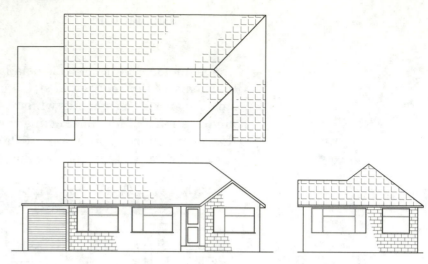

Fig. 7.23 An orthographic projection of a bungalow

When the **Zoom** tool icon is selected the Command Line shows:

> **Command: _zoom**
> **All/Center/Dynamic/Extents/Left/Previous/Vmax/Window/<Scale (X/XP)>:**

Fig. 7.23 shows an orthographic projection of a small bungalow, which has been drawn in AutoCAD R13. The three illustrations Figures 7.24, 7.25 and 7.26 show the R13 graphics window after a **Zoom Window**, a **Zoom Extents** and a **Zoom Scale 0.5**. Another feature is the **Aerial Window**, which appears with a *left-click* on **Aerial View** in the **View** pull-down menu (Fig. 7.27). When the

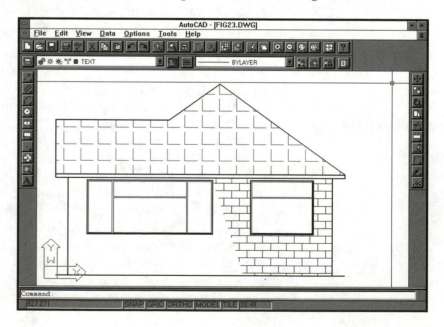

Fig. 7.24 A **Zoom** Window

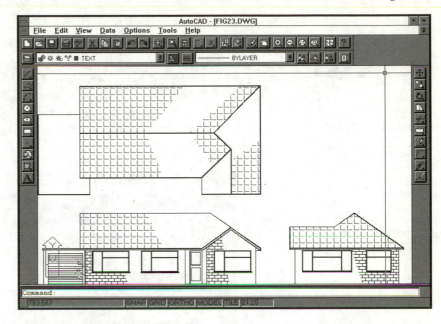

Fig. 7.25 Result of a **Zoom Extents** command

Aerial View window is called to the graphics window, zooms are shown within its area with thick black outlines as can be seen in Fig. 7.28.

The **Aerial View** is of value when working in very large drawings, because the **Aerial View** shows the whole of a drawing, whereas the operator may be working in a small part of the drawing in the graphics window itself shown within the black rectangle in **Aerial View**.

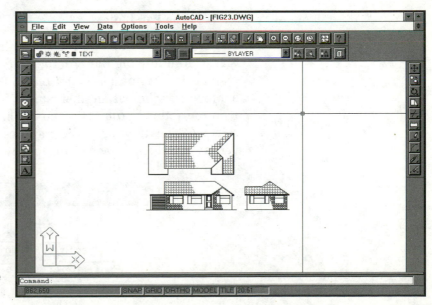

Fig. 7.26 Result of a **Zoom Scale 0.5** command

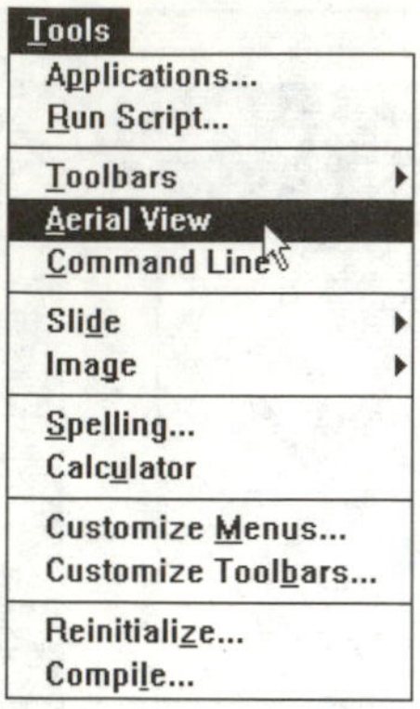

Tools
Applications...
Run Script...

Toolbars   ▶
Aerial View
Command Line

Slide   ▶
Image   ▶

Spelling...
Calculator

Customize Menus...
Customize Toolbars...

Reinitialize...
Compile...

Fig. 7.27 **Aerial View** selected from the **View** pull-down menu

Fig. 7.28 The **Aerial Window** showing the area zoomed in a window

Notes

1. You will find that you will need to use the **Zoom** tool frequently, particularly when constructing or modifying large, intricate drawings or small details in a drawing.
2. The two **Zoom** tools **Window** and **Previous** will be those most frequently used. It is often quicker to *enter* **w** (for Window) or *enter* **p** (for Previous) rather than selecting the tool icons.

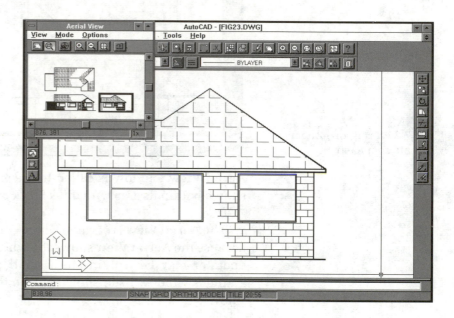

The Pan tools

Left-click on the **Pan Point** tool icon in the **Standard Toolbar** (Fig. 7.29) and following the prompts appearing at the Command Line pan the drawing by a *left-click* on a point in the screen, followed by another *left-click* at another point. Fig. 7.30 shows the result of panning and the prompts at the Command Line when **Pan Point** is selected. The drawing in the graphics window can be panned in a variety of directions, according to which of the **Pan** tools is selected.

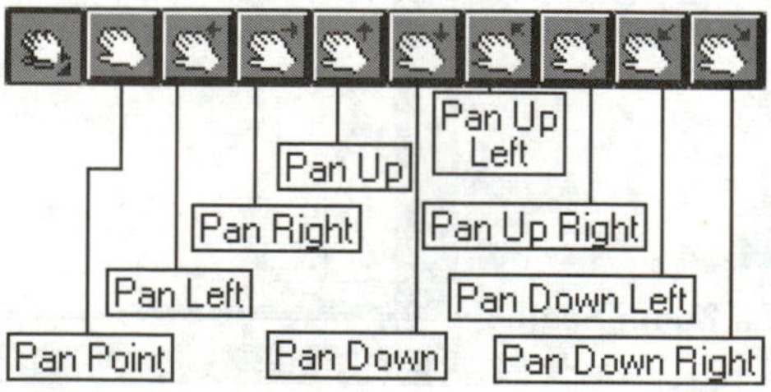

Fig. 7.29 The flyout of the **Pan** tool in the **Standard Toolbar**

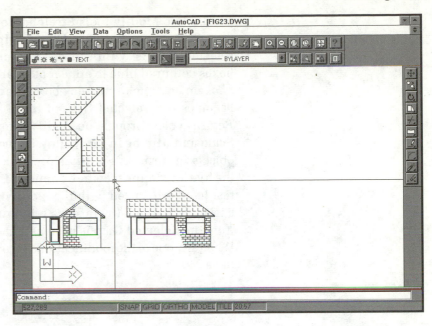

Fig. 7.30 A result of using the **Pan Point** tool

Grips

Left-click on **Grips...** in the **Options** pull-down menu (Fig. 7.31). The **Grips** dialogue box appears (Fig. 7.32). Make sure that the **Enable Grips** box is checked (cross in its area) and set the **Grip Size** as desired. Note that **Unselected Grips** are blue and **Selected** are red. These two colours can be changed if wished.

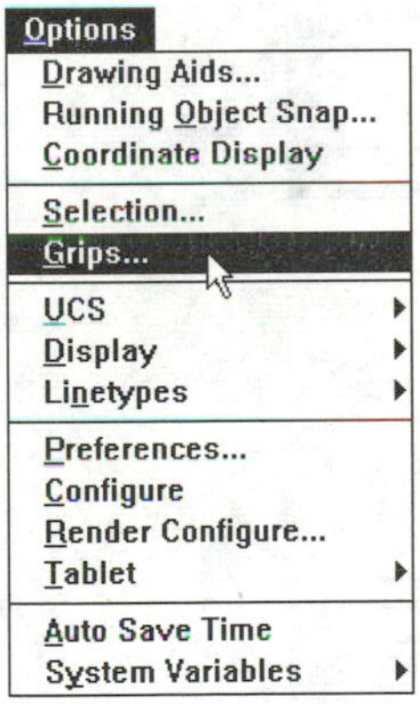

Fig. 7.31 Selecting **Grips...** from the **Options** pull-down menu

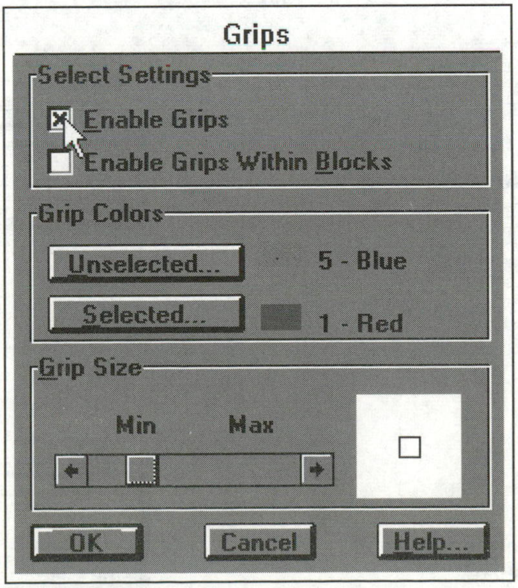

Fig. 7.32 The **Grips** dialogue box

The five **Modify** tools **Stretch**, **Move**, **Rotate**, **Scale** and **Mirror** are associated with **Grips**. When **Grips** are enabled, a *left-click* on selected objects within the R13 graphics window cause grip pick boxes coloured blue to appear at intersections of the objects. A *left-click* on any one of the pick boxes and it changes colour to red and becomes the **Selected Grip** of those at the intersections. Pressing *Return* cycles through the **Modify** commands **Stretch**, **Move**, **Rotate**, **Scale** and **Mirror** in turn, allowing each of the tools to modify the objects in turn. As *Return* is pressed, the prompts associated with the five tools appear at the Command Line. Figs 7.33 to 7.37 show the results of grips used with the modifying of an object in the form of a triangle in the R13 graphics window. In each case a *rubber band* from the **Selected Grip** is used as a base point for the modification. When any one of the modifications is completed, a *left-click* completes the action.

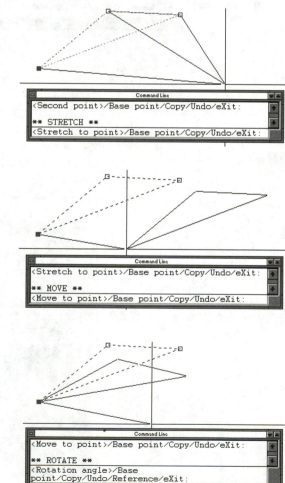

Fig. 7.33 The **Stretch** feature of the **Grid** modify sequence

Fig. 7.34 The **Move** feature of the **Grips** sequence

Fig. 7.35 The **Rotate** feature of the **Grips** sequence

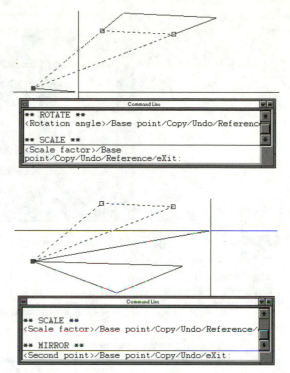

Fig. 7.36 The **Scale** feature of the **Grips** sequence

Fig. 7.37 The **Mirror** feature of the **Grips** sequence

The Redraw and Regen tools

A *left-click* on **Redraw** or **Redraw All** in the **View** pull-down menu (Fig. 7.38) clears unwanted details from the screen, such as blips (if in use), marks due to erasing and moving etc. *Entering* **r** (for Redraw) is probably a quicker method of redrawing the screen. *Entering* **regen** at the Command Line regenerates the screen completely. A longer time is required for regeneration than for redrawing. Regenerating is sometimes necessary after zooming to small areas of the screen in order that objects such as circles and arcs are clearly portrayed.

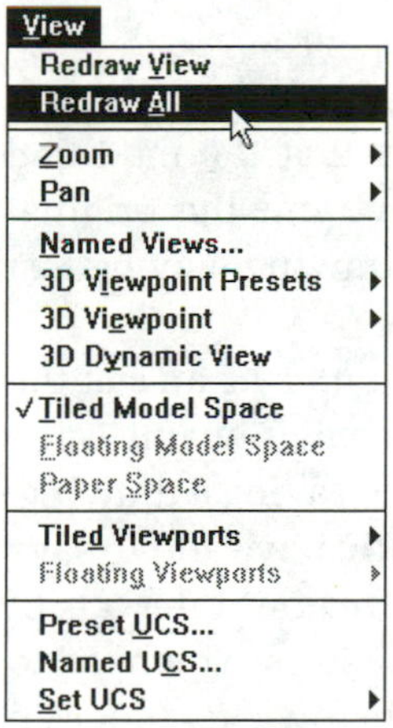

Saving your work

There are several methods of saving your work.

1. Personally I prefer calling up the **Save Drawing As** dialogue box (Fig. 7.39) with a *left-click* on **Save As...** in the **File** pull-down menu. Then either accept the file name showing in the **File Name** box, by a *left-click* on the **OK** button, or *entering* a new filename, followed by a *left-click* on the **OK** button.
2. *Left-click on* **Save** in the **File** pull-down menu, saves the drawing to its existing filename.

Fig. 7.38 Selecting **Redraw All** in the **View** pull-down menu

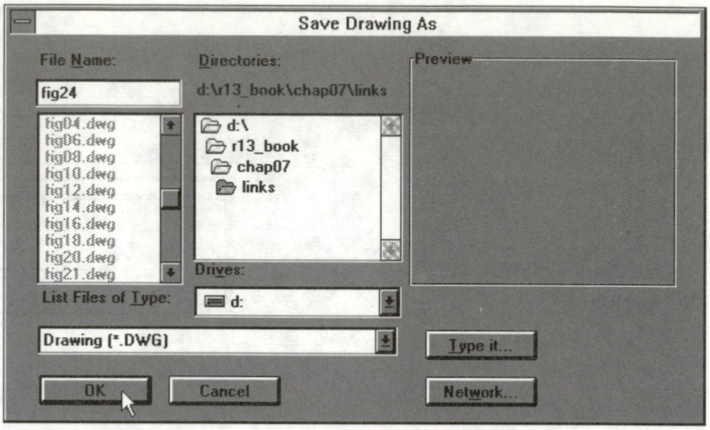

Fig. 7.39 The **Save Drawing As** dialogue box

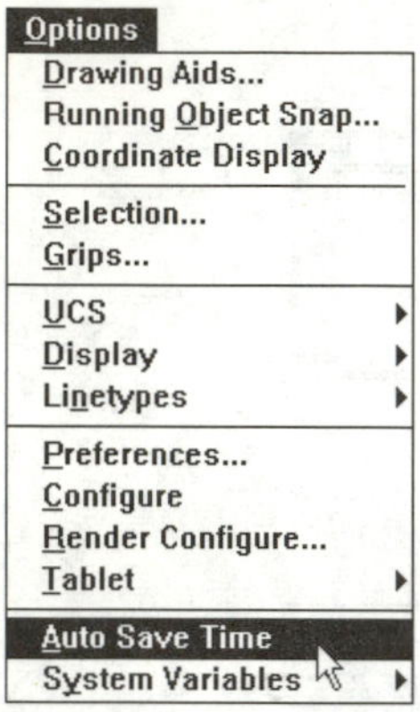

Fig. 7.40 Selecting **Automatic Save** in the **Options** pull-down menu

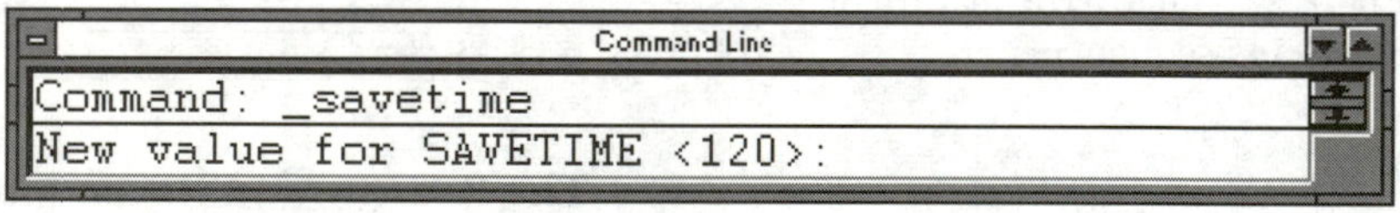

Fig. 7.41 The Command Line showing the prompt when **Automatic Save** is selected

3. *Entering* **s** (for Save) at the Command Line has the same result.
4. Set the **Automatic Save** time (Fig. 7.40) by *entering* a figure representing a length of time at the Command Line in response to the **Automatic Save** prompt **New value for SAVETIME <120>:** (Fig. 7.41). A suggested **Automatic Save** time would be 15 minutes.

Notes

1. There are dangers in setting **Automatic Save**. If the operator is modifying an existing drawing with the idea that the modified drawing is to be saved with a new filename, and the original drawing's filename unchanged, the original drawing may be lost with automatic save in operation.
2. The same problem exists when using **Save** or *entering* an **s** at the Command Line, although if certain that the current filename is the one you wish to use, this is a quicker method of saving a drawing.
3. My own method of saving is to ignore **Automatic Save** and to save through the **Save Drawing As** dialogue box at regular intervals of about 15 minutes, but this may not suit all operators. You need to find the method of saving best suited to your own methods of working in AutoCAD.

Questions

1. What is a **Construction Line**?
2. What is a **Ray**?
3. What is the purpose of **Construction Lines** and **Rays**?

4. How many types of **Point** are there?
5. What differences result from using the **Divide** tool compared with using the **Measure** on an object?
6. What is the **major axis** of an ellipse?
7. What decides the width of the lines forming the shapes produced by using the tool **Rectangle**?
8. What is the effect of calling **Dynamic Zoom**?
9. What is the purpose of the **Pan** tool?
10. What is meant by a **Selected Grip**?

Exercises

1. Construct the outlines given in Fig. 7.42 using the appropriate tools.

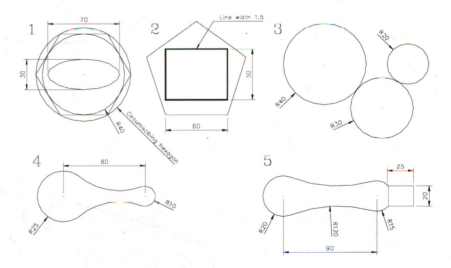

Fig. 7.42 Exercise 1

2. Construct the drawing given in Fig. 7.43. You will need to use the tools: **Circle** (including the **TTR** prompt), **Ellipse**, **Trim**, **Polar Array**, and **Polyline Edit**.
    Do not attempt including the dimensions.
3. Construct the drawing of a Plate given in Fig. 7.44. Use the tools: **Circle** (including **TTR**), **Polyline** (Width 1), **Fillet** (set to 20), and **Polyline Edit**.
4. Construct the drawing given in Fig. 7.45. You will need to use the tools: **Circle**, **Pline** (of Width 1) using the **Tangent Osnap**, **Mirror**, **Trim**, **Fillet** (Radius 20) and **Polyline Edit**.
5. Construct the drawing of a bolt shown in drawing 4 of Fig. 7.46. Fig. 7.46 shows the stages involved in completing the drawing of a bolt.

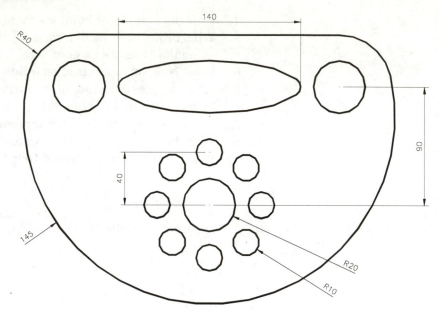

Fig. 7.43 Exercise 2

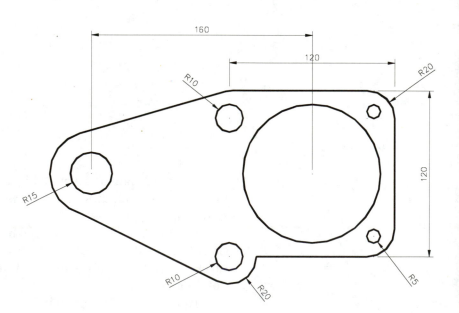

Fig. 7.44 Exercise 3

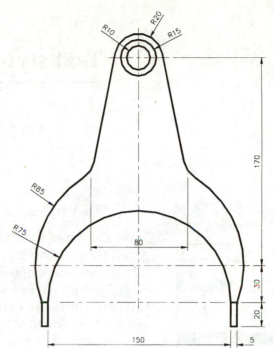

Fig. 7.45 Exercise 4

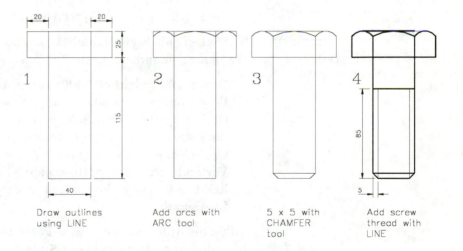

1	2	3	4
Draw outlines using LINE	Add arcs with ARC tool	5 x 5 with CHAMFER tool	Add screw thread with LINE

Fig. 7.46 Exercise 5

CHAPTER 8

Text styles and types of drawing

Text styles

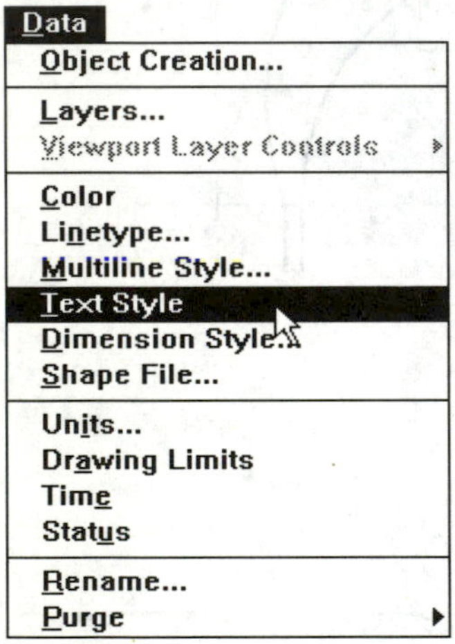

There is a large number of different fonts which can be used in AutoCAD R13 drawings. These include the native AutoCAD fonts (in files with the extension ***.shx**), Postscript fonts (in files with an extension ***.pfb**), Windows TrueType fonts (in files with an extension ***.ttf**) and which are found in the Windows\Support directory. To add text to an AutoCAD drawing, the style of the text, determined by the font to be used, is set by either a *left-click* on the **Text Style...** in the **Data** pull-down menu (Fig. 8.1) or by *entering* **style** at the Command Line. To set the text to the font **Romand** at the Command Line:

> **Command:** *enter* style *Return*
> **Text style name (or ?) <STANDARD>:** *enter* romand *Return*

The **Select Font Style** dialogue box appears Fig. 8.2). *Double-click* on the name **romand.shx** in the list box.

> **New Style. Height <0.0000>:** *enter* 10 *Return*
> **Width factor <1.0000>:** *Return* (to accept 1.0000)
> **Obliquing angle <0>:** *Return* (to accept N)
> **Backwards? <N<:** *Return* (to accept N)
> **Upside-down? <N>:** *Return* (to accept N)
> **Vertical? <N>:** *Return* (to accept N)
> **ROMAND is now the current text style**
> **Command:**

Either the AutoCAD fonts or the Postscript fonts available in R13 can be called from the **Select Font Style** dialogue box, which comes up with the fonts in the **r13\common\fonts** directory showing in the list box. If a Windows TrueType font is required, the pop-up list under **List Files of Type** must be set to ***.ttf**. Only TrueType fonts will then show in the list box with the ending ***.tff**.

Fig. 8.1 Selecting **Text Style** from the **Data** pull-down menu

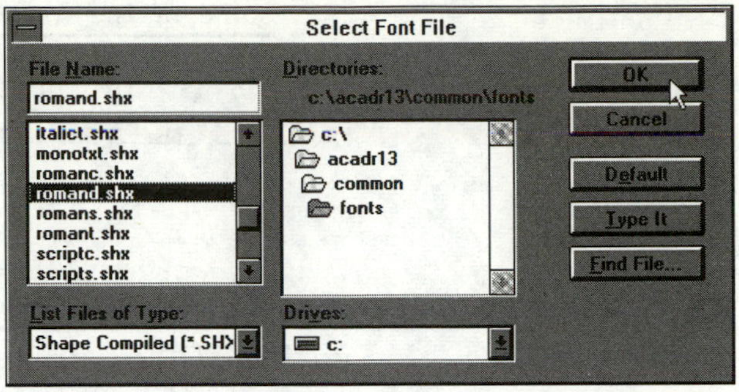
Select Font File
File Name:
romand.shx
italict.shx
monotxt.shx
romanc.shx
romand.shx
romans.shx
romant.shx
scriptc.shx
scripts.shx
Directories:
c:\acadr13\common\fonts
c:\
acadr13
common
fonts
List Files of Type:
Shape Compiled (*.SH>
Drives:
c:
OK
Cancel
Default
Type It
Find File...

Fig. 8.2 The **Select Font Style** dialogue box with **romand.shx** selected

When all the style parameters have been set for the chosen text font, the text can be added to the drawing. Some examples of the variety of text styles available are shown in Figures 8.3 to 8.5. These illustrations shows only a few of the Windows TrueType fonts, some of the available Postscript fonts and some of the AutoCAD fonts.

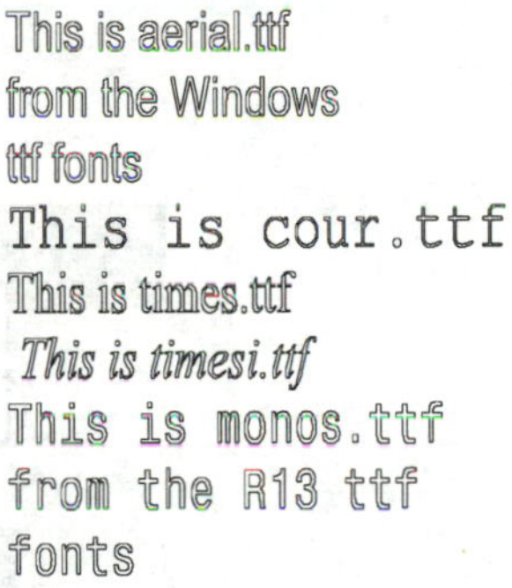
This is aerial.ttf
from the Windows
ttf fonts
This is cour.ttf
This is times.ttf
This is timesi.ttf
This is monos.ttf
from the R13 ttf
fonts

Fig. 8.3 Some Windows and AutoCAD TrueType fonts

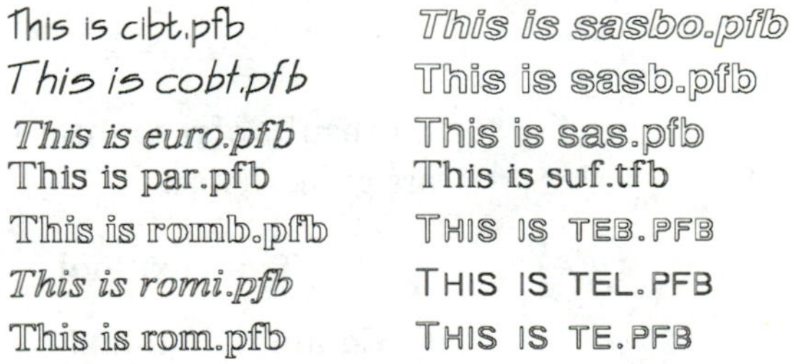
This is cibt.pfb
This is cobt.pfb
This is euro.pfb
This is par.pfb
This is romb.pfb
This is romi.pfb
This is rom.pfb
This is sasbo.pfb
This is sasb.pfb
This is sas.pfb
This is suf.tfb
THIS IS TEB.PFB
THIS IS TEL.PFB
THIS IS TE.PFB

Fig. 8.4 Some of the Postscript fonts

Adding text to a drawing

There are three **Text** tools, found on the **Text** flyout of the **Draw** toolbar (Fig. 8.6). These are the **Text** tool, the **Dtext** tool and the **Single-Line Text** tool. The prompts at the Command Line for the three tools are different and the reader is advised to experiment with

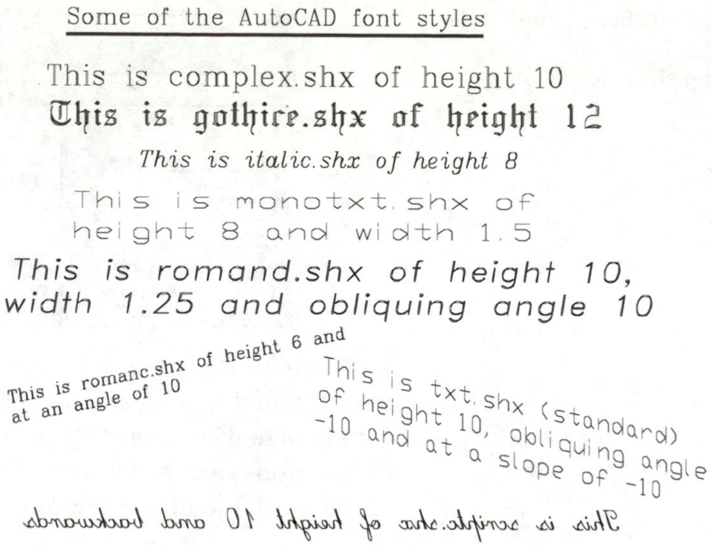

Some of the AutoCAD font styles

This is complex.shx of height 10

𝕿𝖍𝖎𝖘 𝖎𝖘 𝖌𝖔𝖙𝖍𝖎𝖈𝖊.𝖘𝖍𝖝 𝖔𝖋 𝖍𝖊𝖎𝖌𝖍𝖙 12

This is italic.shx of height 8

This is monotxt.shx of
height 8 and width 1.5

*This is romand.shx of height 10,
width 1.25 and obliquing angle 10*

This is romanc.shx of height 6 and
at an angle of 10

This is txt.shx (standard)
of height 10, obliquing angle
-10 and at a slope of -10

This is scriptc.shx of height 10 and backwards (mirrored)

Fig. 8.5 Some AutoCAD fonts
of different sizes, widths,
obliquing angles and rotation
angles

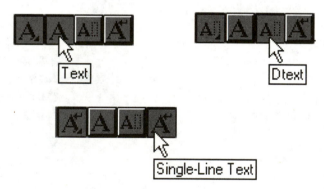

Fig. 8.6 The three **Text** tool
icons on the **Text** flyout of the
Draw toolbar

the results of responses to the variety of prompts, examples of which
are given below:

The Text tool

**Command:_mtext
Attach/Rotation/Style/Height/Direction/<Insertion point>:**

If an insertion point is selected on screen, a prompt asking for a
second point is requested. A text editor appears in the R13 graphics
window, into which text is keyed. When the **OK** button is selected,
the text appears within the box within the insertion point and the
second point.

The Dtext tool

Command_dtext
Justify/Style/<Start point>: *pick* required point on screen
Rotation angle <0>: *Return* (accept the angle of 0)
Text: *enter* required text

As each letter is typed, so it appears within a box on the screen. The D of Dtext means Dynamic – the text is dynamically appearing as it is keyed at the keyboard.

The Single-Line Text tool

Command_text
Justify/Style/<Start point>: *pick* required point on screen
Rotation angle <0>: *Return* (accept the angle of 0)
Text: *enter* required text

The text does not appear on screen until *Return*.

Spelling checker

If text is entered with the aid of the **Text** tool, when the box selected from the **Mtext** prompts appears, the **Edit MText** dialogue box appears, into which the text is entered (Fig. 8.8). When using the **Dtext** tool, the text appears on screen as it is being typed. To amend bad spelling *left-click* on the **Spelling...** tool icon in the **Standard Toolbar** (Fig. 8.7), followed by a *left-click* within the text. This brings up the **Check Spelling** dialogue box (Fig. 8.9) with the text entered in the drawing and showing. The spelling of words can be checked and changed by use of the buttons within the dialogue box from the suggestions which appear in the **Suggestions:** list box. A *left-click* on the word in the **Suggestions:** list which is considered to be a suitable spelling, followed by a *left-click* on the **Change** button, amends the word in the drawing and the next mis-spelt word in the text appears in the **Current word** box.

Note: Whichever style of font is set, it is that font which will appear no matter which of the three text tools are used, unless the **Style**

Fig. 8.7 The **Spelling...** tool icon in the **Standard** toolbar

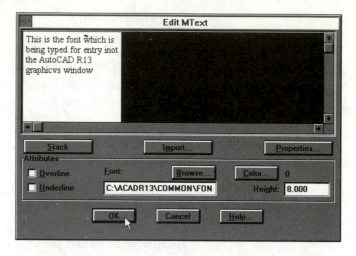

Fig. 8.8 The **Edit MText** dialogue box

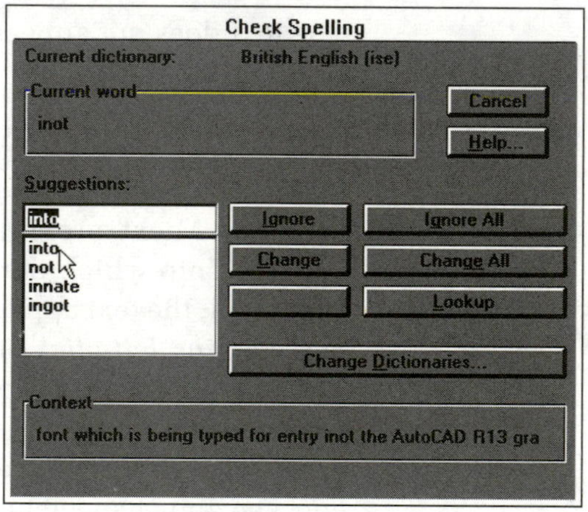

Fig. 8.9 The **Check Spelling** dialogue box

prompt of a text tool is called, when a new style can be set from that prompt. Each of the three text tool prompts allows this resetting of style.

Types of drawing

Four of the common forms of 2D technical drawings which can be constructed in R13 are introduced in this chapter. By far the most common of these is orthographic projection, which is used extensively in the engineering and building industries. The other three forms of drawing described in this chapter are pictorial – isometric, cabinet and planometric.

Orthographic projection

Orthographic projections are the most common form of technical drawings in the engineering and building industries. In general there are two forms of this type of projection – first angle projection and third angle projection. In the USA, third angle orthographic projection is that most commonly used, but elsewhere in the world, both angles of projection will be found in about equal proportions.

The theory behind this form of projection is based upon two imaginary planes, crossing at right angles, one horizontal and the other vertical. Planes crossing at right angles are said to be orthogonal to each other, hence the term orthographic. The two planes form four angles – first, second, third and fourth, but it is only the first and third angles which are pertinent to orthographic projection. The left-hand drawing of Fig. 8.10 is a pictorial view of the two planes and the right-hand drawing shows an edge view of the planes, together with arrows showing the directions from which objects placed within the planes are viewed for the purposes of this form of projection.

Fig. 8.11 shows the general principles of obtaining a first angle projection of a simple bracket. The object is placed within the first angle of the H.P. and V.P. and is then viewed from the front and from above. What is seen from the directions of viewing is cast on to the planes, a Front view on to the V.P. and a Plan on to the H.P. A second V.P. is introduced on to which an end view is drawn. The three planes are rotated so that they all lie in the same plane – that of the drawing sheet, or in the case of a computer that of the screen of the monitor. Fig. 8.12 shows the resulting three views on the rotated planes (left-hand drawing) and the resulting projection when the imaginary planes are withdrawn (right-hand drawing).

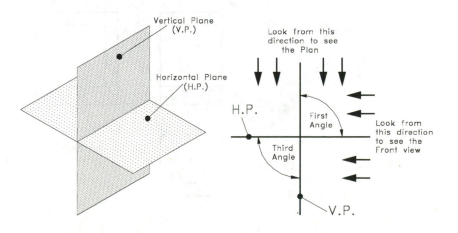

Fig. 8.10 The H.P. and V.P. on which orthographic projection is based

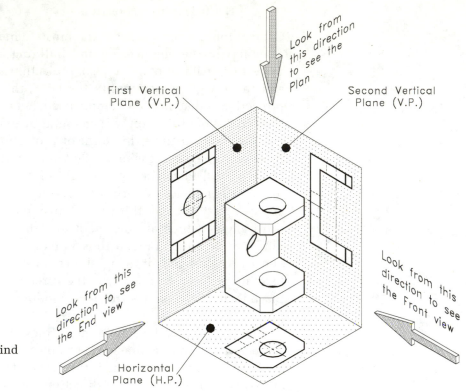

Fig. 8.11 The theory behind
first angle orthographic
projection

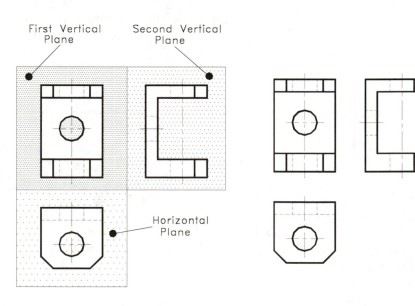

Fig. 8.12 The first angle
projection when the planes
have been rotated and then
removed

Third angle orthographic projection

Fig. 8.13 shows the general principles governing Third Angle projection. The object is placed within the third angle of the H.P. and V.P. and viewed from the front and from above. What is seen is cast upon the planes. A second V.P. allows an end view to be added. The three planes are then rotated so as to lie all in the same plane (Fig. 8.14 left-hand drawing) and the imaginary planes then withdrawn (right-hand drawing of Fig. 8.14).

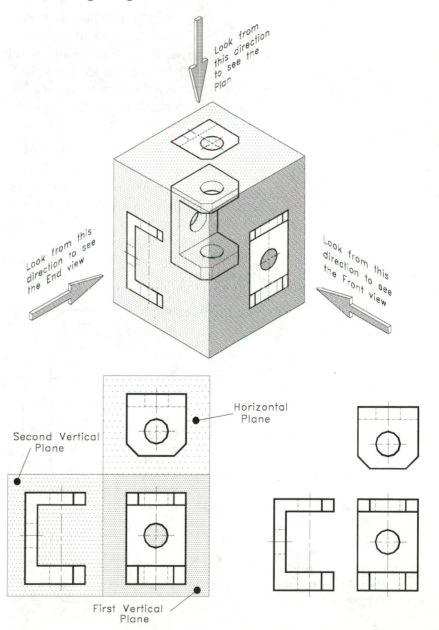

Fig. 8.13 The theory behind third angle orthographic projection

Fig. 8.14 The third angle projection when the planes have been rotated and then removed

First and third angles compared

Note the following differences between first and third angle projections:

1. In first angle, the plan is below the front view.
2. In third angle, the plan is above the front view.
3. In first angle the plan and the end view face outwards from the front view.
4. In third angle, the plan and end view face inwards towards the front view.
5. There is no limit to the number of views of a single object that can be drawn. Theoretically there is a maximum of six, but by the insertion of further V.Ps and/or H.Ps, many more than 6 views can be obtained. Fig. 8.15 shows the theoretical 6 views.
6. Views are not usually named. Their positions in relation to each other makes naming unnecessary. This rule does not apply to views which are sections (see Chapter 9).

Number of views required

When constructing an orthographic projection, the aim should be to fully and completely describe the object being drawn in as few views as possible without detracting from the fact that it is important to maintain accuracy and to ensure that a full understanding of the meaning of the drawing is not sacrificed. Thus some objects, such as thin plates, may require only one view – a front view, some may require only two, others three or more.

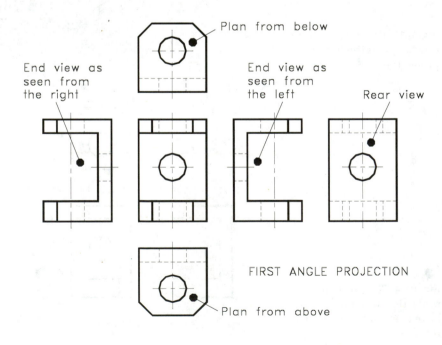

Fig. 8.15 The theoretical six views of an object in first angle projection

Lines in technical drawings

AutoCAD R13 contains a large number of different line types. Apart from these, the common line types used in technical drawings for engineering are shown in Fig. 8.16. Note that outlines are normally two or three times the thickness of other lines. A general rule is that outlines in drawings designed for plotting on A3 sheets should be about 0.7 units and other lines about 0.3 units. The **Polyline** tool is of value here.

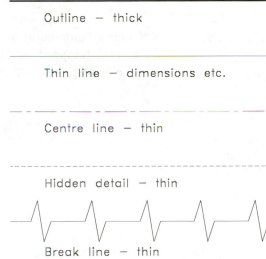

Outline — thick

Thin line — dimensions etc.

Centre line — thin

Hidden detail — thin

Break line — thin

Fig. 8.16 Types of lines in engineering drawings

Outline: Thick line.

Thin line: For features such as dimension lines, hatching lines, etc.

Centre line: A thin line made up from long and short lines alternating with each other. Should be drawn through all circles, spheres, cylinders and similar features.

Hidden detail: Thin lines. A broken dashed line drawn through features not seen from the outside of the object being drawn.

Break line: Thin lines drawn at a break in a drawing.

An example of a third angle orthographic projection

To draw a third angle orthographic projection of the hanger shown in Fig. 8.17 follow the procedures:

1. Open your A3 sheet prototype drawing file (Chapter 5) – Fig. 8.18.
2. Make Layer **CONSTRUCTION** the current layer – Fig. 8.19.
3. *Left-click* on the **Construction Line** tool icon (Fig. 8.20) and draw construction lines as shown in Fig. 8.21. The arithmetic for the positions of the construction lines should be worked out on a piece

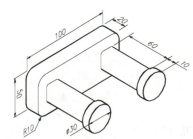

Fig. 8.17 The hanger for the orthographic projection example

Fig. 8.18 Opening an A3
prototype drawing file

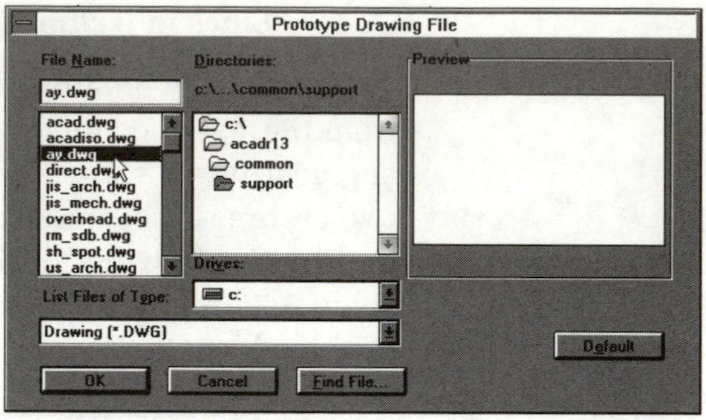

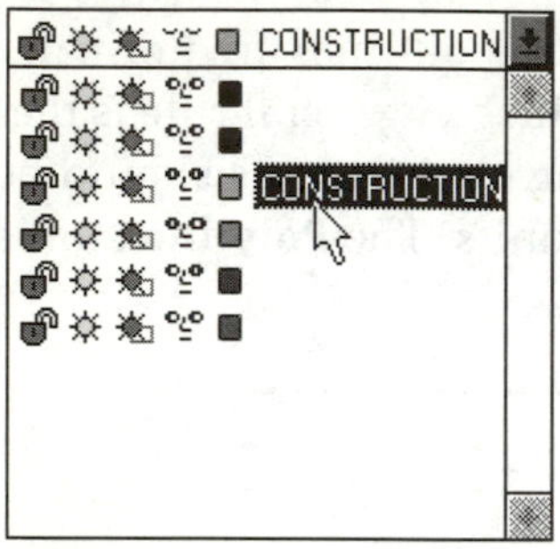

Fig. 8.19 Make
CONSTRUCTION the current
layer

of paper beforehand to attempt obtaining a well laid out set of
views. Attempt at equal spacing between views with sufficient
space at sides, top and bottom of the drawing sheet.

Fig. 8.20 The **Construction
Line** tool icon in the **Line**
flyout of the **Draw** toolbar

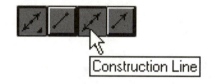

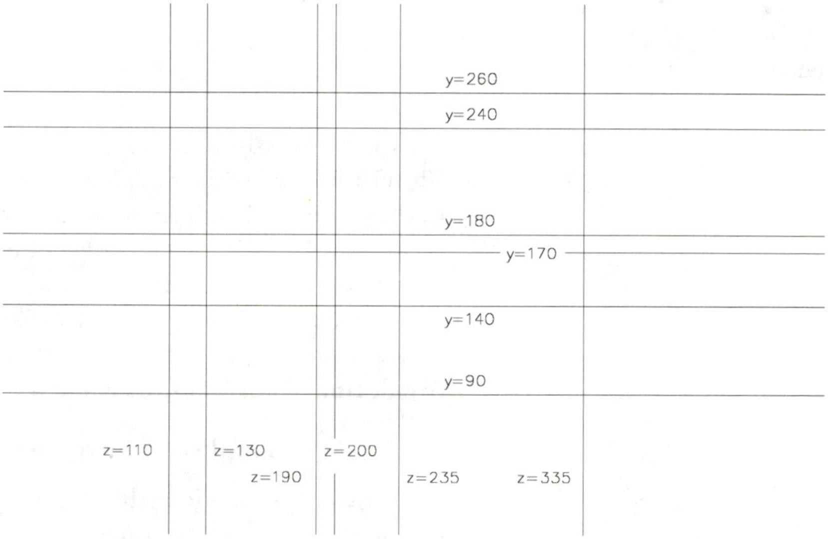

Construction Line

Fig. 8.21. Construction lines
for the orthographic projection
example

4. Make sure that **Grid** and **Snap** are on − Fig. 8.22.

Fig. 8.22 *Double-click* on
SNAP or **GRID** to toggle on/off

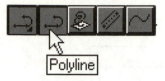

Fig. 8.23 The **Polyline** tool icon in the **Polyline** flyout of the **Draw** toolbar

Fig. 8.24 Adding the outlines of views and plans with the Polyline tool

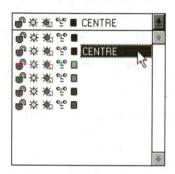

Fig. 8.25 Make layer **CENTRE** current

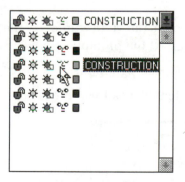

Fig. 8.26 Turn layer **CONSTRUCTION** off

Fig. 8.27 The drawing with added centre and hidden detail lines and with the **CONSTRUCTION** layer off

5. *Left-click* on the **Polyline** tool icon (Fig. 8.23). Set the **Pline** width to 0.7 and construct the three views based on the already drawn construction lines (Fig. 8.24). If **ORTHO** is set on (see Fig. 8.23) the plines may be easier to draw. Use the **Arc** prompt of the **Pline** prompts to construct the circles – two half-circles based upon **Snap** points. Use the **Fillet** tool to produce the radiused corners.

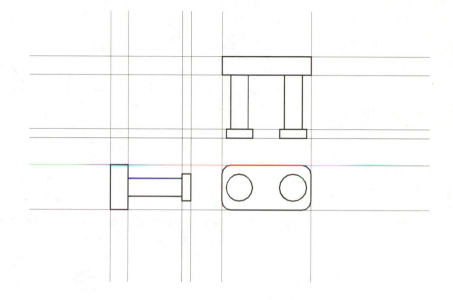

6. Make the **CENTRE** layer current (Fig. 8.25) and add centre lines, then make the **HIDDEN** layer current and add hidden detail. Then turn off the **CONSTRUCTION** layer (Fig. 8.26). The resulting drawing now appears as in Fig. 8.27.
7. With the **Polyline** tool set to width 0 add a border line and a title block area. With text of height 8 add a title and after resetting the text height to 6 add the angle of projection – Fig. 8.28.

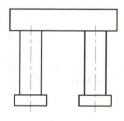

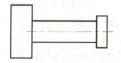

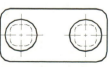

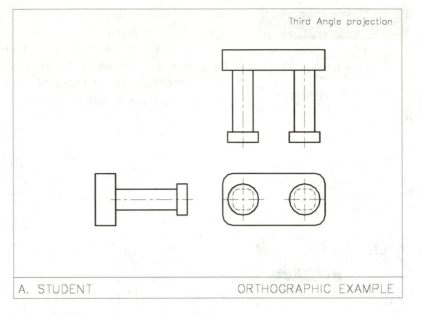

Fig. 8.28 The finished
orthographic projection

Notes

1. In this example the text style is **SIMPLEX**, set in the prototype drawing file (Chapter 5).
2. Dimensions have not been included with the drawing. This is because dimensioning will be dealt with in a later chapter (Chapter 10).

Amending the acad.pgp file

Double-click on the **MS-DOS Prompt** icon in the **Main** window of the Windows **Program Manager** (Fig. 8.29). At the prompt:

   C:\> *enter* edit c:\acadr13\support\acad.pgp *Return*

Or use the name of the directory in which the **acad.pgp** file is held.

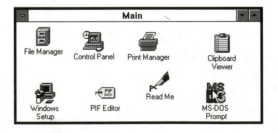

Fig. 8.29 *Double-click* on the
MS-DOS icon in the **Main**
window

   The **MS-DOS Editor** appears on screen with the contents of the acad.pgp file showing. The first part of the file contains details of abbreviations for 2D tools and shows:
   ; Command alias format:
   ; <Alias>,*<Full command name>

; Sample aliases for AutoCAD Commands
; These examples reflect the most frequently used commands.
; Each alias uses a small amount of memory, so don't go
; overboard on systems with tight memory.

A,   *ARC
C,   *CIRCLE
CP,   *COPY
DV,   *DVIEW
E,   *ERASE
L,   *LINE
LA,   *LAYER
LT,   *LINETYPE
M,   *MOVE
MS,   *MSPACE
P,   *PAN
PS,   *PSPACE
PL,   *PLINE
R,   *REDRAW
T,   *MTEXT
Z,   *ZOOM

If you wish to construct your drawings using tool abbreviations instead of selecting tool icons, you could add to the abbreviations included in the **acad.pgp** file. However, if others are using the computer at which you are working, their permissions to do this must be sought. Each abbreviation added to the file uses some memory, which other operators may find troublesome when constructing large drawings. Because I am the sole user of the computer at which I work, I have added the following 2D abbreviations:

AR,	*ARRAY	DO,	*DONUT	PE,	*PEDIT
B,	*BLOCK	EL,	*ELLIPSE	RO,	*ROTATE
BH,	*BHATCH	EP,	*EXPLODE	S,	*STRETCH
BR,	*BREAK	EX,	*EXTEND	SC,	*SCALE
CF,	*CHAMFER	F,	*FILLET	ST,	*STYLE
CH,	*CHANGE	IN,	*INSERT	TR,	*TRIM
D,	*DIM	MI,	*MIRROR	W,	*WBLOCK
DI,	*DISTANCE	OF,	*OFFSET		

Isometric drawing

The **Grid** and **Snap** settings for constructing isometric drawings are best set in the **Drawing Aids** dialogue box (Fig. 8.30). As can be seen in Fig. 8.30:

Snap is on, **Grid** is on (check boxes with crosses).
Y Spacings for **Snap** (5) and **Grid** (10) have been *entered*.
Isometric Snap/Grid is on (check box with cross).
Left Isoplane is current (check circle showing).

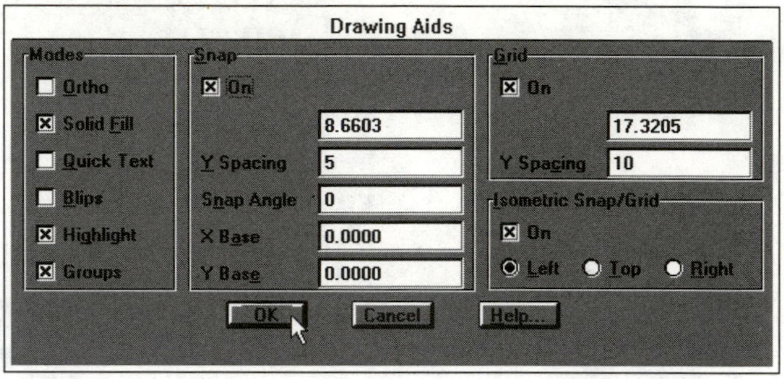

Fig. 8.30 The **Drawing Aids** dialogue box showing typical settings for constructing isometric drawings

Isoplanes

AutoCAD R13 recognises three isoplanes – **Left**, **Top** and **Right**. Isoplanes are shown in Fig. 8.31. The easiest method of setting the required isoplane is to press the **Ctrl** and the **E** key. Repeated pressing of **E** while holding down **Ctrl** toggles between the three isoplanes.

With the settings shown in Fig. 8.30, the AutoCAD R13 graphics window will appear as in Fig. 8.32.

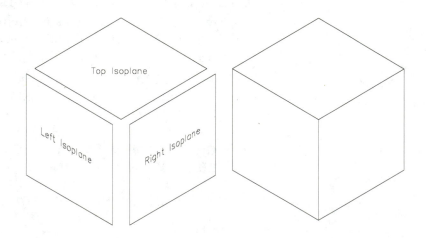

Fig. 8.31 The three Isoplanes and a cube drawn in isometric using all three isoplanes

Constructing an isometric drawing

To construct an isometric drawing of the frame in the orthographic projection of Fig. 8.33, proceed as follows:

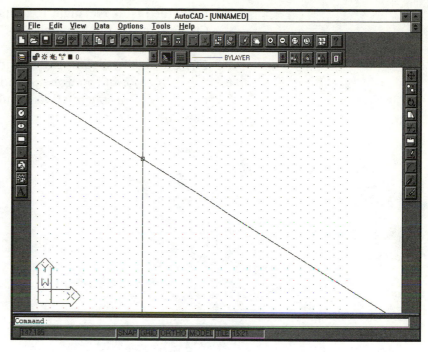

Fig. 8.32 The R13 graphics window setup for isometric drawing

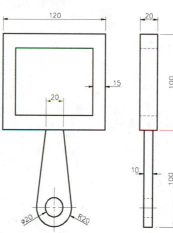

Fig. 8.33 An orthographic projection of the isometric drawing example

1. Open your A3 sheet prototype drawing file.
2. In the **Drawing Aids** dialogue box *enter* **settings** as shown in Fig. 8.30.
3. Press **Ctrl/E** until Isoplane Right shows at the Command Line. Press **Ctrl/D** until relative coordinates show in the Coordinate Window.
4. Select the **Polyline** tool (or *enter* **pl** *Return*) and following the relative coordinate figures in the Coordinate Window, draw the outer rectangle of 120 by 100 units.

5. Draw the inside rectangle 15 units inside the outer.
6. **Ctrl/E** to obtain the Isoplane Top. With **Polyline** add lines of the top edge.
7. **Ctrl/E** to obtain Isoplane Left and add plines for the left-hand edge.
8. Add plines for inner edges, amending the Isoplane with **Ctrl/E** as necessary. The construction should now look like the left-hand drawing of Fig. 8.34.

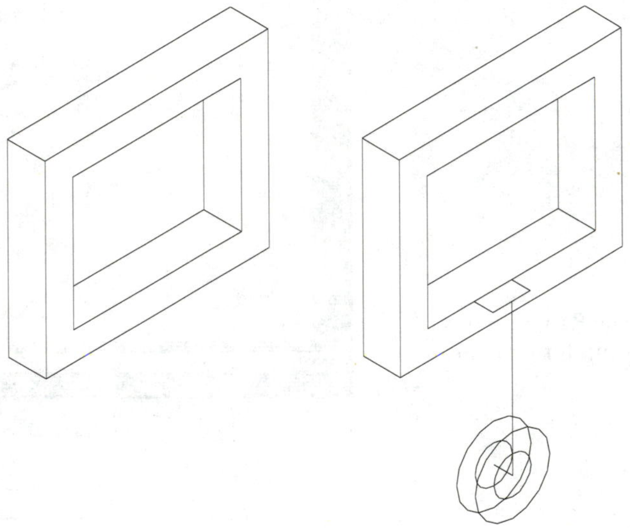

Fig. 8.34 First stages of the isometric drawing example

9. Construct lines to position the top of the handle and draw another line to give the centre of the arc for the bottom of the handle.
10. Guided by the lines (item 9) draw isometric ellipses for the handle end and its hole. The construction now appears as in the right-hand drawing of Fig. 8.34.
11. Draw plines for the handle edges using the **Osnap Tangent** to ensure accurate tangency to the outer ellipses – left-hand drawing of Fig. 8.35.
12. With **Trim** and **Erase** complete the drawing – right-hand Fig. 8.35.

Notes

1. With the aid of the **Polyline Edit** tool, together with the **Break** tool, the outlines of isometric drawings can be thickened as shown in Fig. 8.36, to give an appearance of depth to the drawing.
2. Isometric drawing is not a 3D method, although the resulting drawing may have a 3D appearance. Isometric drawings are a 2D method of constructing pictorial views. True 3D drawing will be described later in Chapters 14 and 15.

Fig. 8.35 The final stages of
the isometric drawing
example

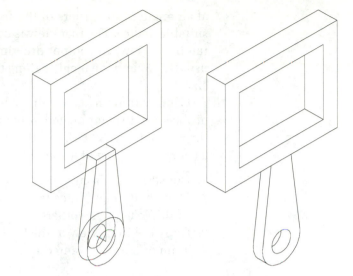

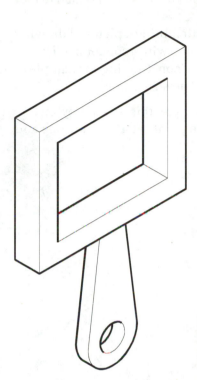

Fig. 8.36 Outer lines of the
isometric example thickened
to width 1 with the aid of the
Polyline Edit tool

3. Fig. 8.37 Shows a simple exploded isometric drawing constructed
    in the AutoCAD R13 graphics window.

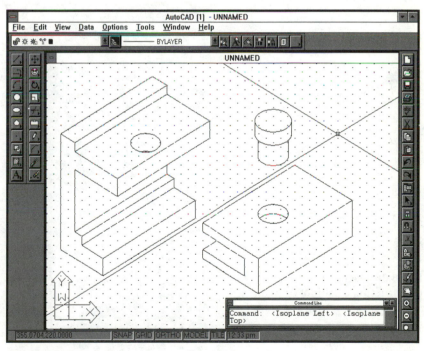

Fig. 8.37 An example of a
simple exploded isometric
drawing in the R13 graphics
window

Cabinet drawing

Cabinet drawing is a form of oblique drawing. In oblique drawing,
a front view of the object being drawn is constructed. Lines are taken

at an angle from corners of the front view at 30°, 45°, 60°, or other suitable angles. The rear view is completed by copying from parts of the front view. In cabinet drawing, the lines taken at an angle are usually 45° and the lengths along the 45° lines are then scaled to half size.

Cabinet drawing is of value when attempting a pictorial drawing of objects with complicated front views and with a common thickness throughout. Fig. 8.38 shows the stages in constructing an example of a cabinet drawing of a shaped block. The stages are:

1. Construct the front view. In this example, this was a polyline.
2. Draw half-length lines from suitable points at 45°. Draw one and multiple copy the others.
3. Copy the front view to the back.
4. Trim or erase unwanted lines.

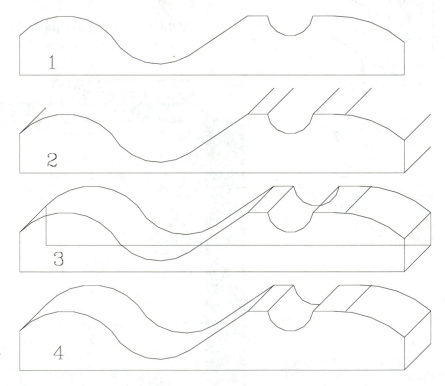

Fig. 8.38 Stages in constructing a cabinet drawing

Planometric drawing

Planometric drawing is another form of pictorial drawing suitable for showing layouts of buildings, street areas etc. in a pictorial form. The stages in constructing a pictorial drawing are:

1. Draw a plan either at an angle of 30° or 45° to the horizontal, or drawn horizontally and rotated through 30° or 45°.

2. Draw verticals at appropriate corners of the plan.
3. Add other lines to complete the drawing.

   To construct a planometric in R13, set the **Snap Angle** in the **Drawing Aids** dialogue box at either 30 or 45, whichever you consider most suitable for your drawing. Make sure than **Isometric Snap/Grid** is off. Then use **Grid** and **Snap** to assist in the construction of the plan. Fig. 8.39 shows a setting for exhibition stands in a hall drawn in this form of pictorial drawing. The stages in constructing Fig. 8.39 were:

1. *Enter* **Snap Angle** 30.
2. Construct the plan with **Grid** and **Snap** on. Use **Offset** for partition thicknesses.
3. *Enter* **Snap Angle** 0.
4. Set **Osnap Endpoint** on. Turn **Ortho** on. Turn **Snap** off.
5. Draw a vertical. **Multiple Copy** to other corners.
6. Add plines between top edges.
7. **Trim** or **Erase** unwanted lines.

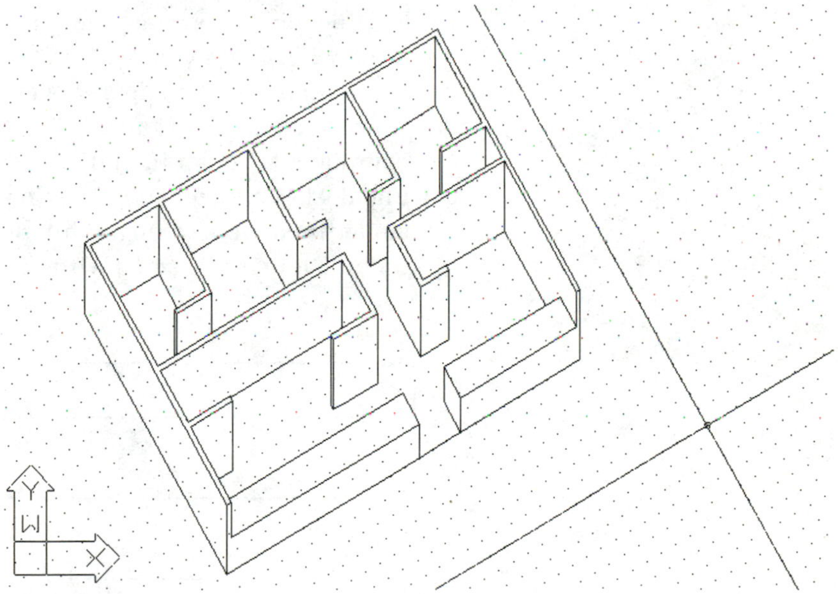

Fig. 8.39 An example of a planometric drawing

Questions

1. Orthographic projection is based upon two planes orthogonally placed to each other. Which of the four angles formed by the two planes are used in orthographic projections?

2. In first angle projection in which direction does the front of the plan face?

3. And in third angle projection?

4. What governs the number of views needed to fully describe an item by orthographic projection?

5. Why is it necessary to open a prototype drawing before commencing any construction in R13?

6. When turning a layer off, how can you tell it is off?

7. What is the purpose of the **acad.pgp** file?

8. What are the angles commonly employed for isometric drawing?

9. What is meant by the term **cabinet drawing**?

10. Why is it necessary to change the **Snap Angle** back to zero after constructing the plan of a planometric drawing in R13?

Exercises

1. Construct a first angle orthographic projection of the hanger shown in Fig. 8.17. The methods of construction for this exercise will be very similar to those describing the third angle example starting on the same page as Fig. 8.17. Do not include any dimensions with your drawing

2. Fig. 8.40 is a first angle orthographic projection of a component from a machine. Construct a third angle projection of the component. Do not include the dimensions.

3. Fig. 8.41 is an isometric drawing of a bracket. Construct a third angle three-view orthographic projection of the bracket. Do not include any dimensions with your drawing.

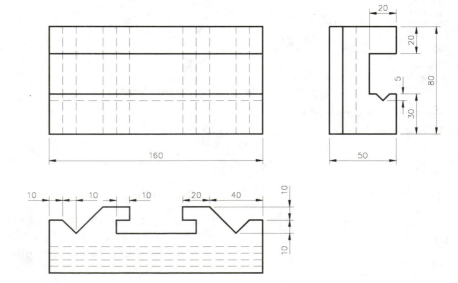

Fig. 8.40 Exercise 2

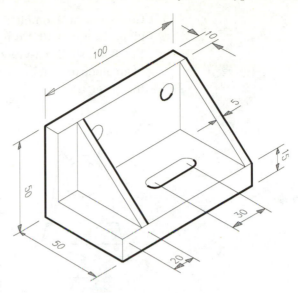

Fig. 8.41 Exercise 3

4. Fig. 8.42 is an isometric drawing of a link from a machine part, drawn on a 20 mm grid. Construct a three view orthographic projection of the part in either first or third angle projection. Do not include any dimensions.

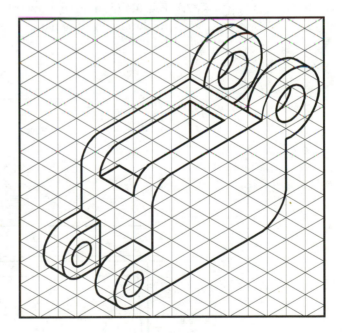

Fig. 8.42 Exercise 4

5.　Construct an isometric drawing of the orthographic projection given in Fig. 8.40. Do not include any dimensions.

6.　Fig. 8.43 is a three-view first angle orthographic view of the case of an electric pencil sharpener. Construct an isometric drawing of the case.

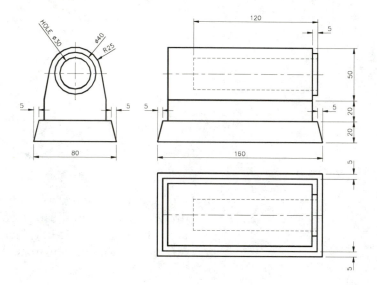

Fig. 8.43 Exercise 6

7.　Fig. 8.44 is a three-view third angle projection of a table. Working to the given dimensions construct an isometric drawing of the table.

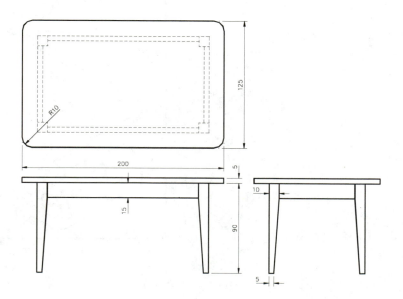

Fig. 8.44 Exercise 7

8. The two right-hand drawings of Fig. 8.45 show a two-view orthographic projection of an ornament. Stages 1, 2 and 3 show how the front view was obtained. Using any suitable sizes construct a cabinet drawing of the ornament.

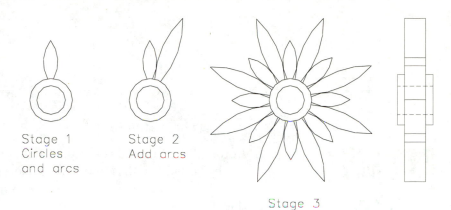

Fig. 8.45 Exercise 8

9. Fig. 8.46 is an orthographic projection of a model made in wood to show forms of moulding. Construct a cabinet drawing of the model.

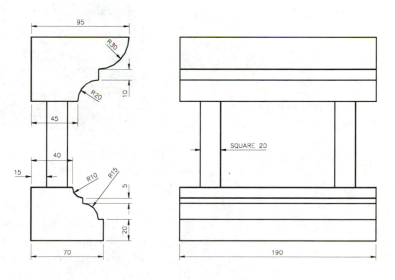

Fig. 8.46 Exercise 9

10. Working to any convenient sizes, contruct a planometric drawing similar to that given in Fig. 8.40.

CHAPTER 9

Hatching

The Hatch tool

AutoCAD R13 includes a large number of hatching patterns, which can be added to a drawing with the aid of the **Hatch** tool (Fig. 9.1). A *left-click* on the tool brings up the **Boundary Hatch** dialogue box (Fig. 9.2).

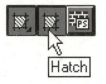

Fig. 9.1 The **Hatch** tool icon from the **Hatch** flyout of the **Draw** toolbar

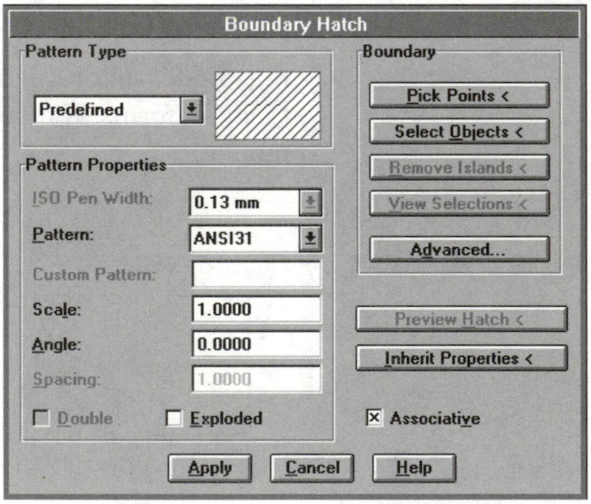

Fig. 9.2 The **Boundary Hatch** dialogue box

The dialogue box appears on screen with the ANSI31 hatch pattern showing in the **Pattern Type** box. Repeated *left-clicks* in the area of the pattern allows cycling through the available hatch patterns. As the pattern in the **Pattern Type** box changes so its name appears in the **Pattern:** box, together with the current **Scale:** and **Angle:** boxes showing the scale and angle of the hatch pattern. The available patterns can also be seen by a *left-click* on the arrow against the **Pattern:** box. A drop-down list of pattern names appears which can be scrolled down or up to select a name. The 65 to 70 hatch patterns which are included in R13 are a mixture of engineering, materials, architectural, decorative and ground feature patterns. Some of the patterns are shown in Fig. 9.3. In addition the operator

Fig. 9.3 Some of the hatch patterns available in R13

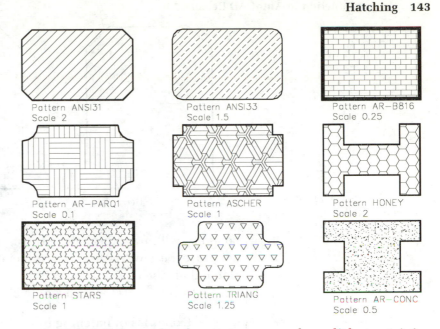

can devise his/her own hatch patterns, or purchase disks containing a number of patterns in files.

Associative hatching

Left-clicks in the box to the left of **Associative** will set the check cross on or off. If on (cross present) hatching automatically adjusts to any change in the associated boundaries. Fig. 9.4 gives an example of the advantage of having **Associative** hatching on. As the upper window frame in the drawing is moved to a new position the hatching automatically adjusts to the changed boundaries. Fig. 9.5 is another example, showing that a hatched area can itself be moved within its

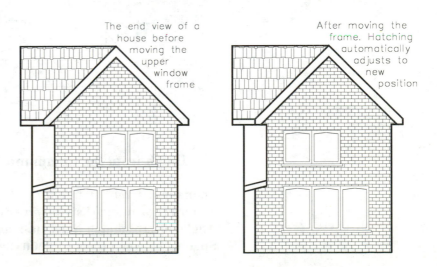

Fig. 9.4 An example of the advantage of using **Associative** hatching

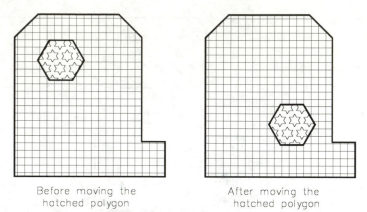

Before moving the
hatched polygon

After moving the
hatched polygon

Fig. 9.5 Another example of **Associative** hatching

boundary within another hatched area – all the hatching automatically adjusts to the new conditions if **Associative** is set on in the **Boundary Hatch** dialogue box. In this example, the polygon and its hatching can be treated as if it were a single object.

Examples of hatching in engineering drawings

Fig. 9.6 shows the hatching of areas in a sectional view using the normal **ANI31** hatch pattern set to **Scale** 2 and using the **Pick Points** boundary selection button for picking the areas to be hatched. In this example **Associative** hatching was set off (no cross in its box).

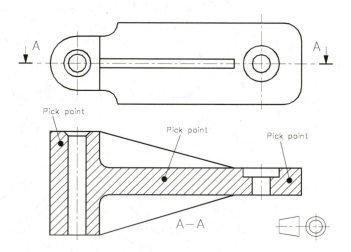

Pick point

Pick point

Pick point

A – A

Fig. 9.6 An example of a sectioned view

Hatch from the Command Line

Command: *enter* hatch *Return*
Pattern (? or name/U,style): *enter* u *Return*
Angle for crosshatch lines <0>: *enter* 45 *Return*
Spacing between lines <1.0000>: *enter* 3 *Return*

Double hatch area? <N>: *Return*
Select boundaries or RETURN for direct hatch:
Select objects: *Return*
Retain polyline ? <N>: *Return*
From point: *pick*
Arc/Close/Length/Undo/<Next point>: *pick*
Arc/Close/Length/Undo/<Next point>: *pick*
Arc/Close/Length/Undo/<Next point>: *pick*
Arc/Close/Length/Undo/<Next point>: *pick*
Arc/Close/Length/Undo/<Next point>: *enter* c *Return*
From point or RETURN to apply hatch: *pick*
Command:

And the area which has been defined by the polyline drawn during the sequence of prompts is hatched, without the polyline appearing on screen. Fig. 9.7 shows some areas hatched in this manner, without the bounding polyline.

Fig. 9.7 Examples of hatching without boundaries

When the response to the prompt **Pattern (? or name/U,style):** is a **?** a list of the hatch pattern names appears in a text window. This list may be of interest to the reader because it gives meaning to the variety of hatch patterns. The list starts as follows:

ANGLE   **Angle steel**
ANSI31   **ANSI Iron, Brick, Stone masonry**
ANSI32   **ANSI Steel**
ANSI33   **ANSI Bronze, Brass, Copper**
ANSI34   **ANSI Plastic, Rubber**
ANSI35   **ANSI Fire brick, Refractory material**
ANSI36   **ANSI Marble, Slate, Glass**

> **ANSI37   ANSI Lead, Zinc, Magnesium, Sound/Heat/Elec Insulation**
> **ANSI38   ANSI Aluminium**

and continues to list all the patterns available in R13.

Explode

When an area is hatched it usually forms a single object, unless the **Exploded** box is checked (cross appearing in box) with a *left-click*. If not exploded a hatched area can be modified in various ways as a single object – it can be erased, moved, copied, scaled, rotated etc. Even if the **Exploded** box is not checked at the time the hatching is originated it can be exploded with the use of the **Explode** tool or by *entering* explode at the Command Line, followed by a *left-click* within the hatched area.

Text within a hatched area

Any text within a hatched area can be treated as if it is an object and chosen with a *left-click* on the **Select Objects** button in the **Boundary Hatch** dialogue box. Text is surrounded with an invisible boundary which allows it to be chosen as an object within hatched areas.

Fig. 9.8 An example of a hatched area containing text

Questions

1. In which toolbar would you expect to find the **Hatch...** tool icon?
2. What is meant by **Associative** hatching?
3. What happens when the cursor is placed over the **Pattern Type:** box in the **Boundary Hatch** dialogue box, followed by a *left-click*?
4. What is the difference between using the **Pick Points** and using the **Select Objects** buttons in the **Boundary Hatch** dialogue box?
5. Look at Fig. 9.5 on page 144. Was the polygon with its **STAR** hatch pattern moved as a single object or in a window?

Plate I Selecting the **AutoCAD R13** icon from the **Program Manager** window

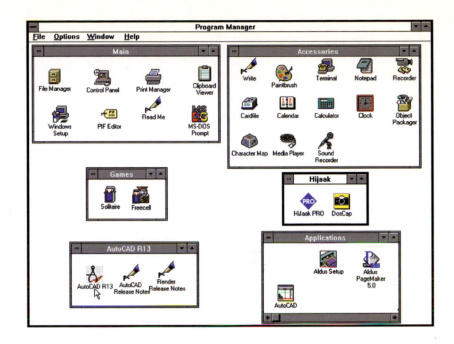

Plate II The **AutoCAD** window that first appears when **AutoCAD R13** is selected

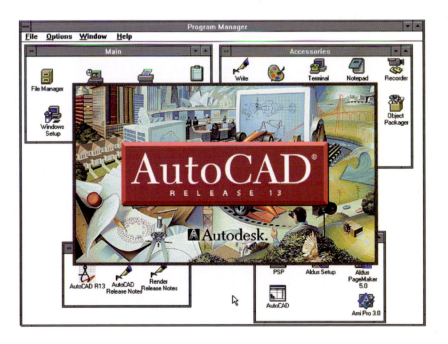

Plate III Selecting a
drawing to open from the
Select File dialogue box

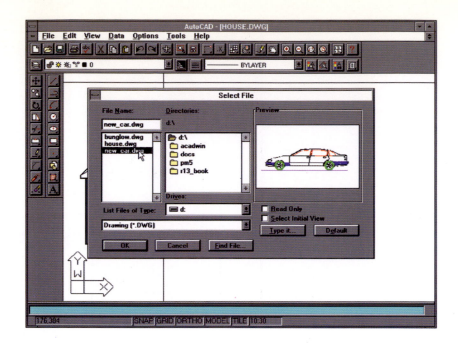

Plate IV The **Aerial View**
window showing which
part of the drawing has
been magnified using
Zoom

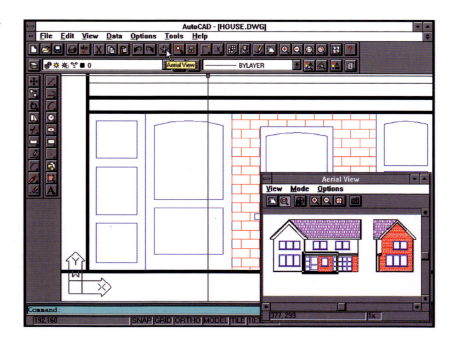

Plate V The **Boundary Hatch** dialogue box; AutoCAD is configured here to display an on-screen menu and no toolboxes

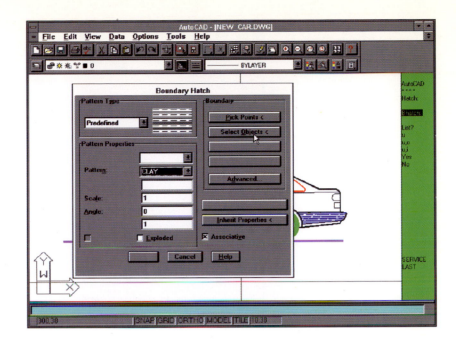

Plate VI A **Help** window

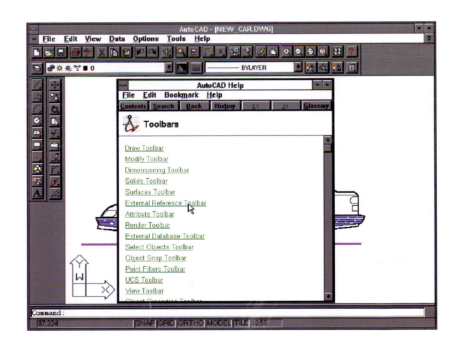

Plate VII A 3D model in
a distance perspective
view (**Dview**)

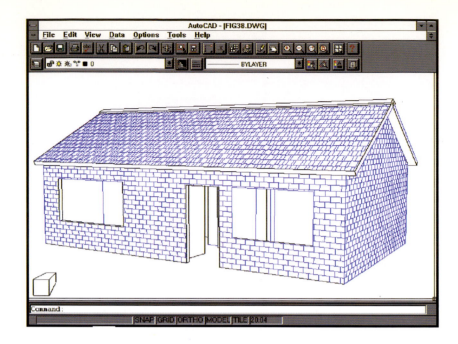

Plate VIII A 3D model
constructed in a four-
viewport graphics
window

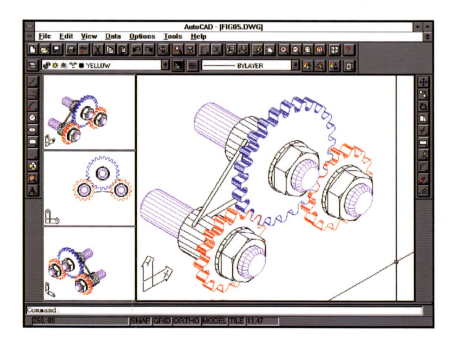

Plate IX The 3D model in Plate VIII in a single viewport with the **Clipboard Viewer**

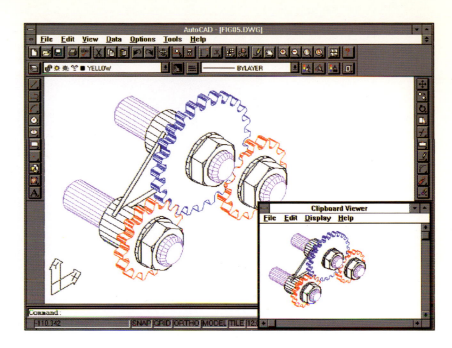

Plate X A rendering of the 3D model shown in Plate VIII

Plate XI A 3D model
after the tool **Shade** has
been selected and applied

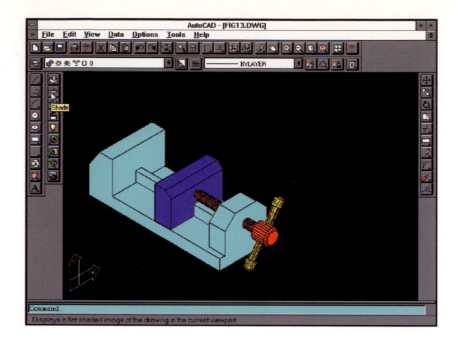

Plate XII The 3D model
shown in Plate XI
rendered in several
materials

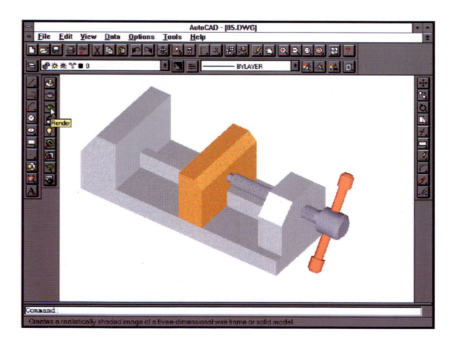

Plate XIII The same
rendering as in Plate XII
displayed with a different
screen colour configuration

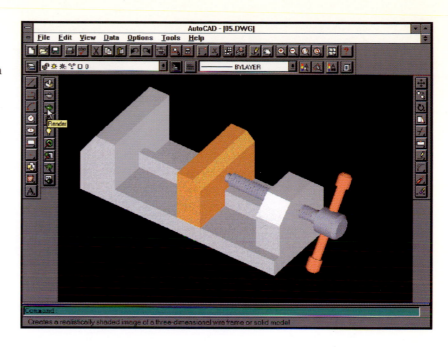

Plate XIV An exploded
view of a part from a pump
device after rendering

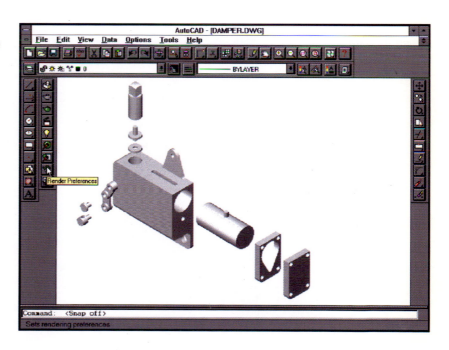

Plate XV A rendering of
an exploded 3D model

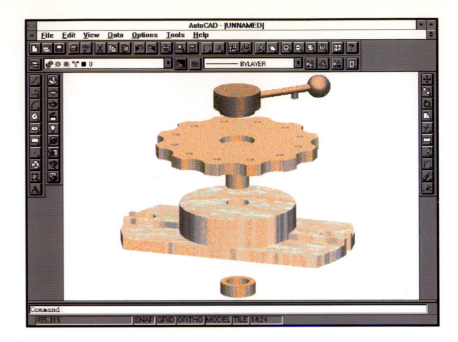

Plate XVI A rendering in
colour materials

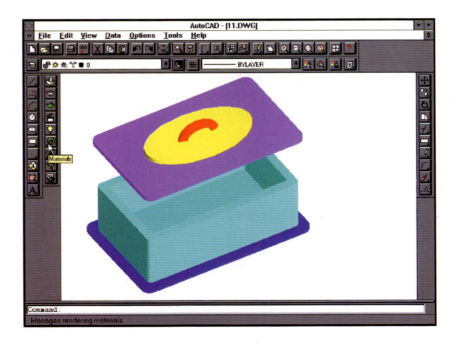

6. Why are parts of the Front sectional view of Fig. 9.6 (page 144) not hatched?

7. What happens to any hatched areas when the **Explode** button of the **Boundary Hatch** dialogue box has been selected?

8. How can you make sure that text within a hatched area is not covered by the hatch lines?

Exercises

1. Working to the dimensions given, construct the three view orthographic projection of a stand given in Fig. 9.9 with the Front view in section.

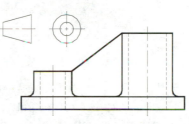
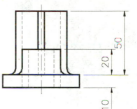
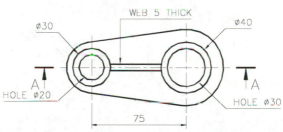

WEB 5 THICK

Ø30   Ø40

A   A
HOLE Ø20   HOLE Ø30

75

Fig. 9.9 Exercise 1

2. Fig. 9.10 is the side view of a car with some hatching applied to the sides and bumpers. Choose any car design and construct a similar side view which incorporates some hatching patterns.

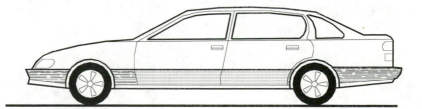

Fig. 9.10 Exercise 2

3.   The outlines of Fig. 9.11 have been formed from plines of varying thicknesses. Either copy the given pattern or construct a similar pattern which includes a hatched border.

Fig. 9.11 Exercise 3

4.   Fig. 9.12 is another pattern which includes hatched areas. Copy the given pattern to any convenient sizes.

Fig9.12 Exercise 4

5.   Fig. 9.13 is a design which includes some text. Either copy the given pattern or construct a similar drawing to your own design.

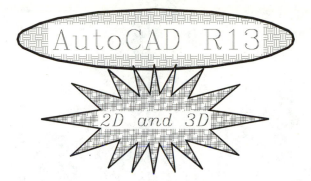

Fig. 9.13 Exercise 5

6.   Fig. 9.14 is a front view and end view of a building. Working to any suitable sizes copy the given drawing.

Fig. 9.14 Exercise 6

7.   Copy the design given in Fig. 9.15. The upper drawing shows how the design was developed.

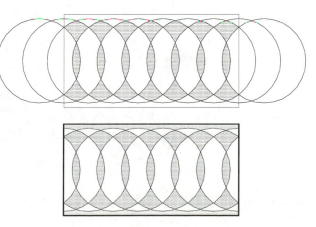

Fig. 9.15 Exercise 7

8.   Another hatched design. Working to sizes of your choice copy the given pattern design.

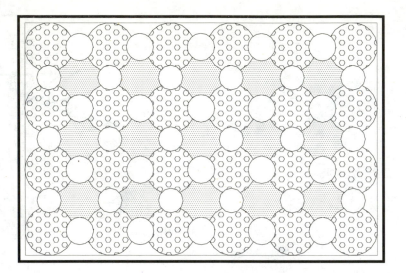

Fig. 9.16 Exercise 8

9.   Fig. 9.17 is a first angle, orthographic projection of a lathe turret tool holder. Working to the dimensions given with the drawing copy the plan and end view and include a sectional front view.

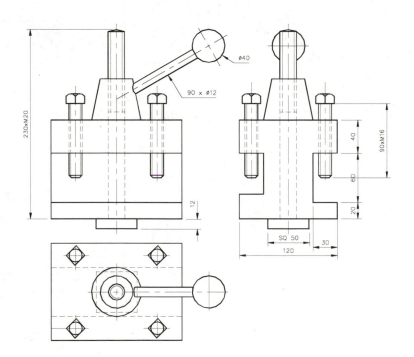

Fig. 9.17 Exercise 9

10. A sectional drawing through a wall is given in Fig. 9.18 Copy the
     drawing to any suitable sizes.

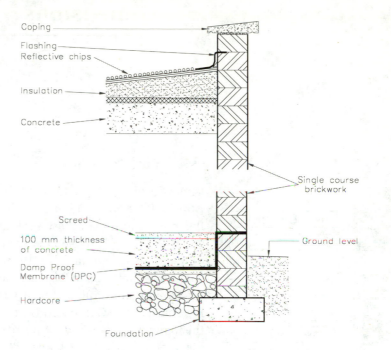

Fig. 9.18 Exercise 10

CHAPTER 10

Dimensions

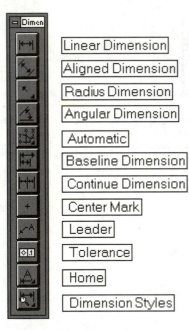

Introduction

Dimensioning of any form of technical drawing is important and AutoCAD R13 includes comprehensive dimensioning systems. Only the most common of these systems will be described in this chapter and the reader is advised to experiment with the various methods of dimensioning available with the software. As with other tool/command methods in R13, dimensioning tools can be selected from the **Dimension** toolbar (Fig. 10.1), or entries can be made from the keyboard at the Command Line. As shown in Fig. 10.1, only four of the icons include outward pointing arrows showing that flyouts are associated with those icons. These four flyouts are shown in Fig. 10.2. To set the parameters for dimensioning, a *left-click* on the **Dimension Styles...** tool icon (Fig. 10.2) brings the **Dimension Styles** dialogue box on screen (Fig. 10.3).

Fig. 10.1 The **Dimension** toolbar showing the names of the tools which can be selected from the icons

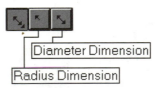

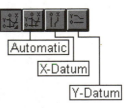

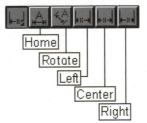

Fig. 10.2 The four flyouts of the **Dimension** toolbar

The Dimensions Styles dialogue box

The dialogue box in which dimensioning parameters are set is shown in Fig. 10.3. *Left-click* on the arrow to the right of the **Current:** box and a pop-up list drops down showing the dimension styles available in the software (Fig. 10.4). We will be using the **STANDARD** style.

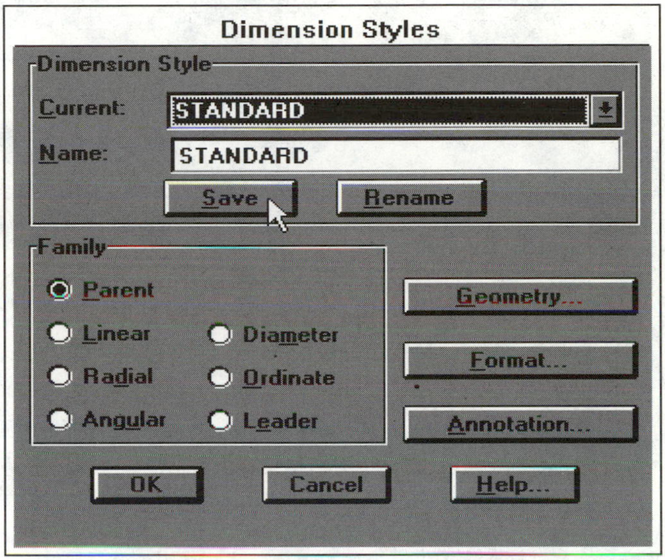

Fig. 10.3 the **Dimensions Style** dialogue box

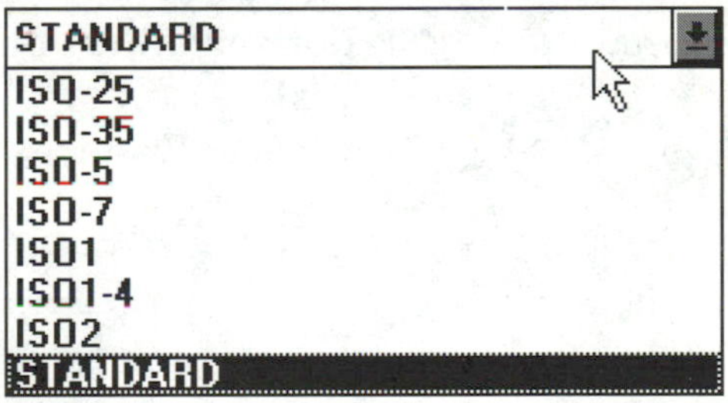

Fig. 10.4 The available dimension styles

Left-click on the **Geometry** button and the **Geometry** dialogue box appears (Fig. 10.5), in which settings for dimension lines, extension lines, arrow heads and centre marks can be set, together with the colour for the dimensions. In this box, our settings are:

Dimension Line Spacing	1
Extension Line Extension	3
Extension Line Origin Offset	3
Arrowheads	Closed Filled arrows, 4 long
Center mark	Line
Overall Scale	1

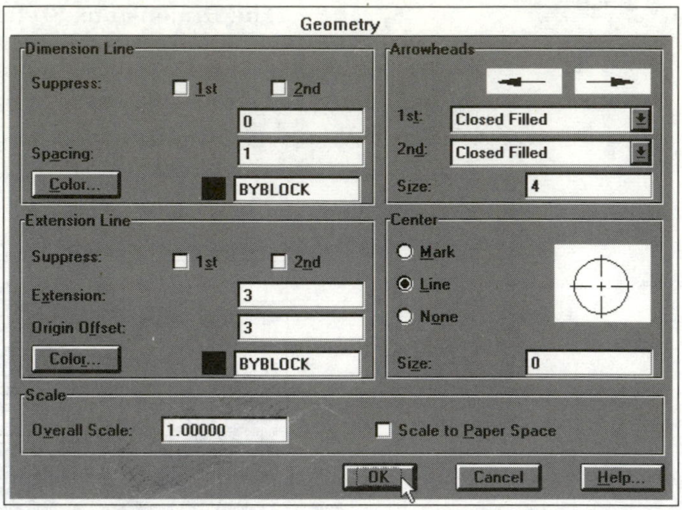

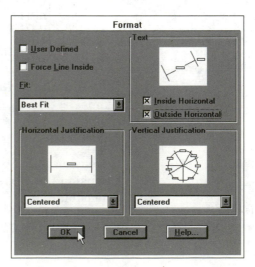

Fig. 10.5 The **Geometry** dialogue box

Closed Filled
None
Closed
Dot
Closed Filled
Oblique
Open
Origin Indication
Right Angle
User Arrow...

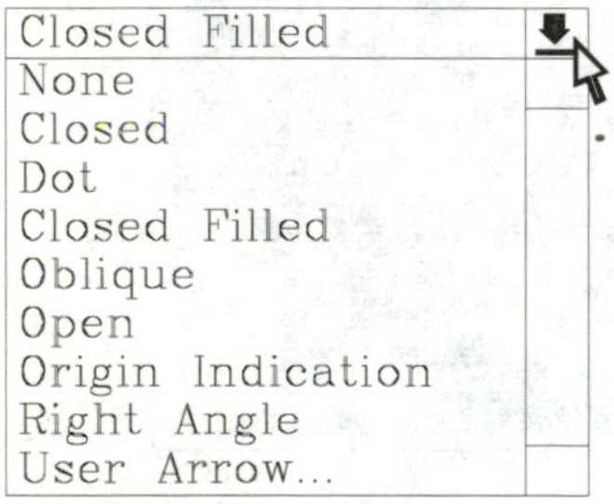

Fig. 10.6 The pop-up list showing different arrowheads

In the **Geometry** dialogue box, a *left-click* on the arrow button to the right of the **1st** and **2nd Arrowheads** list brings down a pop-up list showing the types of arrowhead from which a selection can be made (Fig. 10.6). Or, repeated *left-clicks* on either arrow icon scrolls through the arrowheads.

Left-click on the **Format** button and the **Format** dialogue box appears (Fig. 10.7), in which settings for the positioning of various forms of dimensions can be set. In this box our settings are:

Fit   Leader
Horizontal Justification   Centred
Text   Outside
Vertical Justification   Centred

Fig. 10.7 The **Format** dialogue box

Horizontal Justification

Vertical Justification

Fig. 10.8 The pop-up lists showing different justifications

Fit

Fig. 10.9 The pop-up list showing fits

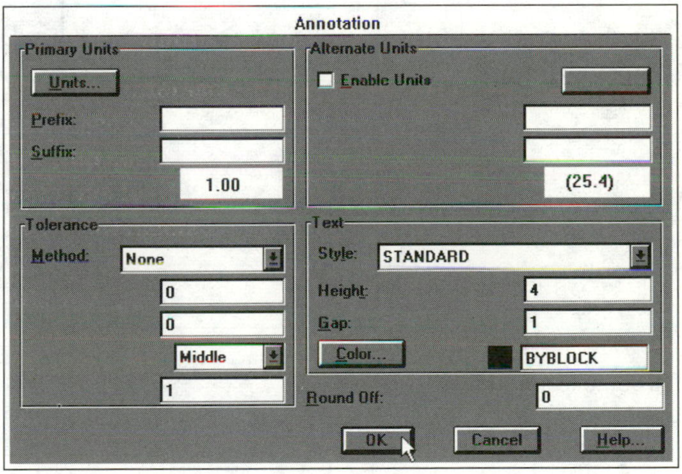

Fig. 10.10 The **Annotation** dialogue box

Left-click on the **Annotation** button and the **Annotation** dialogue box appears (Fig. 10.10), in which settings for a prefix, a suffix, tolerances and text are set. In this box our settings are:

Prefix	none
Suffix	none
Tolerances	none
Alternate Units	none
Text	4 high with a gap of 1

Left-click on either **Horizontal Justification** or the **Vertical Justification** list arrows in the **Format** dialogue box brings down the pop-up lists from which justifications can be set (Fig. 10.8). A *left-click* on the **Fit** list box arrow brings up the pop-up list shown in Fig. 10.9, from which a selection can be made.

Prefixes and/or suffixes (e.g. mm, in, ft etc.) can be set in the **Annotation** dialogue box (Fig. 10.10), as also can the parameters for tolerances connected with dimensions.

Examples of dimensions

Fig. 10.11 shows some of the different types of dimensioning possible with AutoCAD R13. The examples given in this illustration do not show all the possibilities of different ways in which dimensions can be shown in drawings. The reader is advised to experiment with different settings so as to judge for themselves which are the best settings for dimensions to be included in the drawings being constructed.

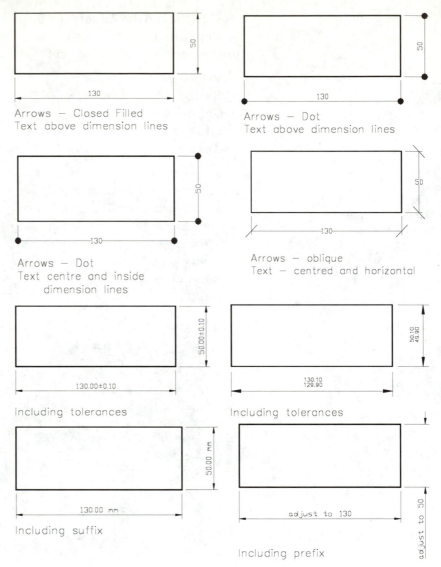

Fig. 10.11 Some examples of different settings for dimensioning

Geometric tolerances

Geometric tolerancing of dimensioning features (new to AutoCAD), is included in R13. Fig. 10.12 shows the meanings of 12 of the most

Fig. 10.12 The main geometrical tolerance symbols

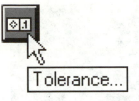

Fig. 10.13 The **Tolerance** tool icon from the **Draw** toolbar

used geometric tolerancing symbols. To add a geometric tolerance to a dimension, first add the dimension to the drawing with which the tolerance is to appear. Then *left-click* on the **Tolerance** tool icon in the **Dimensions** toolbar (Fig. 10.13). The **Symbol** dialogue box then appears (Fig. 10.14). Then *left-click* on the symbol to be added to the dimension and up comes the **Geometric Tolerance** dialogue box (Fig. 10.15). Insert the required figures. A *left-click* in any of the **MC** boxes brings up the **Material Condition** box (Fig. 10.16). Select the required symbol. When all the geometrical symbol parameters have been added in the **Geometric Tolerance** dialogue box, a *left-click* on the **OK** button brings the prompt **enter tolerance location:** at the Command Line. A *left-click* near the dimension causes the required tolerance box, such as that shown in Fig. 10.17, to appear in the position which has been selected by the *left-click*. Some examples of simple geometric tolerances are shown in Fig. 10.18.

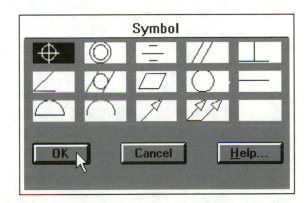

Fig. 10.14 The **Symbol** dialogue box

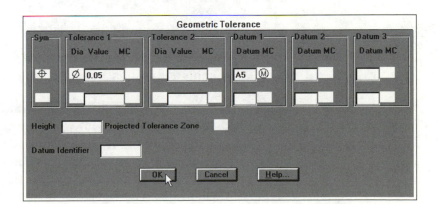

Fig. 10.15 The **Geometric Tolerance** dialogue box

Fig. 10.16 The **Material Condition** dialogue box

Fig. 10.17 The symbol as it would appear in the drawing

Fig 10.18 Some examples of geometric tolerances

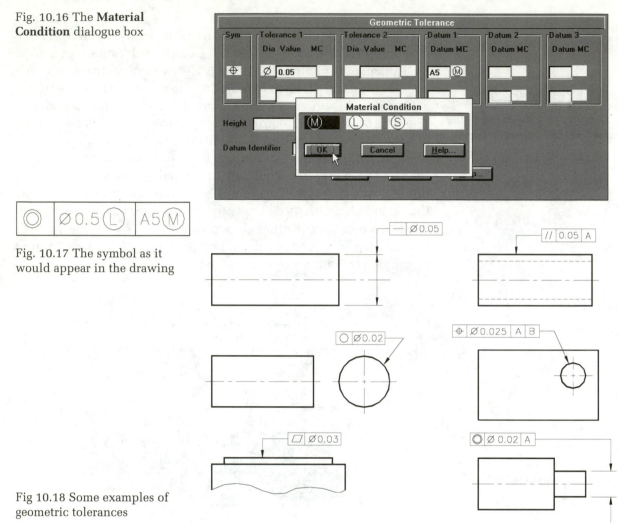

Command Line prompts when adding dimensions

Left-click on the **Linear Dimension** tool icon (see Fig. 10.1). The prompts and responses appearing at the Command Line are given in Fig. 10.19.

A second example involving the **Angular Dimension** and the **Radial Dimension** tool is given in Fig. 10.20. The angle was dimensioned with the aid of the **Angular Dimension** tool (Fig. 10.1 on page 152) and the circle with the aid of the **Diameter Dimension** tool from the **Radial** flyout of the **Draw** toolbar (see Fig. 10.2 on page 152). Note the similarities between the two sets of prompts given in Figs. 10.19 and 10.20. Other forms of dimensioning use a similar set of prompts to those given with these two illustrations. The reader is advised to

```
Command_dimlinear
First extension line origin or RETURN to select: pick
Second extension line origin: pick
Dimension line location (Text/Angle/Horizontal/Vertical/Rotated): enter h ⏎
Dimension line location (Text/Angle): enter t ⏎
Dimension text<100>: enter %%c100 ⏎
Dimension line location (Text Angle): enter a ⏎
Enter text angle: enter 10 ⏎
```

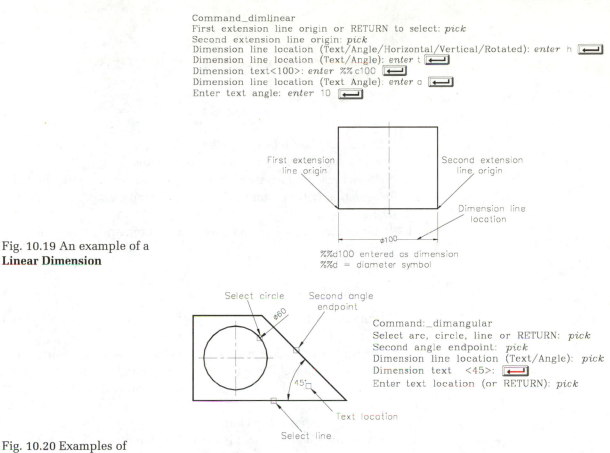

Fig. 10.19 An example of a
Linear Dimension

Fig. 10.20 Examples of
dimensioning with the aid of
Angular Dimension and
Radial Dimension

experiment with dimensioning tools and see for him/her self the
prompts involved with each tool.

The %%symbol calls

When entering text in AutoCAD R13 for any text or for dimensions,
if it is necessary to include the symbols for diameter, degrees or the
plus/minus tolerance symbols, *enter* %% in front of **c** (for diameter),
d (for degrees) and **p** (for plus/minus). If a percentage symbol is
needed then it must be preceded with '%%'. Thus:

%%c   symbol for diameter (Ø)
%%d   symbol for degrees (°)
%%p   symbol for plus/minus (±)
%%%   symbol for %

From the above:

%%c50   = Ø50
%%p0.5 mm = ±0.5 mm
%%d50   = 50°
100%%%   = 100%

Notes

1. Dimensions should be treated as single objects. They can be acted upon by tools such as **Stretch**, **Move**, **Scale**.
2. If a drawing which has been dimensioned is scaled or stretched, the dimensions will automatically adjust to the new scale or stretch sizes.
3. R13 includes dimension editing tools, which are not described in this book.

Questions

1. In which toolbar would you expect to find dimensioning tool icons?
2. In which dialogue box are the parameters for dimensioning set?
3. How would you set dimensioning to the standard ISO methods?
4. How many types of arrowheads for dimensions would you expect to find in R13?
5. What is a **geometric tolerance**?
6. How are diameter symbols included with a dimension which has to be entered from the keyboard?

Exercises

1. Copy the outlines given in Fig. 10.21 and add the dimensions which are included with the outlines.
2. Construct the three view first angle orthographic projection given in Fig. 10.22 and add all necessary dimensions to the sizes given with the drawing.

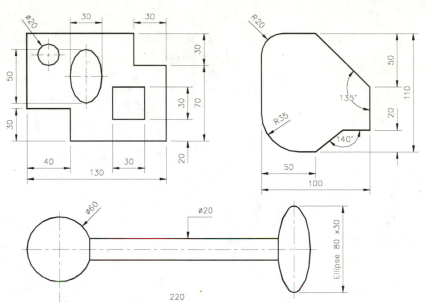

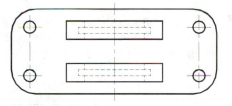

Fig. 10.21 Exercise 1

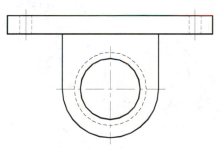

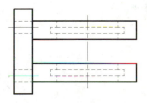

Fig. 10.22 Exercise 2

<u>Sizes</u>

Backplate 170 x 70 x 15
Holes in backplate ⌀10
Each support 85 x 80 x 15
Supports are 20 apart
Holes in supports ⌀50
Slots in supports 5 x 5

3. A third angle orthographic projection of a square pipe, a cylindrical pipe and a transition piece is given in Fig. 10.23. Copy the given drawing and add all necessary dimensions.

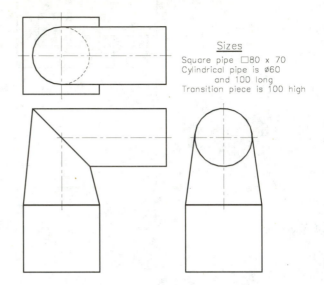

Sizes
Square pipe □80 x 70
Cylindrical pipe is ⌀60
and 100 long
Transition piece is 100 high

Fig. 10.23 Exercise 3

4. A 20-button digitising puck is shown in two views in Fig. 10.24. Copy and dimension the drawing. Don't worry that you won't see such a puck.

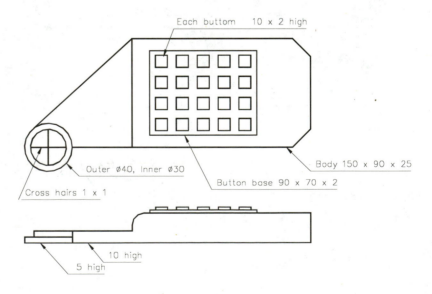

Each buttom   10 x 2 high

Outer ⌀40, Inner ⌀30

Body 150 x 90 x 25

Button base 90 x 70 x 2

Cross hairs 1 x 1

10 high

5 high

Fig. 10.24 Exercise 4

CHAPTER 11

The Edit menu and types of file

Introduction

The commands in the **Edit** pull-down menu must not be confused with the tools in the **Modify** toolbar, which some may regard as editing tools. A *left-click* on **Edit** in the menu bar brings down the menu shown in Fig. 11.1.

Edit	
Undo	Ctrl+Z
Redo	Ctrl+A
Cut	Ctrl+X
Copy	Ctrl+C
Copy View	
Paste	Ctrl+V
Paste Special...	
Properties...	
Links...	
Insert Object...	

Fig. 11.1 The **Edit** pull-down menu

Undo and Redo

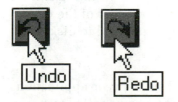

Fig. 11.2 The **Undo** and **Redo** tool icons found in the **Standard** toolbar

These two tools (commands) can be either selected from the **Edit** menu or by *left-clicks* on their tool icons in the **Standard** toolbar (Fig. 11.2). **Undo** undoes the last action taken by the operator. Repeated calls on **Undo** will undo until all actions taken during the current drawing session are undone. **Redo**, on the other hand, only redoes the very last undone action. I find it easier to undo an action – say the drawing of a single line – by *entering* **u** at the Command Line.

Object linking and embedding

Object linking and embedding (OLE) technology allows graphic images (objects) such as AutoCAD drawings (from files with the extension ***.dwg**), bitmaps (from files with the extension ***.bmp**), Windows metafiles (from files with the extension ***.wmf**) and other types of graphics, as well as text from documents produced by Windows applications, to be either linked or embedded into most applications running under Windows. This includes Windows AutoCAD R13 into which graphics and text can be linked or embedded and from which drawings can be linked or embedded into documents produced in Windows by applications such as word processing or desk top publishing programs.

Linking and embedding are different forms of placing objects from one application to another.

Linked objects

If an original graphics object such as an AutoCAD drawing is linked to a document produced by a desk top publishing program (DTP) and is changed in any way, the changes can be immediately reflected in the document. For example a change in the diameter of a circle in a linked AutoCAD drawing can be quickly changed in the DTP document with the aid of link tools in the DTP program.

Embedded objects

If an object such as an AutoCAD drawing is embedded in a document produced by a DTP (or other program), changes in the AutoCAD drawing cannot be reflected in the document. The data for the drawing becomes embedded in the data for the document and becomes part of the document file when the document is saved to disk.

Pasted objects

Graphics and text from other applications can be pasted to or from AutoCAD R13 drawings. Pasted objects become part of the data in the file of the drawing or document when it is saved to disk.

The Windows Clipboard

Linking, embedding and pasting is carried out between applications with the aid of the Windows **Clipboard**. This can be called to screen by a *double-click* on the **Clipboard Viewer** icon (Fig. 11.3). There is no need to call the **Clipboard** on to the screen because objects being linked, embedded or pasted between applications are carried out in

Fig. 11.3 The **Clipboard Viewer** icon in the **Main** window of the Windows **Program Manager**

the background without the **Clipboard** having to be visible. The reader is advised, however, to view the **Clipboard** until reasonably conversant with the operations of linking, embedding and pasting.

Examples of OLE and pasting

First example

In this example the drawing from Fig. 15.5 (page 231) is linked to a document produced with the aid of the DTP PageMaker 5. The procedure to obtain the link followed the pattern:

1. Load the drawing, which is to be linked into the AutoCAD graphics window.
2. *Left-click* on **Copy View** in the **Edit** menu (Fig. 11.1).
3. The drawing is automatically copied to the **Clipboard** (Fig. 11.4).

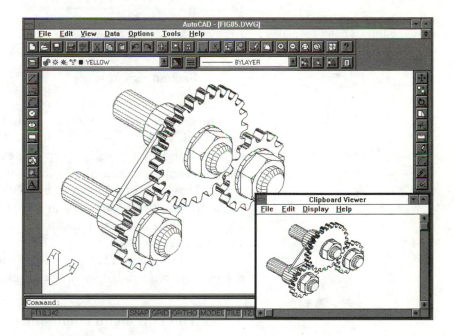

Fig.11.4 The AutoCAD drawing as it appears in the **Clipboard**

4. Select **Paste Link** from the PageMaker **Edit** pull-down menu and the linked drawing appears in the PageMaker document (Fig. 11.5). Text and other details can be added to the document in PageMaker as wished. If a change is now made to the AutoCAD drawing, the change can be made effective in the PageMaker document with the aid of the **Links** command from the PageMaker **File** menu.

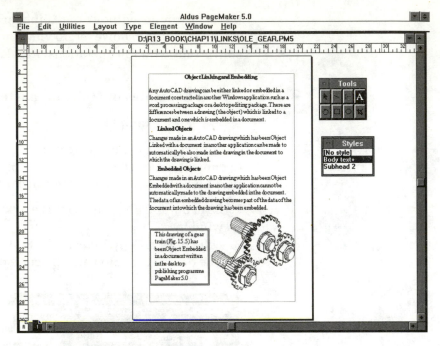

Fig. 11.5 The AutoCAD drawing linked to a Pagemaker document

Second example

In a paintbox application open one of the bitmaps from the Windows directory. Then **Copy** the bitmap from the paintbox screen into the **Clipboard**. In AutoCAD, *left-click* on **Paste** in the **Edit** pull-down menu and the bitmap will appear in the AutoCAD graphics window. Fig. 11.6 includes examples of three of the Windows bitmaps (files with extension *.bmp) pasted into AutoCAD.

All linked, embedded or pasted objects can be re-sized, once they are in the window of the application. The method is to move the cursor, under mouse control, on to any one of the tiny squares at the corners of the object. Then hold down the mouse button and *drag* the object to its required size. An example is included in Fig. 11.6.

The Edit menu commands

The Copy command

If an AutoCAD drawing is to be embedded (i.e. not linked) into a document from another application, use **Copy** from the **Edit** menu. The Command Line will show the prompts:

> **Command:_copyclip**
> **Select objects:** *enter* w (for Window) *Return*
> **First corner:** *pick* **Other corner:** *pick*
> **Select objects:** *Return*
> **Command:**

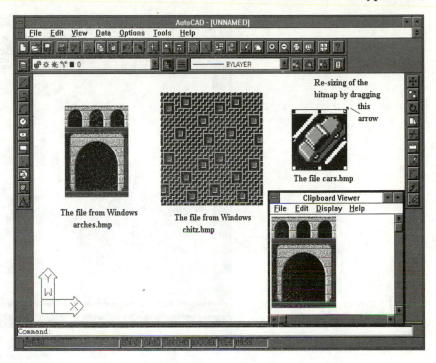

Fig. 11.6 Three Windows
bitmaps pasted into AutoCAD

and the windowed area of the drawing is copied to the **Clipboard**,
ready for pasting into a document from another application. Any
changes made in the AutoCAD drawing cannot however be reflected
in the object now embedded in the other application. The data of the
object becomes part of the data for the file of the document in the
other application.

The Cut command

Using this command allows part of an AutoCAD drawing to be cut
from the drawing before being copied into the **Clipboard**. Fig. 11.7
shows an example in the **Clipboard**. Those parts selected with the
Cut command have been cut from the drawing in the **Clipboard**.

The Paste Special command

Brings up the **Paste Special** dialogue box, showing details of features
already on the **Clipboard**. Selection from the items showing will
paste them on to the screen. Fig. 11.8 shows the dialogue box with
details of some text in the **Clipboard**.

The Insert Object command

Brings up the **Insert New Object** dialogue box (Fig. 11.9), with a list
of applications from which objects can be inserted into the AutoCAD

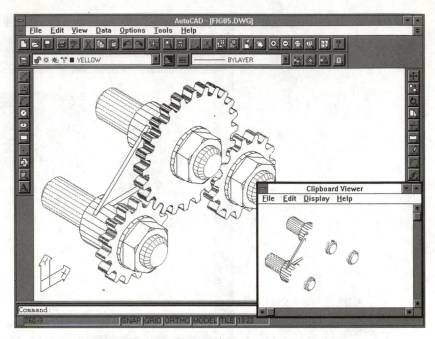

Fig. 11.7 An example of the use of the **Cut** command from **edit**

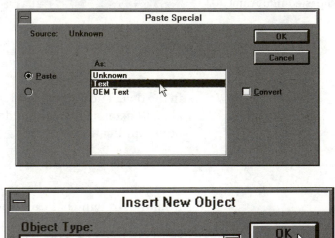

Fig. 11.8 The **Paste Special** dialogue box

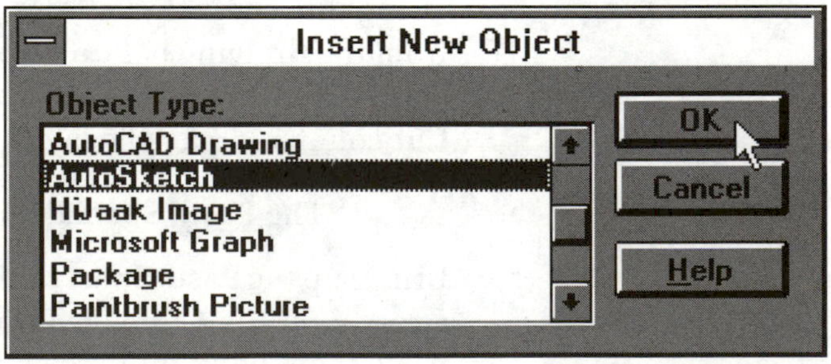

Fig. 11.9 The **Insert New Object** dialogue box

graphics window. As an example, selecting **AutoSketch** from the applications in the list box, brings up the AutoSketch **Select File** dialogue box. Selection of a drawing file from that dialogue box allows it to be inserted into the AutoCAD window.

Modify Ellipse

Properties

Color...	BYLAYER	Handle:	5F
Layer...	0	Thickness:	0
Linetype...	HIDDEN	Linetype Scale:	1

Center

Pick Point <

X: 215
Y: 195
Z: 0

Major Radius: 95
Minor Radius: 42.72001872
Radius Ratio: 0
Start Angle: 0
End Angle: 360

Major Axis Vector

X: 95
Y: 0
Z: 0
Area: 12750

OK   Cancel   Help...

Fig. 11.10 The **Modify Ellipse** dialogue box

The Links command

A dialogue box appears showing the links already in the AutoCAD graphics window.

The Properties comamnd

Allows the amendment of objects in the graphics window. A *left-click* on **Properties**, followed by another *left-click* on an object on screen – in the example shown in Fig. 11.10, an ellipse – brings up the **Modify Ellipse** dialogue box. Objects have their own dialogue boxes, depending upon which type of object is selected.

File types

DXF files

DXF files (**D**ata e**X**change **F**iles) are a form of file format for exchanging drawing files between CAD software systems. Most modern CAD software packages contain a DXF system for saving and loading DXF drawing files. The format was originated by Autodesk, the publishers of AutoCAD, but the format has been universally accepted as the standard for the exchange of drawing files between CAD systems. In AutoCAD R13, both 2D and 3D drawing data can be saved to DXF format files.

Saving a drawing to DXF

To save an AutoCAD drawing to DXF format:

1. Either *left-click* on the **Open** tool from the **Standard** toolbar (Fig. 11.11), or *left-click* on **Open...** in the **file** pull-down menu (Fig. 11.12). From the **Select File** dialogue box which then appears, select the drawing file to be loaded (Fig. 11.13).

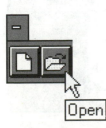

Fig. 11.11 The **Open** tool icon from the **Standard** toolbar

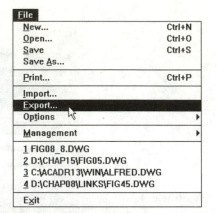

Fig. 11.12 The **File** pull-down menu

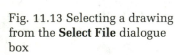

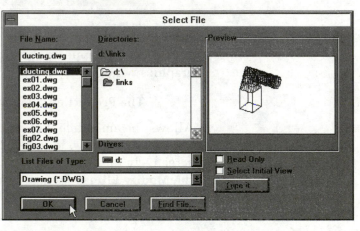

Fig. 11.13 Selecting a drawing from the **Select File** dialogue box

2. *Left-click* on **Export...** in the **File menu** (Fig. 11.12).
3. In the **Export Data** dialogue box which then appears, select ***.DXF** from the pop-up list under **List Files of Type:** (Fig. 11.14). *Enter* a suitable filename in the **File Name:** box, followed by a *left-click* on the **OK** button of the dialogue box.
4. The file will be saved with the extension ***.dxf**.

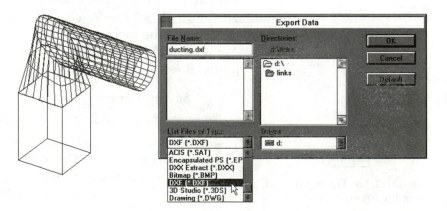

Fig. 11.14 Saving the drawing to **DXF format**

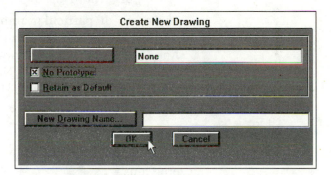

Fig. 11.15 The **New** tool icon
from the **Standard** toolbar

Loading a DXF file

If an attempt is made to load a DXF file into a prototype drawing screen, the attempt will fail. DXF files can only be loaded into a screen without set drawing parameters (limits, grid, snap, etc.). So to load a DXF file:

1. *Left-click* on the **New** tool icon in the **Standard** toolbar (Fig. 11.15) or *left-click on* **New...** in the **File** pull-down menu (Fig. 11.12).
2. The **Create New Drawing** dialogue box appears (Fig. 11.16). Make sure the **No Prototype** box is checked with a cross. If it isn't, *left-click* in the box to see that it is checked. Then *left-click* on the **OK** button of the dialogue box.

Fig. 11.16 The **Create New Drawing** dialogue box

3. *Left-click on* **Import...** in the **File** pull-down menu (Fig. 11.12).
4. In the **Import File** dialogue box which then appears (Fig. 11.17), select ***.DXF** from the **List Files of Type:** pop-up list, another *left-click* on the required DXF file name in the **File Name:** list box and a third *left-click* on the **OK** button of the dialogue box. The required DXF drawing will then appear.

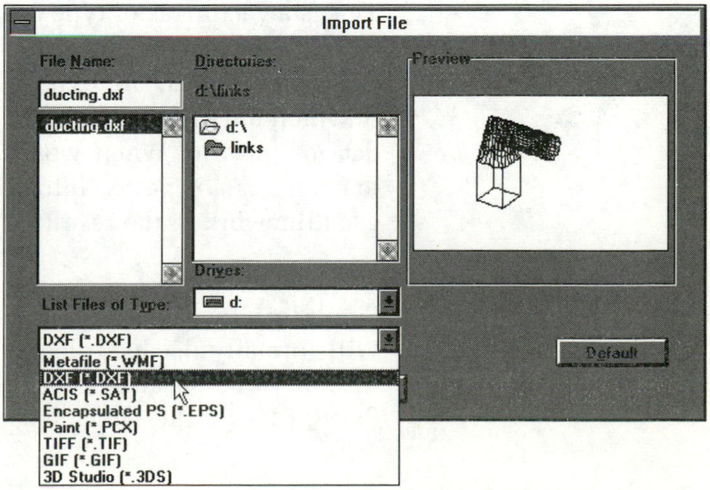

Fig. 11.17 The **Import File** dialogue box

Other types of file

It will have been noticed that AutoCAD drawings can be exported in a variety of file types (see the pop-up list in Fig. 11.14). We are not concerned here with most of these formats, but attention should be paid to the following:

Encapsulated Postscript *.EPS

The type of EPS file which can be exported from AutoCAD R13 is one which can be loaded into documents produced with other applications. The reader is advised to experiment with exporting and then importing EPS files.

3D Studio *.3DS

These are of particular importance to those who are using the Autodesk software **3D Studio** for producing photo-like renderings of AutoCAD R13 3D model drawings. Until R13, only DXF files could be exported to 3D Studio. Now there is no need to export the 3D drawing in DXF format before being able to load a drawing constructed in AutoCAD into 3D Studio.

Bitmap *.BMP

Can be of value when using paint type programs or other graphics programs.

Importing graphics of other file types

See the pop-up list showing in Fig. 11.17. For the purposes of this book, the reader may wish to experiment with importing graphics of the following file types.

Metafile *.WMF

This is a vector/raster type format. AutoCAD drawing files contain vector information in which the mathematical data of all objects such as lines, arcs, circles is retained in the file. Raster files are those in which only the positions of the pixels on screen are held in the data of the file. When working in some applications, AutoCAD drawings can be pasted into documents in WMF format to produce good linework in the resulting graphics.

Paint *.PCX

Similar to bitmap files and can usually be pasted into other documents. Will normally also load cleanly into Macintosh systems. I find these files of value because PCX files are usually smaller than bitmap (BMP) files for the same object.

Questions

1. What is the meaning of the term **object**?
2. What is the difference between object **linking** and object **embedding**?
3. Which command is used for linking AutoCAD drawing to a document produced with the aid of the Windows application **Write**?
4. Which command is used if an AutoCAD drawing is to be embedded in a document produced with the aid of a DTP application?
5. Why is the Windows **Clipboard** used when linking or embedding graphics or text between applications?
6. What is the difference between linking or embedding and pasting?
7. What happens when the command **Cut** is used?
8. What is a **DXF** file?
9. Which firm originated the DXF file format?
10. What steps must first be taken before an AutoCAD drawing can be saved to DXF format?

CHAPTER 12

Blocks and Insertions

Introduction

Any AutoCAD drawing with the filename extension **.dwg** can be inserted into any other AutoCAD drawing. Inserting drawings into other drawings with the aid of the **Insert Block...** tool not only allows parts of drawings to be added to other drawings, but also allows the speedy construction of circuit drawings such as those for electric, electronic, pneumatic and gate circuits from drawings which have been built up in *libraries* of symbols. Such libraries of symbols can either be built up by the operator or purchased ready to use as collections of symbol drawing files on disks. Here we are only concerned with operator constructed libraries.

Libraries of symbols

Libraries of drawings symbols can run into many hundreds, if not thousands of symbol files. A small library of symbols for nuts and bolts is illustrated in Fig. 12.1. The library was constructed with the aid of the **Block** tool (Fig. 12.2). The method of using this tool is given in Fig. 12.3. The stages are:

1. Construct a drawing of the required symbol.
2. *Left-click* on the **Block** tool icon in the **Draw** toolbar. A dialogue box **Create Drawing File** appears. *Enter* the required drawing filename in the **File Name:** box of the dialogue box, followed by a *left-click* on its **OK** button.
3. Respond to the prompts in the Command Line as indicated in Fig. 12.3.
4. When the drawing has been selected, it disappears from the screen.
5. *Enter* **oops** at the Command Line and the drawing reappears.

The symbol drawing is saved to the filename entered in the dialogue box in the directory which has been chosen to hold the files for the particular library of symbols. In the example given in Fig. 12.3 the

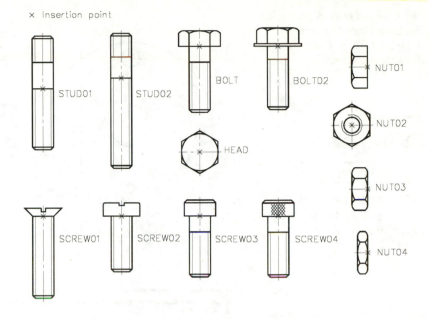

Fig. 12.1 A small library of nuts and bolts

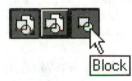

Fig. 12.2 The **Block** tool icon from the **Block** flyout of the **Draw** toolbar

drawing was saved as **d:\chap12\links\bolts\bolt02.dwg**. The filenames of the symbols in this library are given in Fig. 12.1.

An example of the insertion of symbols from this library is given in Fig. 12.4. This shows that the symbols represented by **Bolt02.dwg** and **Head.dwg** have been inserted as blocks in position in a third angle projection of a clutch system with the aid of the **Insert Block...** tool. To insert the drawing **Bolt02**, either *left-click* on the **Insert Block...** tool icon (Fig. 12.5), or *enter* insert at the Command Line.

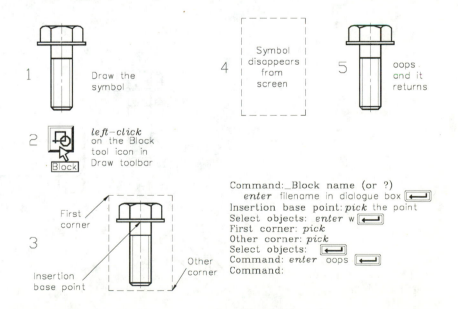

Fig. 12.3 The stages in constructing a symbol for a library

Fig. 12.4 An example of using
the **Insert** tool to place a
drawing from a library into a
drawing on screen

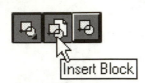

Fig. 12.5 The **Insert Block...**
tool icon from the **Block** flyout
of the **Draw** toolbar

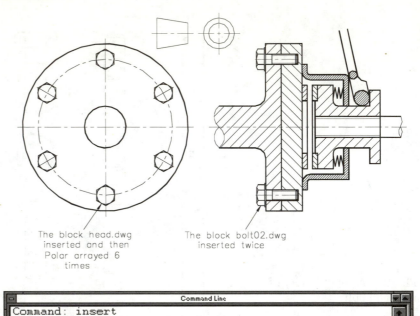

The block head.dwg
inserted and then
Polar arrayed 6
times

The block bolt02.dwg
inserted twice

Fig. 12.6 The prompts which
appear in the Command Line
window when insert is
entered from the keyboard

```
Command Line
Command: insert
Block name (or ?): c:\bolts\bolt
  Insertion point: X scale factor <1> / Corner / XYZ:
  Y scale factor (default=X):
  Rotation angle <0>:
```

Fig. 12.6 shows the Command Line prompts when insert is *entered*
from the keyboard.

Fig. 12.7 illustrates the results of a number of different responses
to the prompts appearing at the Command Line when the command

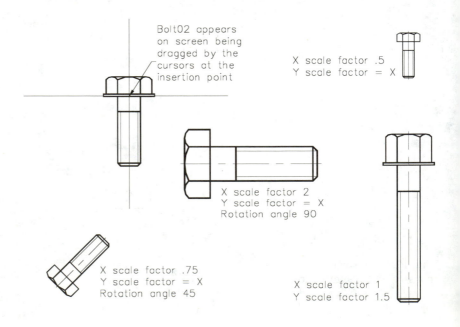

Bolt02 appears
on screen being
dragged by the
cursors at the
insertion point

X scale factor .5
Y scale factor = X

X scale factor 2
Y scale factor = X
Rotation angle 90

X scale factor .75
Y scale factor = X
Rotation angle 45

X scale factor 1
Y scale factor 1.5

Fig. 12.7 The process of
inserting a block

insert is entered. When the **Insert Block** tool icon is selected, the **Insert** dialogue box appears (Fig. 12.8). Entries can be made in the various boxes of the dialogue box. If **File...** is selected, the **Select Drawing File** dialogue box comes up, from which the selection of a drawing file can be made.

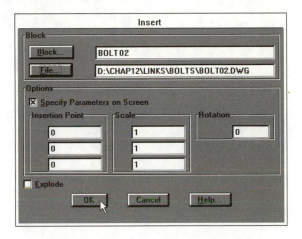

Fig. 12.8 The **Insert** dialogue box

Blocks in a drawing

Whenever a block is placed in a drawing, it can be called to the screen again, either by a *left-click* on **Blocks...** in the **Insert** dialogue box, or by *entering* the block name at the Command Line. Fig. 12.9 shows the **Defined Blocks** dialogue box, from which a block already within a circuit diagram of an electronics circuit drawing can be selected. Only the names of the blocks which have already been inserted in the current drawing will show in the dialogue box. An AutoCAD text window will appear with block names in response to a **?** *entered* at the Command Line.

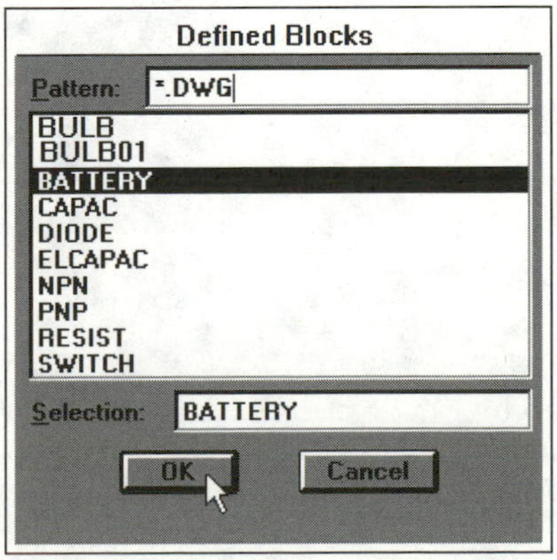

Fig. 12.9 The **Defined Blocks** dialogue box

Electric and electronic circuit diagram drawings

Fig. 12.10 shows a small library of electric/electronic circuit diagram symbols which have been saved as drawing files in a directory **c:\electric**. Fig. 12.11 shows the stages in the construction of a very simple electronics circuit by insertion of symbol drawings from the drawing files in this directory. Fig. 12.12 is a circuit diagram for a

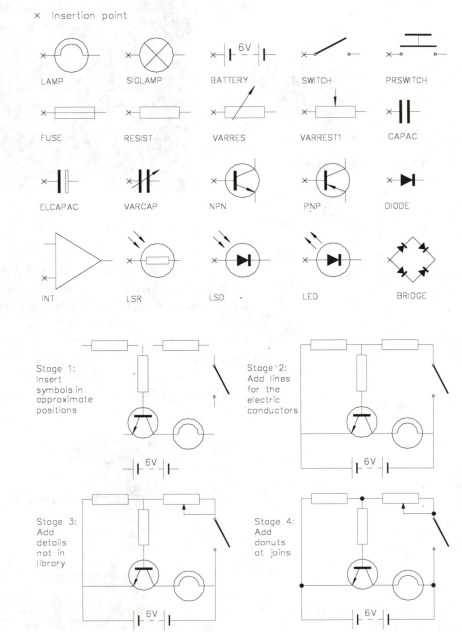

Fig. 12.10 A small library of electric/electronic circuit diagram symbols

Fig. 12.11 Stages in the construction of a simple electronics ciruit diagram from block symbols in a library

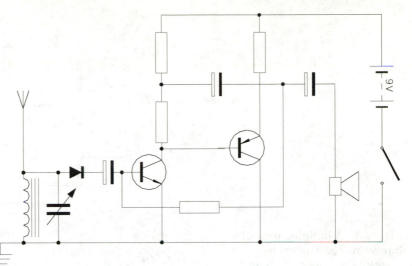

Fig. 12.12 A circuit diagram for a simple electronics transistor radio

somewhat more complicated electronics circuit diagram. The method of constructing any such diagram will be similar to that employed to construct the diagram in Fig. 12.11.

Other examples of libraries

Fig. 12.13 is a small library of symbols from which building plans can be constructed and Fig. 12.14 is an example of a building plan

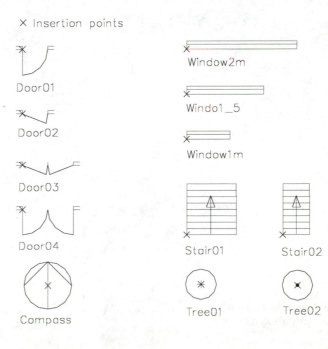

Fig. 12.13 A library of building plan symbols

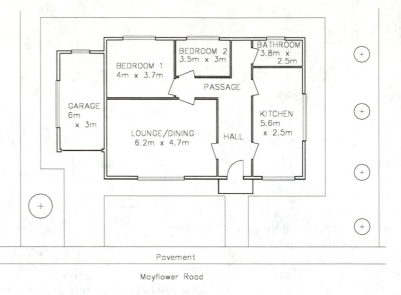

Fig. 12.14 A building plan of a bungalow constructed by insertion of symbol drawings from the library of Fig. 12.13

of a bungalow in part of its grounds constructed by insertion of symbols from the library.

Fig. 12.15 is a small library of symbols of components of pneumatics circuits and Fig. 12.16 is a diagrammatic drawing which includes the pneumatic circuit for controlling the depth of a hole to be drilled in a block of metal.

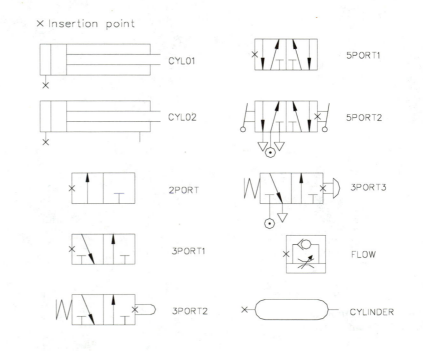

Fig. 12.15 A small library of pneumatics circuit symbols

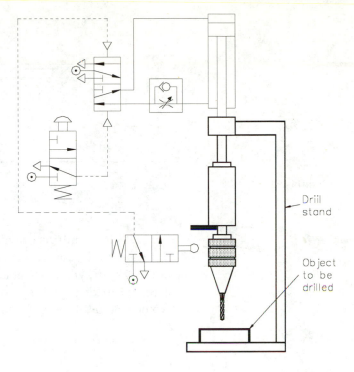

Drill
stand

Object
to be
drilled

Fig. 12.16 A diagrammatic
drawing of a drill with its
pneumatic circuit diagram to
control the depth of drilled
holes

Questions

1. What is the difference between a block saved to a drawing file and a block already in a drawing?
2. What is a **library** of circuit symbols?
3. Is there a limit to the number of symbols which can be saved in a library?
4. Why use the **oops** command (or tool) when a block has been saved to a filename on disk?
5. Why is an insertion point necessary when saving a block?

Exercises

1. Fig. 12.17 is a sectional view through an engineering part in which a top is to be fitted to a base with the aid of studs held in place with nuts and washers placed in the two spaces in the sectional view. Construct a drawing of a suitable stud, a suitable nut and a washer, save them to disk as symbols then copy the given drawing to the dimensions given and insert the studs, nuts and washers in the spaces.

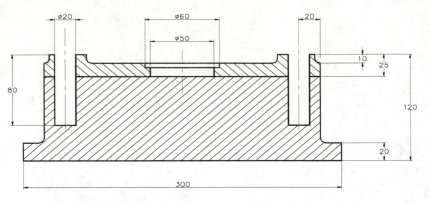

Fig. 12.17 Exercise 1

2. Fig. 12.18 is an outline drawing of a plan of a bungalow. With Fig. 12.13 as a guide, construct and save to disk, a sufficient number of building plan symbols to enable the building plan to be completed by the insertion of your symbols. The completed plan is to include two bedrooms, a living room, a bathroom and a kitchen.

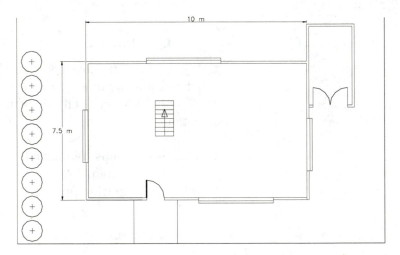

Fig. 12.18 Exercise 2

3. Copy Fig. 12.19 to any suitable scale and using Fig. 12.10 as a guide, construct and save to disk, a sufficient number of electric/electronics symbols to complete the drawing of Fig. 12.19 by insertion of your symbols.

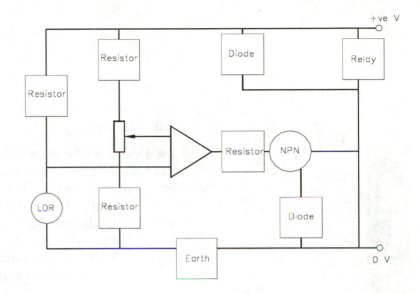

Fig. 12.19 Exercise 3

4. With Fig. 12.15 as a guide, construct a sufficient number of pneumatics symbols to be inserted into a drawing allowing the construction of the completed circuit partly given in Fig. 12.20.

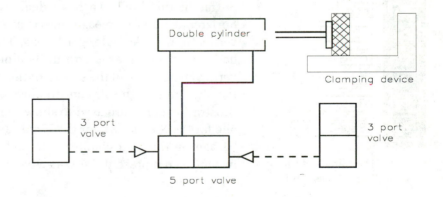

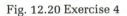

Fig. 12.20 Exercise 4

CHAPTER 13

The Surfaces toolbar

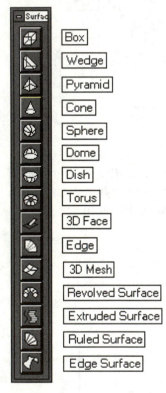

Box

Wedge

Pyramid

Cone

Sphere

Dome

Dish

Torus

3D Face

Edge

3D Mesh

Revolved Surface

Extruded Surface

Ruled Surface

Edge Surface

Fig. 13.1 The names of the tools in the **Surfaces** toolbar

Introduction

Fig. 13.1 shows the **Surfaces** toolbar, together with the names of the tools in the toolbar. These tools are used for the construction of 3D (three-dimensional) drawings. It is probable that once the reader becomes familiar with 3D construction methods in AutoCAD R13 that he/she will mainly be using tools from the **Solids** toolbar for the construction of most 3D drawings, but the **Surfaces** tools are very suitable for some 3D constructions and the reader is advised to practise and experiment with the **Surfaces** tools.

3D coordinates x,y,z

This and the following two chapters deal with 3D constructions, in which a third coordinate axis Z is used in addition to the two coordinate axes X and Y of 2D (two-dimensional) drawing construction. So far in this book we have dealt with constructions in which horizontal units of measurement are taken along an X axis with vertical units taken along a Y axis. The Z axis is perpendicular to both the X and Y axes and units along the Z axis are taken as if vertical to the face of the screen of the computer. A pictorial view of the directions of the 3D coordinate axes is given in Fig. 13.2. In this illustration cones are used to show the coordinate axes directions – one for the X axis, two for the Y axis and three for the Z axis. It will be seen in the next chapter that such cones will be used in some instances to represent the axes when constructing 3D solid models.

Methods of 3D drawing

Drawing with lines

Fig. 13.3 is a 3D drawing of a simple rectangular block, drawn with the aid of the **Line** tool from the **Draw** toolbar and using the absolute coordinates method of construction (see page 43). The Command

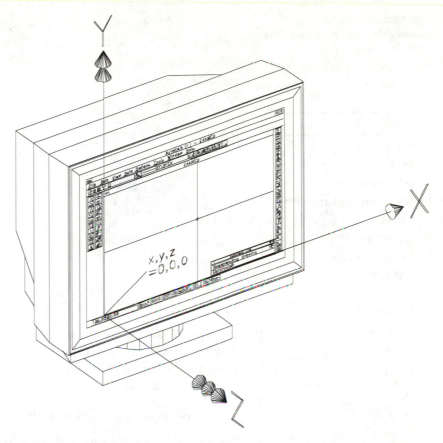

Fig. 13.2 The directions of the
x, y and z coordinate axes

Line sequence is included in the illustration. Note that those coordinates
for the line points of the base, which is on the XY plane, have only
the x,y figures, while those of the top of the outline require all three
of the x,y,z coordinates.

Using Filters

If working with a two-button mouse, pressing the **Shift** key of the
keyboard and the right mouse button will normally bring the **Filters**
menu on screen – Fig. 13.4. Filters could have been used for
positioning the endpoint of lines in the example given in Fig. 13.3.
Take the line in the prompt sequence:

Line From point: 210,210,50

The same point could have been gained by:

Line From point: 210,210

followed by **Shift** + *right-click* which brings up the **Filters** menu.
Select **.XY** from the menu with a *left-click*. **(need Z)** appears at the
Command Line. *Enter* the z coordinate (50) and the required point

Fig. 13.3 Drawing a
rectangular outline using **Line**
with absolute coordinates

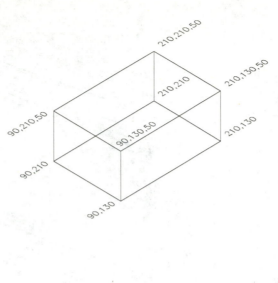

```
Command:_line
From  point: 90,130
To  point: 210,130
To  point: 210,210
To  point: 90,210
To  point: 90,130
To  point: 90,130,50
To  point: 210,130,50
To  point  210,210
To  point  Return
Command: Return
From  point: 210,130,50
To  point: 210,210,50
To  point: 210,210
To  point: Return
Command: Return
From  point: 210,210,50
To  point: 90,210,50
To  point: 90,210
To  point: Return
Command: Return
From  point: 90,130
To  point: 90,130,50
To  point: Return
Command: Return
```

From
Endpoint
Midpoint
Intersection
Apparent Intersection
Center
Quadrant
Perpendicular
Tangent
Node
Insertion
Nearest
Quick,
None
.X
.Y
.Z
.XZ
.YZ
.XY

Fig., 13.4 The **Filters** menu

210,210,50 is located. This may seem a long-winded method, but
with practice it takes less time than entering the full x,y,z coordinates.
The other filters in the menu can be used as appropriate when
constructing in 3D.

Isometric 3D Viewpoint Presets

Fig. 13.3 shows a view as if looking from above and from the south
east corner of the XY plane. This viewing position was obtained with
the aid of the **3D Viewpoint Presets**, which can be selected either
from the **View** pull-down menu (Fig 13.5) or from tool icons in the
Standard toolbar (Fig. 13.6). All four **Isometric** preset viewing

Fig. 13.5 The **3D Viewpoint
Presets** from the **View** pull-
down menu

View	
Redraw View	
Redraw All	
Zoom	▶
Pan	▶
Named Views...	
3D Viewpoint Presets	**Plan View** ▶
3D Viewpoint	**Top**
3D Dynamic View	**Bottom**
✓**Tiled Model Space**	**Left**
Floating Model Space	**Right**
Paper Space	**Front**
Tiled Viewports	**Back**
Floating Viewports	**SW Isometric**
Preset UCS...	**SE Isometric**
Named UCS...	**NE Isometric**
Set UCS	**NW Isometric**

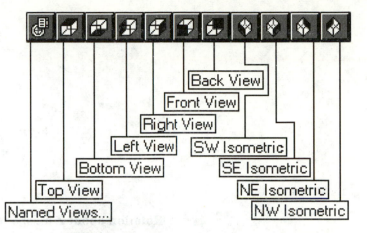

Fig. 13.6 The **3D Viewpoint Presets** tool icons in the **Standard** toolbar

positions are shown in Fig. 13.7. The 3D letter E for showing the four isometric views were drawn with the aid of the **Box** tool from the **Surfaces** toolbar. See page 184.

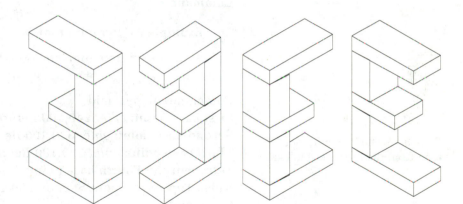

Fig. 13.7 The four isometric viewing positions: NW, NE, SW, SE

Using the Surfaces tools

Example 1 – Box tool

Left-click on the **Box** tool icon (Fig. 13.8). The Command Line changes to:

Fig. 13.8 The **Box** tool icon from the **Surfaces** toolbar

Command: ai_box
Initializing... 3D Objects loaded.
Corner of box: *enter* 100,100 *Return*
Length: *enter* 50 *Return*
Cube/<Width>: *enter* 75 *Return*
Height: *enter* 75 *Return*

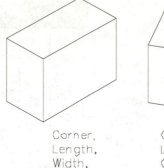

Fig. 13.9 Example 1

Rotation about Z axis: *enter* 0 *Return*
Command: *Return*
Corner of box: *enter* 300,100 *Return*
Length: *enter* 70 *Return*
Cube/<Width>: *enter* c (for Cube) *Return*
Rotation about Z axis: *enter* 30 *Return*
Command:

Example 2 – Pyramid tool

Left-click on the **Pyramid** tool icon (Fig. 13.10). The Command Line changes to:

Fig. 13.10 The **Pyramid** tool icon from the **Surfaces** toolbar

Command: ai_pyramid
First base point: *enter* 240,100 *Return*
Second base point: *enter* 320,100 *Return*
Third base point: *enter* 320,180 *Return*
Tetrahedron/<Fourth base point>: *enter* 240,180 *Return*
Ridge/Top/<Apex point>: *enter* 280,140,75 *Return*
Command:

Fig. 13.11 Example 2. The results of using different prompts in the **Pyramid** command set

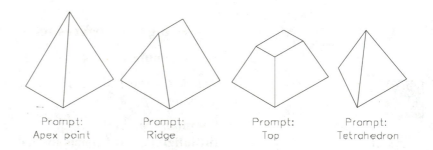

This example uses the **Apex point**, which is the default prompt. To determine the axis the coordinate point must be given in terms of *x,y,z* – that is all three coordinates must be given. Fig. 13.11 shows

pyramids drawn using the four different prompts of the tool command set.

Example 3 – Cone tool

Fig. 13.12 The **Cone** tool icon from the **Surfaces** toolbar

Command: ai_cone
Base center point: *enter* 125,160 *Return*
Diameter/<Radius> of base: *enter* 35 *Return*
Diameter/<Radius> of top <0>: *Return*
Height: *enter* 75 *Return*
Number of segments <16>: *enter* 12 *Return*
Command:

Radius
at top=0
Segments=12

Radius
of base=40
of top=25
Segments=16

Radius
of base=25
of top=25
Height=60

Fig. 13.13 Example 3. Using three different sets of prompts

Example 4 – Sphere tool

Fig. 13.14 The **Sphere** tool icon from the **Surfaces** toolbar

Command: ai_sphere
Center of sphere: *enter* 150,200,75 *Return*
Diameter/<Radius> : *enter* 75 *Return*
Number of longitudinal segments <16>: *enter* 12 *Return*
Number of latitudinal segments <16>: *enter* 8 *Return*
Command:

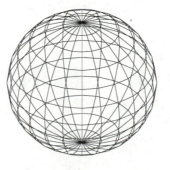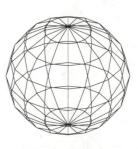

Longitudinal 24
Latitidunal 16

Longitudinal 12
Latitidunal 8

Fig. 13.15 Example 4

Example 5 – Dome and Dish tools

Fig. 13.16 The **Dome** tool icon from the **Surfaces** toolbar

Command: ai_dome
Center of dome: *enter* 100,150 *Return*
Diameter/<Radius> : *enter* 40 *Return*
Number of longitudinal segments <16>: *Return*
Number of latitudinal segments <16>: *enter* 8 *Return*
Command:

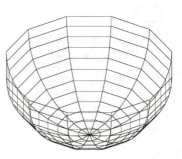

```
    Dome                  Dish
Logitudinal 16       Longitudinal 12
Latitudinal 8        Latitudinal 16
```

Fig. 13.17 Example 5. A **Dome** and a **Dish**

Example 6 – Torus tool

Fig. 13.18 The **Torus** tool icon from the **Surfaces** toolbar

Command: ai_torus
Center of torus: *enter* 150,125 *Return*
Diameter/<Radius> of torus: *enter* 60 *Return*
Diameter/<Radius> of tube: *enter* 10 *Return*
Segments around tube circumference <16>: *enter* 8 Return
Segments around torus circumference <16>: *Return*
Command:

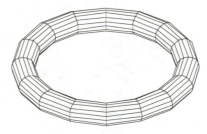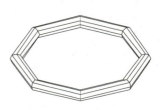

```
Tube segments 16      Tube segments 8
Torus segments 16     Torus segments 8
```

Fig. 13.19 Example 6. Two surfaces constructed with the **Torus** tool

3D surface meshes

The 3D objects shown above are made up from 3D surface meshes, in the form of rectangles the length and width of which are determined by the segment numbers requested by the prompts associated with the tools. Those surface meshes and other features behind the 3D surface meshes facing the direction of viewing can be hidden from view by calling the command **hide** as follows:

Command: *enter* hide *Return*
Regenerating drawing.
Command:

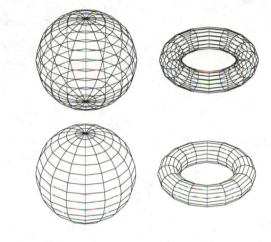

Fig. 13.20 A **Sphere** and a **Torus** before **Hide** (upper drawings) and after **Hide** (lower drawings)

Example 7 – 3D Face tool

Fig, 13.21 The **3D Face** tool icon from the **Surfaces** toolbar

Left-click on the **3D Face** tool icon (Fig. 13.21). The Command Line changes to:

Command: _3dface
First point: *enter* 100,100 *Return*
Second point: *enter* 100,100,100 *Return*
Third point: *enter* 200,100,100 *Return*
Fourth point: *enter* 200,100 *Return*
Third point: *Return*
Command: *Return*
First point: *enter* 100,100 *Return*
Second point: *enter* 100,250 *Return*
Third point: *enter* 200,250 *Return*
Fourth point: *enter* 200,100 *Return*
Third point: *Return*

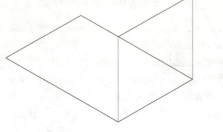

Fig. 13.22 Example 7. Before and after **Hide**

Command: *enter* hide *Return*
Regenerating drawing.
Command:

Example 8 – Edge tool

Fig. 13.24 shows an example of lines in a Tabsurf/Edgesurf model hidden with the aid of the **Edge** tool. (Fig. 13.23).

Fig. 13.23 The **Edge** tool from the **Surfaces** toolbar

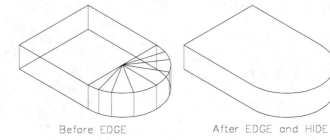

Fig. 13.24 Example 8

Before EDGE   After EDGE and HIDE

Example 9 – Revolved Surface tool

With the **Polyline** tool from the **Draw** toolbar construct an outline such as that shown in Fig. 13.26. Then *left-click* on the **Revolved Surface** tool icon (Fig. 13.25). The Command Line changes to:

Fig. 13.25 The **Revolved Surface** tool icon from the **Surfaces** toolbar

Command: _revsurf
Select path curve: *left-click* on the polyline
Select axis of revolution: *left-click* on the axis of revolution

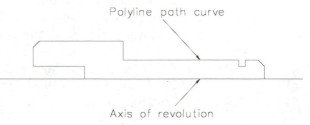

Polyline path curve

Axis of revolution

Fig. 13.26 The path curve and axis of revolution for a **Revolved Surface**

Start angle <0>: *Return*
Included angle (+=ccw, –=cw) <Full circle>: *Return*
Command:

The **Revolved Surface** mesh density depends upon two variables which need to be set before calling the command. These are **Surftab1** and **Surftab2**. They are called by:

Command: *enter* surftab1 *Return*
New value for SURFTAB1 <6>: *enter* 16 *Return*
Command:

With **Surftab2** amended in the same manner. Example 9 was constructed with **Surftab1** set to 16 and **Surftab2** set to 2.

Fig. 13.27 shows the resulting revolved surface as viewed from the **SE Isometric Viewpoint**.

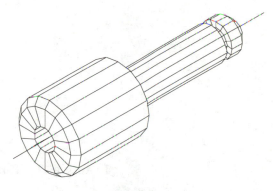

Fig. 13.27 Example 9. The **Revolved Surface** as viewed from the **SE Isometric Viewpoint**

Example 10 – Extruded Surface tool

With the aid of the **Polyline** tool from the **Draw** toolbar, draw an outline such as that shown in Fig. 13.28. Then *left-click* on the **Extruded Surface** tool icon (Fig. 13.29). The Command Line changes to:

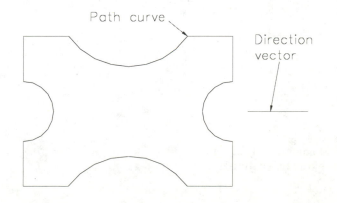

Fig. 13.28 Example 10. Path curve and direction vector

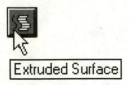

Fig. 13.29 The **Extruded Surface** tool icon from the **Surfaces** toolbar

Command: _tabsurf
Select path curve: *left-click* on the path curve
Select direction vector: *left-click* on the direction vector
Command:

Fig. 13.30 shows the resulting extruded surface after **Hide**. Note that the upper surface is not a surface mesh.

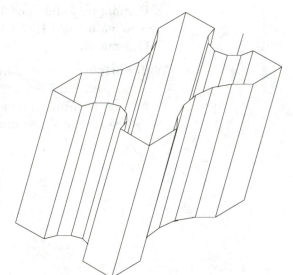

Fig. 13.30 Example 10

Example 11 – Ruled Surface tool

Fig. 13.31 The **Ruled Surface** tool icon from the **Surfaces** toolbar

Draw an arc and a line as shown in Fig. 13.32. One end of the line is at a point 50 units above the XY plane. The arc lies on the XY plane. Then *left-click* on the **Ruled Surface** tool icon (Fig. 13.31). The Command Line changes to:

Command: _rulesurf
Select first defining curve: *left-click* on the arc or the line

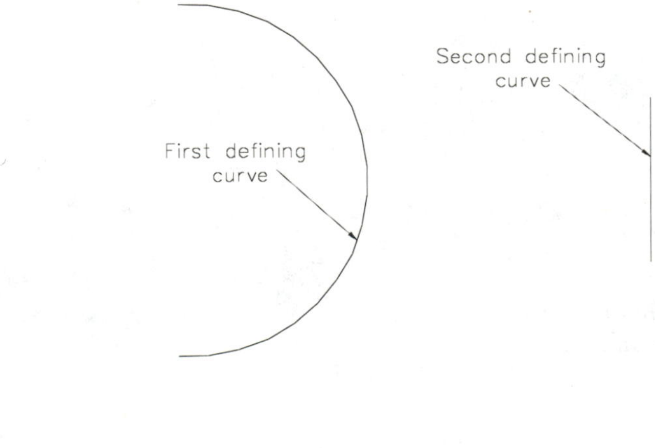

Second defining curve

First defining curve

Fig. 13.32 Example 11. The arc and line of the two defining curves

Select second defining curve: *left-click* on the other arc or line
Command:

In this example **Surftab1** was set to 16 and **Surftab2** set to 2.
The resulting 3D object is shown in Fig. 13.33 after calling **Hide**.

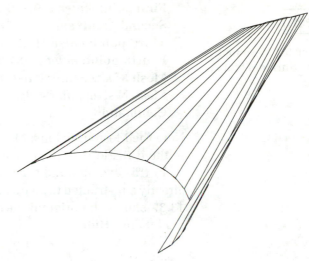

Fig. 13.33 Example 11 as seen
from the **SE Isometric Viewing
Point**

Example 12 – Edgesurf tool

Fig. 13.34 The **Edge Surface**
tool icon from the **Surfaces**
toolbar

With the aid of the **Line** tool from the **Draw** toolbar construct the
rectangle from 100,100 to 100,250,100 to 250,250,50 to 250,100,150
to 100,100. Then *left-click* on the **Edge Surface** tool icon (Fig. 13.34).
The Command Line changes to:

Command: _edgesurf
Select edge 1: *left-click* on an edge
Select edge 2: *left-click* on the second edge
Select edge 3: *left-click* on the third edge
Select edge 4: *left-click* on the last edge
Command:

and the edgesurf surface is formed.
Surftab1 was set to 8 and **Surftab2** set to 2 for this example.

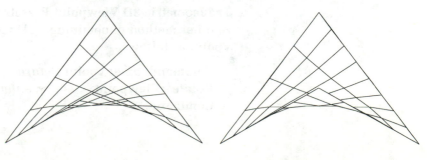

Fig. 13.35 Example 12 before
and after **Hide**

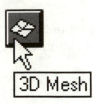

Fig. 13.36 The **3D Mesh** tool icon from the **Surfaces** toolbar

Example 13 – 3D Mesh tool

Left-click on the **3D Mesh** tool icon (Fig. 13.36). The Command Line changes to:

Command: _3dmesh
First point: *enter* 110,120 *Return*
Second point: *enter* 110,220 *Return*
Third point: *enter* 210,220,100 *Return*
Fourth point: *enter* 210,120,100 *Return*
Mesh M size: *enter* 8 *Return*
Mesh N size: *enter* 4 *Return*
Command:

Note the Mesh divisions: **M** in the direction along the X axis and **N** in the direction along the Y axis.

In this example the **Mirror** tool was used to copy the 3D mesh already constructed to give a mirror image joining the first mesh. Fig. 13.37 shows the original mesh on the XY plane and the mirrored model after **Hide**.

Fig. 13.37 Example 13. The original 3D Mesh and after **Mirror**, a second 3D Mesh added

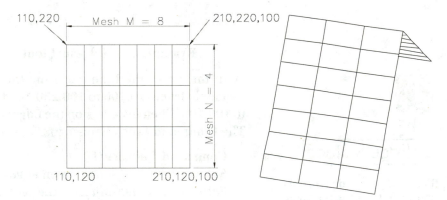

Further 3D tools

The Vpoint tool

The **Isometric 3D Viewpoint Presets** were introduced on page 186 Another method of obtaining a 3D viewing point is to use the tool **Vpoint** as follows:

Command: *enter* vpoint *Return*
Rotate/<Viewpoint><0,0,1>: *enter* –1,–1, 1 *Return*
Command:

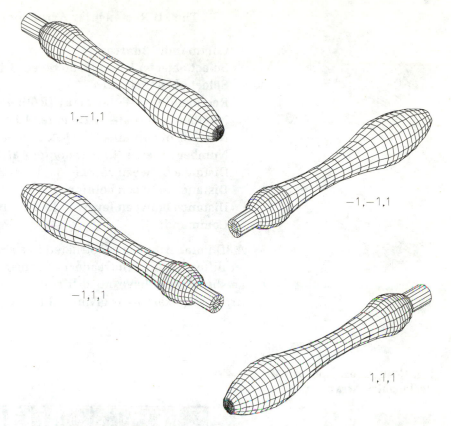

Fig. 13.38 Four **Vpoint**
viewing positions

Fig. 13.38 shows 4 viewpoint positions of a **Revolved Surface** 3D object. Other viewing positions can be obtained by entering different X, Y and Z figures. It is not distance from the object that is given by the coordinate vpoint figures, but the direction in terms of *x,y,z* from which the object is viewed. Thus:

X = –1 is from the left.
X = 1 is from the right.
Z = –1 is from below.
Z = 1 is from above.

The reader is advised to experiment with entering a variety of *x,y,z* figures in response to the **vpoint** prompts.

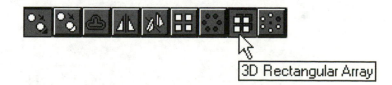

Fig. 13.39 The **3D Rectangular Array** tool icon from the **Copy** flyout of the **Modify** toolbar

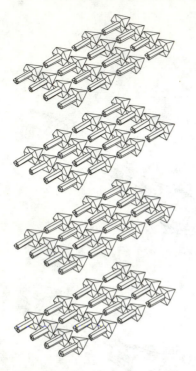

The 3D Rectangular Array tool

Command: _3darray
Select objects: *left-click* on object **1 found.**
Select objects: *Return*
Rectangular or Polar array (R/P): *enter* r *Return*
Number of rows (---)<1>: *enter* 4 *Return*
Number of columns (| | |)<1>: *enter* 4 *Return*
Number of levels (...)<1>: *enter* 4 *Return*
Distance between rows (---): *enter* −30 *Return*
Distance between columns (| | |): *enter* 60 *Return*
Distance between levels (...): *enter* 150 *Return*
Command:

A **3D Polar Array** is constructed in a similar manner. The prompts are different, but if the reader can construct a **3D Rectangular Array**, he/she should have no difficulty with constructing a **3D Polar Array**. An example is given in Fig. 13.42.

Fig. 13.40 An example of a **3D Rectangular Array**

Fig. 13.41 The **3D Polar Array** tool icon from the **Copy** flyout of the **Modify** toolbar

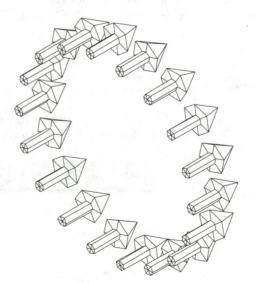

Fig. 13.42 A **3D Polar Array**

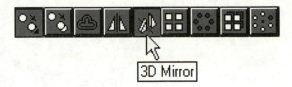

Fig. 13.43 The **3D Mirror** tool icon from the **Copy** flyout of the **Modify** toolbar

The 3D Mirror tool

Command: _mirror3d
Select objects: *enter* w (Window) *Return* **First corner:** *pick*
Other corner: *pick*
Plane by Entity/Last/Zaxis/View/XY/YZ/ZX/<3points>: *pick*
Second point: *pick*
Third point on plane: *Select* .**XY** filter and *pick* first point:
(need Z): *enter* 1 *Return*
Delete old objects <N>:
Command:

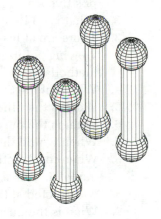

Fig. 13.44 An example of a 3D model acted upon by **3D Mirror** in two directions

The 3D Rotate tool

A similar set of prompts occurs as when the **3D Mirror** tool is in use, except that only two points on the required mirror line are required.

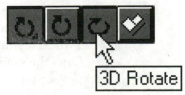

Fig. 13.45 The tool **3D Rotate** from the **Rotate** flyout of the **Draw** toolbar

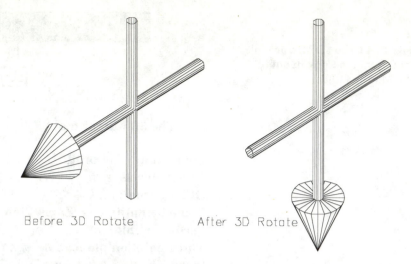

Fig. 13.46 Before and after the use of **3D Rotate**

Before 3D Rotate   After 3D Rotate

Questions

1. In which direction, relative to the monitor screen, does the positive *z* axis point?
2. What is a **Filter** in connection with 3D coordinates?
3. There are at least two methods by which an operator can obtain viewing points in order to view a 3D model. What are two of these methods?
4. Which of the **Surfaces** tools is used to construct a 3D cylinder?
5. What is the difference between a **Dish** and a **Dome**?
6. What is the purpose of the variables **Surftab1** and **Surftab2**?
7. When would the variable **Surftab2** be set to 2?
8. When constructing a 3D extruded surface, the upper surface of the model is not a surface mesh. How could a surface mesh be constructed at the top of an extruded model?
9. What is the purpose of the tool **Hide**?
10. When using the **Vpoint** command from which direction are the viewing points: **−1,−1,1   1,−1,1   −1,1,1   1,1,1**?

Exercises

1. A pictorial view and a third angle orthographic projection of four boxes are given in Fig. 13.47. Construct the boxes in their correct positions relative to each other.
2. Two boxes and a cone make up the 3D model shown in Fig. 13.48. Copy the model to the sizes given in the third angle orthographic projection

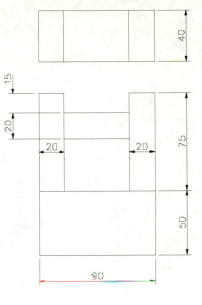

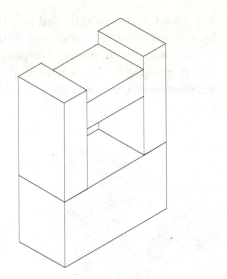

Fig. 13.47 Exercise 1

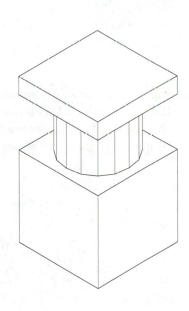

Fig. 13.48 Exercise 2

3.   Fig. 13.49 shows an extruded polyline with its open top covered by a rulesurf surface, together with a third angle orthographic projection of the 3D model. The polyline from which the extrusion was developed was drawn using the Line and Arc prompts of the **Polyline** tool. Construct the model to the dimensions given.

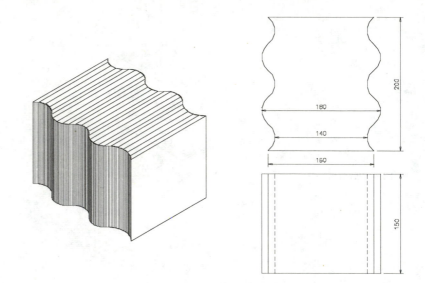

Fig. 13.49 Exercise 3

4.   Fig. 13.50 shows a 3D model resulting from a Revolved Surface of the pline included with the illustration. The **Surftab** settings for the revolved surface were **Surftab1** = 12 **Surftab2** = 2. To the dimensions given construct the model.

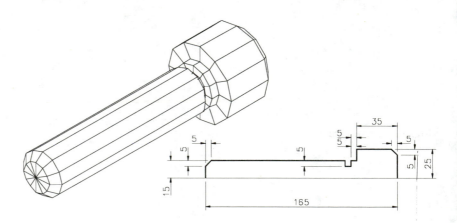

Fig. 13.50 Exercise 4

5. The model shown in Fig. 13.51 is of two identical revolved surfaces crossing each other at right angles. The surfaces were developed from the dimensioned polyline given with the illustration. Construct the model from the information given.

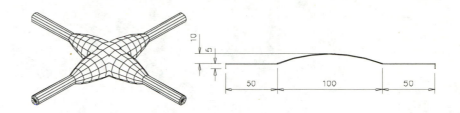

Fig. 13.51 Exercise 5

6. Fig. 13.52 is a 3D Rectangular Array of a revolved surface from the dimensioned pline given with the illustration. The settings for the 3D Array are: **Surftab1** = 9; **Surftab2** = 9; **Distance between rows** = 100; **Distance between columns** = 100; **Distance between layers** = 100.

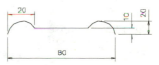

Fig. 13.52 Exercise 6

7. Using the same revolved surface as for Exercise 6 construct the 3D Polar Array given in Fig. 13.53. There are 12 objects in the array and the centre of the array is 60 units below the centre of the revolved surface model.

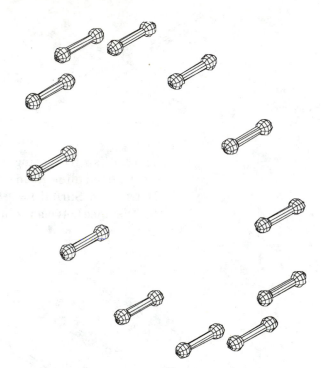

Fig. 13.53 Exercise 7

8. The 3D model shown in Fig. 13.54 was constructed from six 3D Faces to the dimensions given with the illustration. Construct the model to the sizes given.

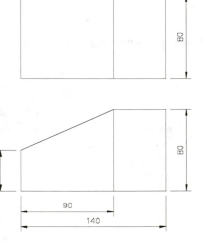

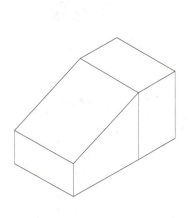

Fig. 13.54 Exercise 8

9. A much harder exercise. Fig. 13.55 shows a 3D model constructed from a **Revolved Surface** (handle), an **Extruded Surface** (file blade) and a **Ruled Surface** (top of blade). To any suitable dimensions attempt the construction of a similar 3D model.

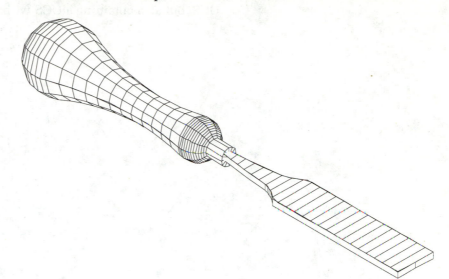

Fig. 13.55 Exercise 9

10. Fig. 13.56 is a 3D model of a tent made up from **3D Faces** (tent sides), **Cones** (poles) and **Polylines** (the ropes). Construct a similar model to any suitable sizes.

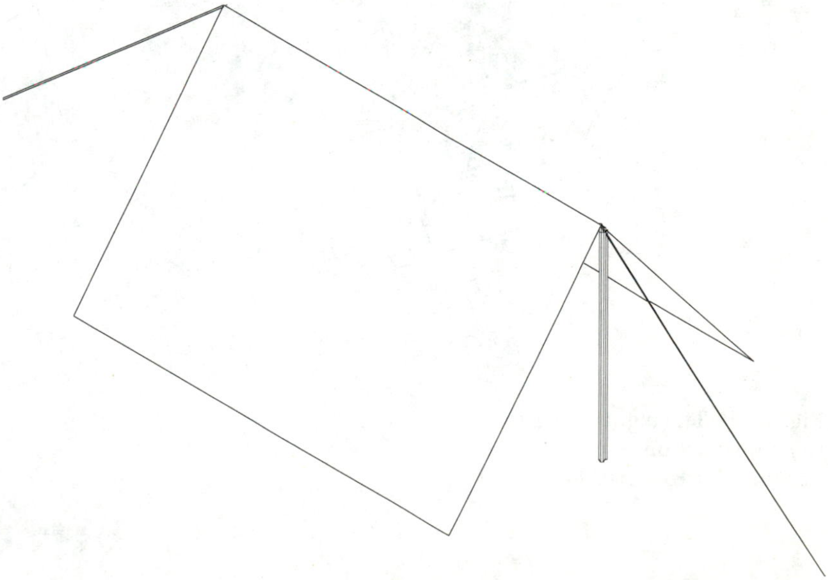

Fig. 13.56 Exercise 10

11. The eight drawings in Fig. 13.57 show the stages in the construction
     of the drawing of a transition piece between a square pipe and a
     cylindrical pipe. Construct the drawing as shown. The construction
     demands constant changes in the UCS using not only the **Preset**
     UCS, but also obtaining a UCS with the **3point** prompt.

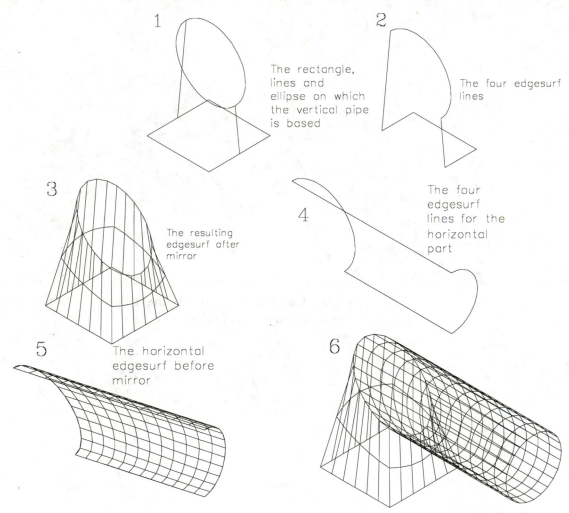

1   The rectangle,
    lines and
    ellipse on which
    the vertical pipe
    is based

2   The four edgesurf
    lines

3   The resulting
    edgesurf after
    mirror

4   The four
    edgesurf
    lines for the
    horizontal
    part

5   The horizontal
    edgesurf before
    mirror

6   The two edgesurfs

Fig. 13.57 The eight stages in
the construction of the
drawing for Exercise 11

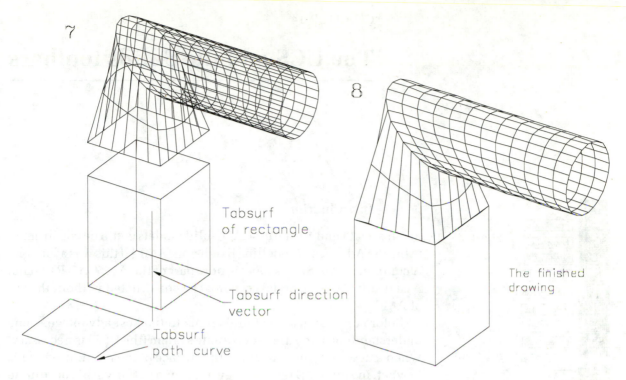

7

8

Tabsurf
of rectangle

Tabsurf direction
vector

Tabsurf
path curve

The finished
drawing

Fig. 13.57 *Continued*

CHAPTER 14

The UCS and the Solids toolbars

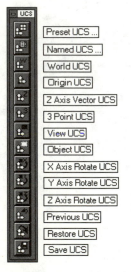

Fig. 14.1 The **UCS** toolbar

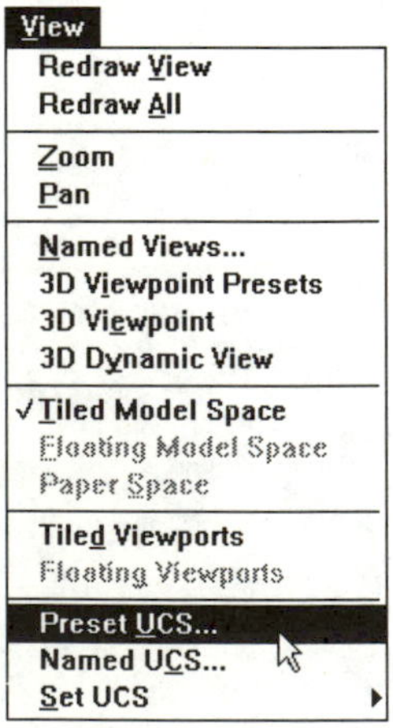

Fig. 14.2 **Preset UCS...** in the **View** pull-down menu

Introduction

In releases 11 and 12 of AutoCAD, solid models could be constructed using the Advanced Modelling Extension (AME) if this was available. A complete set of **Solids** tools is now part of the AutoCAD R13 data. As a result 3D solid models can now be constructed without the aid of AME.

Before one can use the **Solids** tools to the best advantage, some understanding of the **user coordinate system** (the **UCS**) is necessary. When a new drawing is opened, the surface of the monitor screen is in what, in AutoCAD terminology, is known as the **world coordinate system** (**WCS**) – with x coordinate units horizontal and y coordinate units vertical. In the WCS, z units are perpendicular to the screen's surface.

The UCS allows the operator to set up the AutoCAD graphics window at any angle to the WCS.

The user coordinate system

Some of the UCS settings can be preset in the **UCS Orientation** dialogue box be called either by a *left-click* on the **Preset UCS...** tool icon in the **UCS** toolbar (Fig. 14.1) or from the **View** pull-down menu (Fig. 14.2). The dialogue box appears (Fig. 14.3) from which any of nine preset UCS orientations can be chosen. That selected in Fig. 14.3 is the **RIGHT** UCS. Fig. 14.4 shows a 3D solid model in a pictorial view with arrows showing the directions of viewing of four of the UCS orientations – **WCS**, **FRONT**, **RIGHT** and **LEFT**. Fig. 14.5 shows the model as it appears on screen when each of these UCS orientations are selected from the dialogue box.

Note the directions of the X, Y and Z coordinate axes in Figs 14.4 and 14.5.

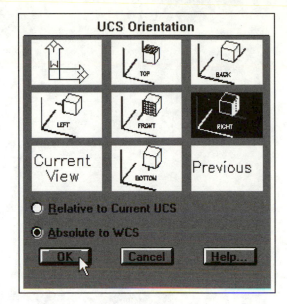

Fig. 14.3 The **UCS Orientation** dialogue box

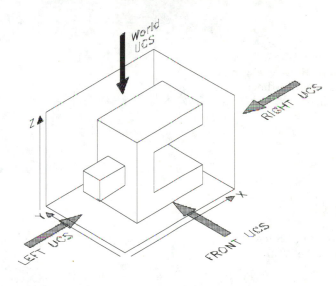

Fig. 14.4 Four of the pre-set **UCS** orientations

The UCS icon

When in the WCS the **UCS** icon (Fig. 14.6) appears at the bottom left-hand corner of the R13 graphics window. The icon can take various forms as indicated in Fig. 14.7. The icon reflects the current orientation of the UCS.

The variable UCSFOLLOW

When setting a new UCS the orientation will not change unless the variable **UCSFOLLOW** is set ON (ON=1) as follows:

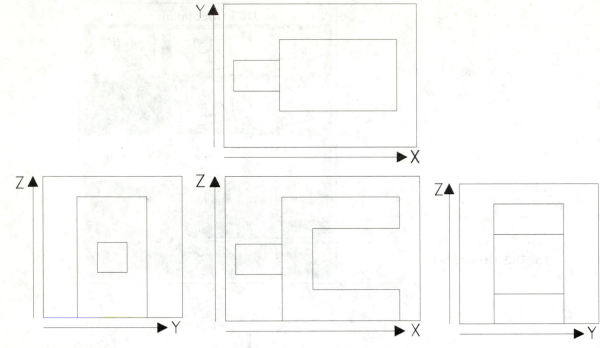

Fig. 14.5 Four of the pre-set **UCS** orientations arranged as if in third angle orthographic projection

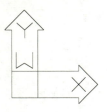

Fig. 14.6 The **UCS** icon as it appears in the WCS

The UCS icon in the WCS

The UCS icon in UCS other than the WCS

The UCS icon in VPOINT −1,−1,1

The UCS icon when the UCS is viewed on its edge

The UCS icon at the Origin of a solid The cross in the icon shows the origin (0,0,0)

Fig. 14.7 The variety of forms which can be taken by the **UCS** icon

Command: *enter* ucsfollow *Return*
New value for UCSFOLLOW<0>: *enter* 1 *Return*
Command:

and the variable is set ON. When ON, any selected or new UCS will be set up. If OFF the UCS becomes inactive.

UCS prompts at the Command Line

There are a variety of UCS tools as shown in Fig. 14.1. These can be selected from the **UCS** toolbar or entered in response to prompts after **ucs** is called at the command line. When any of the tool icons is selected from the toolbar, the responses will be:

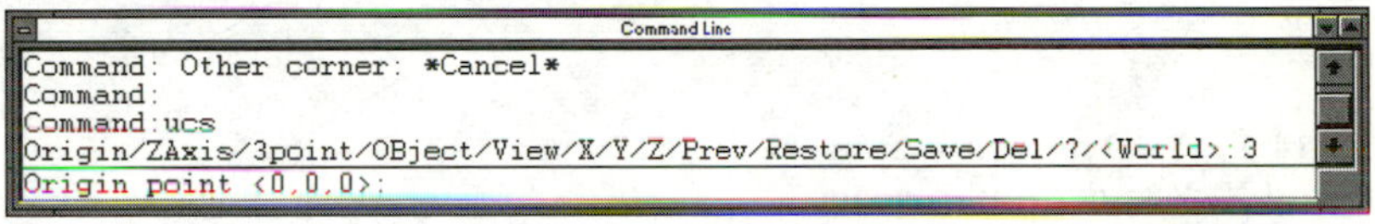

Fig. 14.8 The Command Line window after *entering* **ucs**

```
                              Command Line
Command: Other corner: *Cancel*
Command:
Command:ucs
Origin/ZAxis/3point/OBject/View/X/Y/Z/Prev/Restore/Save/Del/?/<World>:3
Origin point <0,0,0>:
```

Preset UCS...: The **UCS Orientation** dialogue box appears.
Named UCS...: The **UCS Control** dialogue box appears from which previously saved UCS orientations can be selected – Fig. 14.9.
World UCS: The screen changes to the **WCS**.

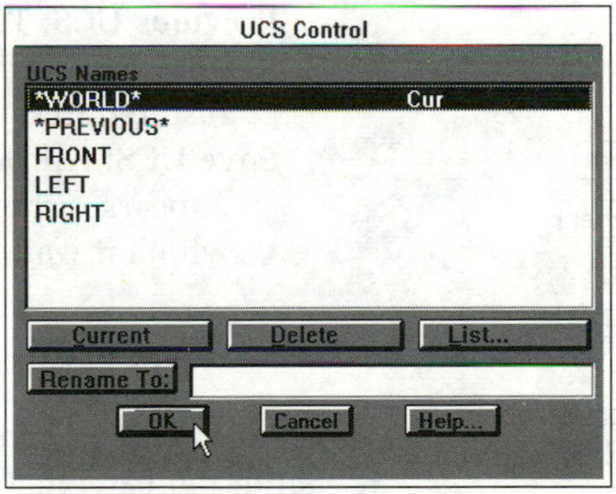

Fig.14.9 The **UCS Control** dialogue box

```
                         UCS Control
UCS Names
*WORLD*                                        Cur
*PREVIOUS*
FRONT
LEFT
RIGHT


            [ Current ]   [ Delete ]   [ List... ]
[ Rename To: ] [                    ]
              [ OK ]  [ Cancel ]  [ Help... ]
```

Origin UCS – the **UCS** icon will appear at a selected origin (0,0,0) – Fig. 14.10. Used in conjunction with the variable **UCSICON** (this is discussed later).
Z Axis Vector UCS: A 3D model can be rotated around a new Z axis selected by either selecting points on the screen or by entering the coordinates of each end of the new Z axis.
3 Point UCS: A new UCS can be chosen by entering three points on a new UCS plane.

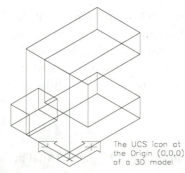

The UCS icon at the Origin (0,0,0) of a 3D model

Fig. 14.10 The **UCS** icon at the Origin of a 3D model

View UCS: When in a UCS at an angle such as can be obtained with the **X**, **Y** and/or **Z Axis Rotate UCS** calls, other details – text or drawings can be placed in a normal position on screen – Fig. 14.11.

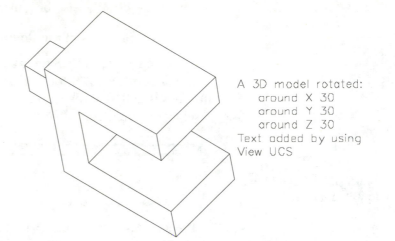

A 3D model rotated:
    around X 30
    around Y 30
    around Z 30
Text added by using
View UCS

Fig. 14.11 A 3D model rotated around X, Y and Z and placed in a **View UCS** position for the addition of text.

Object UCS: A 3D model can be aligned with an object on screen.
X Axis Rotate UCS: A 3D model can be rotated around the X axis.
Y Axis Rotate UCS: A 3D model can be rotated around the Y axis.
Z Axis Rotate UCS: A 3D model can be rotated around the Z axis.
Previous UCS: Takes the screen back to the previous UCS.
Restore UCS: Allows a previously saved and named UCS to be restored to screen.
Save UCS: Allows a UCS to be saved to a name. A saved UCS appears in the **UCS Control** dialogue box with the name to which it was saved.

The Solids toolbar

3D solid models can be constructed with the aid of the tools in the **Solids** toolbar. Fig. 14.12 shows the toolbar, together with the names of the available tools. With some practice and ingenuity, practically any 3D solid model can be constructed with the aid of these tools. Taking each of the tools in turn, the following examples show the results of their use.

Example 1 – Box tool

Left-click on the right hand icon in the **Box** flyout (Fig. 14.13). The Command Line changes to:

Command: _box
Center/<corner of box>: <0,0,0>: *enter* 130,210 *Return*

Fig. 14.12 The **Solids** toolbar with the names of the tool icons in the toolbar

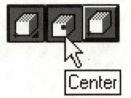

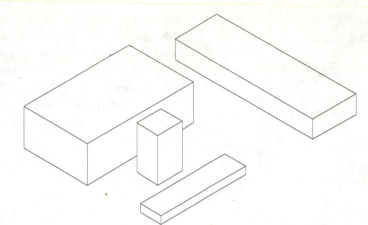

Fig. 14.13 The tool icons from the **Box** flyout of the **Solids** toolbar

Fig. 14.14 Example 1. Some boxes

Cube/Length/<other corner>: *enter* 280,210 *Return*
Height: *enter* 50 *Return*
Command:

Example 2 – Sphere tool

Left-click on the **Sphere** tool icon in the **Solids** toolbar (Fig. 14.12). The Command Line changes to:

Command: _sphere
Center of sphere <0,0,0>: *enter* 120,200 *Return*
Diameter/<Radius>: of sphere: *enter* 60 *Return*
Command:

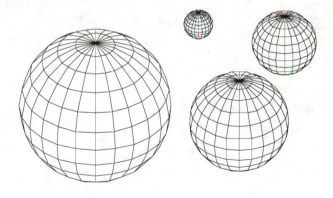

Fig. 14.15 Example 2. Some spheres

Example 3 – Cylinder tool

Either circular or elliptical cylinders can be constructed using the **Cylinder** tool. *Left-click* on the **Elliptical Cylinder** tool icon (Fig. 14.16). The Command Line changes to:

Fig. 14.16 The flyout from the **Cylinder** tool icon in the **Solids** toolbar

Command:_cylinder
Elliptical/<center point> <0,0,0>:_e
<Axis endpoint>/Center: *enter* c (Center) *Return*
Center of ellipse <0,0,0>: *enter* 170,190 *Return*
Axis endpoint: *enter* 240,190
Other axis distance: *enter* 170,160
Center of other end?<Height>: *enter* 100 *Return*
Command:

Fig. 14.17 shows four cylinders formed with the tool – two circular and two elliptical.

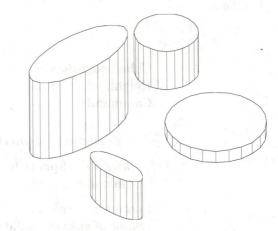

Fig. 14.17 Example 3. Some cylinders

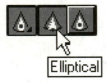

Fig. 14.18 The flyout from the **Cone** tool icon of the **Solids** toolbar

Example 4 – Cone tool

Left-click on the **Elliptical** tool icon from the **Cone** flyout of the **Solids** toolbar (Fig. 14.18). The Command Line changes to:

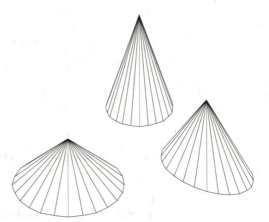

Fig. 14.19 Example 4. Some cones

Command:_cone
<Elliptical>/Center point <0,0,0>:_e
<Axis endpoint 1>/Center: *enter* 255,160 *Return*
Axis endpoint 2: *enter* 255,60 *Return*
Other axis distance: *enter* 285,110 *Return*
Apex/<Height>: *enter* 100 *Return*
Command:

Fig. 14.19 shows a number of cones constructed with the tool – a circular cone and two elliptical cones.

Example 5 – Extrude tool

The action of the **Extrude** tool allows outlines constructed with the **Polyline** tool from the **Draw** toolbar to be extruded into 3D models. As an example the polyline outline of Fig. 14.20 was extruded as follows. *Left-click* on the **Extruded Surface** tool icon from the **Solids** toolbar. The Command Line changes to:

Command:_extrude
Select objects: *left-click* on the outline **1 found**
Select objects: *Return*
Path/<Height of extrusion>: *enter* 75
Extrusion taper angle <0>: *Return*
Command:

Other examples of extrusions are given in Fig. 14.21.

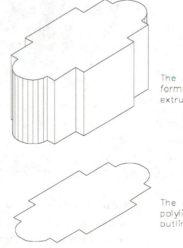

The 3D model formed by extrusion

The orginal polyline outline

Fig. 14.20 Example 5. The original polyline outline and its extrusion

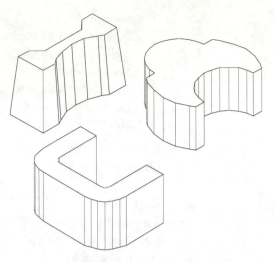

Fig.14.21 More examples of the use of the **Extrude** tool

Example 6 – Revolve tool

This tool is designed to produce revolved surfaces from polyline outlines. Fig. 14.22 shows a polyline outline and the **Revolved Surface** derived from the outline. The revolved surface was produced as follows. After drawing the polyline outline, *left-click* on the **Revolve** tool icon in the **Solids** toolbar. The Command Line changes to:

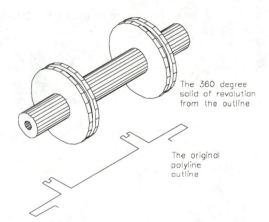

The 360 degree solid of revolution from the outline

The original polyline outline

Fig. 14.22 Example 6. The original polyline outline and its solid of revolution

Command:_revolve
Select objects: *left-click* on the outline **1 found**
Select objects: *Return*
Axis of revolution – Object/X/Y/<Start point of axis>: *Return*
Angle of revolution <full circle>: *Return*
Command:

and the surface of revolution is formed. Other examples are given in Fig. 14.23.

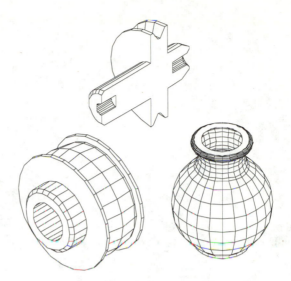

Fig. 14.23 Further examples of solids of revolution

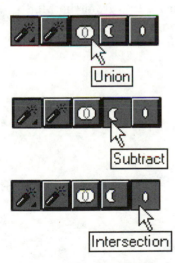

Fig. 14.24 The three Boolean operators from the **Explode** flyout of the **Modify** toolbar

The Boolean operators: Union, Subtract and Intersection

The R13 solids can be joined with the **Union** tool, subtracted from each other with the **Subtract** tool or a 3D solid can be formed from the parts remaining when solids interfere with other with the **Intersection** tool. These three tools (Fig. 14.24) are known as Boolean operators named after the inventor of this particular type of constructional method. The tools are found in the **Explode** flyout of the **Modify** toolbar.

Example 1 – Union tool

Fig. 14.25 shows the effects of the **Union** tool from the **Modify** toolbar on four solids – three boxes and a solid of revolution. *Left-click* on the **Union** tool icon in the **Modify** toolbar. The Command Line then shows:

Command: _union
Select objects: *left-click* on one solid
Select objects: *left-click* on one solid
Select objects: *left-click* on one solid
Select objects: *left-click* on one solid
Select objects: *Return*
4 solids selected.
(A series of statements appear showing the tool's actions)
Command:

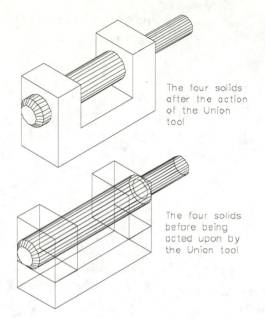

The four solids
after the action
of the Union
tool

The four solids
before being
acted upon by
the Union tool

Fig. 14.25 Example 1. The
action of the **Union** tool on
four solids

Example 2 – Subtract tool

Fig. 14.26 shows the effects of the **Subtract** tool from the **Modify**
toolbar on six solids – a solid of extrusion and five cylinders. *Left-
click* on the **Subtract** tool icon in the **Modify** toolbar. The Command
Line then shows:

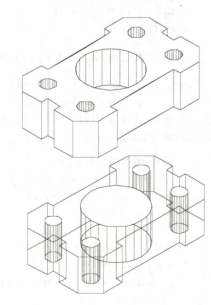

The 6 solids
after the action
of the Subtract tool

The original six
solids before
the action of
the Subtract tool

Fig. 14.26 Example 2. The
action of the **Subtract** tool on
six solids

Command:_subtract
Source of objects...
Select objects: *left-click* on the solid of extrusion
Select objects: *Return*
Objects to subtract from them...
Select objects: *left-click* on a cylinder
Select objects: *left-click* on a cylinder
Select objects: *left-click* on a cylinder
Select objects: *left-click* on a cylinder
Select objects: *left-click* on a cylinder
Select objects: *Return*
6 solids selected.
(A series of statements appear showing the tool's actions)
Command:

Example 3 – Intersection tool

Fig. 14.27 shows the effects of the **Intersection** tool from the **Modify** toolbar on two solids – a box and a cone. *Left-click* on the **Intersection** tool icon in the **Modify** toolbar. The Command Line then shows:

Command:_intersect
Select objects: *left-click* on the box
Select objects: *left-click* on the cone
Select objects: *Return*
2 solids intersected.
(A series of statements appear showing the tool's actions)
Command:

The two solids
after the action
of Intersection

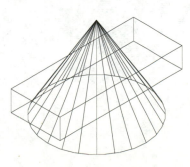

Fig. 14.27 Example 3. The
action of the **Intersection** tool
on two solids

The two solids
before the action
of Intersection

3D solid model exercises

1. Fig. 14.28 is a third angle orthographic projection of the solid model to be constructed for this exercise. Fig. 14.29 shows the stages of construction involving tools from the **Solids** toolbar.

   (a) Construct the solid primitives for the 3D model in the preset **FRONT UCS** called from the **UCS Orientation** dialogue box.

   (b) Switch to the **WORLD UCS** to move the smallest box to its central position with respect to the remainder of the solid.

   (c) Call the **SW Isometric 3D Viewpoint** from the **View menu,** then follow the stages recommended in Fig. 14.29.

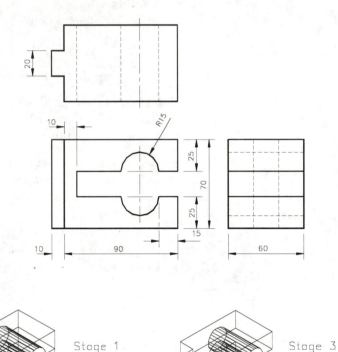

Fig. 14.28 Third angle orthographic projection for Exercise 1

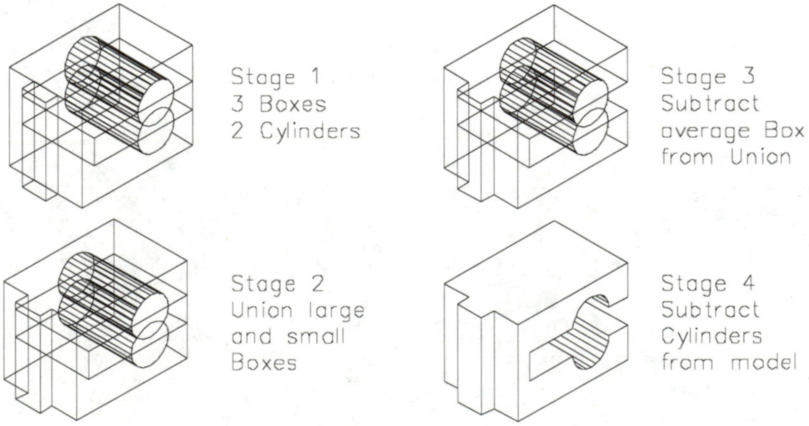

Stage 1
3 Boxes
2 Cylinders

Stage 3
Subtract
average Box
from Union

Stage 2
Union large
and small
Boxes

Stage 4
Subtract
Cylinders
from model

Fig. 14.29 Stages in the construction of the 3D model for Exercise 1

2. Fig. 14.30. The 3D model for this exercise can be constructed as follows:

(a) Preset **FRONT UCS**.
(b) Draw the two plines for the extrusion outlines.
(c) Use the tool **Extrude** from the **Solids** toolbar to form the two extrusions.
(d) With the tool **Cylinder** from **Solids** add the two holes.
(e) Use **Subtract** for **Solids** to subtract the holes from the extrusions.
(f) Call **WORLD UCS**.
(g) Move the smaller extrusion to its central position.
(h) Use **Union** from **Solids** to complete the 3D model.
(i) Select **SW Isometric 3D Viewpoint** to see the model in a pictorial form.

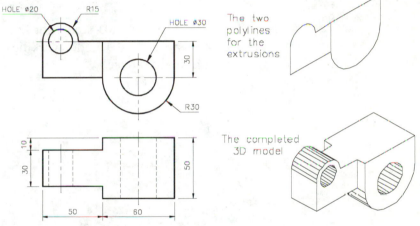

Fig. 14.30 A first angle orthographic projection, the polylino for the extrusions and the completed 3D model for Exercise 2

3. Fig. 14.31. Construct the 3D model following stages as follows:

(a) **FRONT UCS**.
(b) Draw **Polyline** for handle revolved surface.
(c) Draw **Polyline** for handle support.
(d) Draw **Polylines** for webs.
(e) Use **Revolve** from **Solids** to form handle.
(f) Use **Extrude** from **Solids** to form handle support and webs.
(g) **WORLD UCS** to move handle support and webs to central positions.
(h) **RIGHT UCS** to form **Cylinder** and **Box** for head.
(i) **WORLD UCS** to reposition head.
(j) **Union** from **Solids** to join all parts.
(k) **Vpoint** −1,−1.5,1 to obtain pictorial view.
(l) **Hide**.

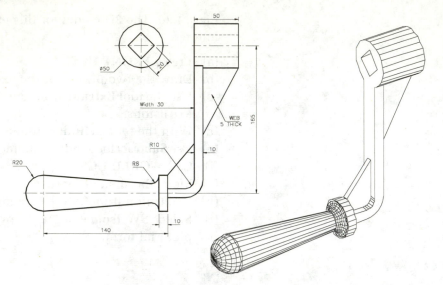

Fig. 14.31 A front view and the finished 3D model for Exercise 3

4. Fig. 14.32 is a 3D model for Exercise 3 of Chapter 8 (page 139). Construct the 3D model working to the dimensions given with the original exercise.

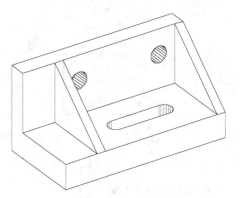

Fig. 14.32 Exercise 4

5. Fig. 14.33 is a 3D model for Exercise 2 of Chapter 8 (page 130). Construct the 3D model working to the dimensions given with the original exercise.

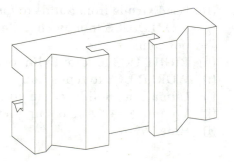

Fig. 14.33 Exercise 5

More advanced examples of 3D models

Figures 14.34 and 14.35 are examples of more complex 3D models constructed with the aid of the tools from the **Solids** toolbar. These two models are included here as examples only and are not intended as exercises for the reader to work, although an attempt to construct them may prove to be interesting.

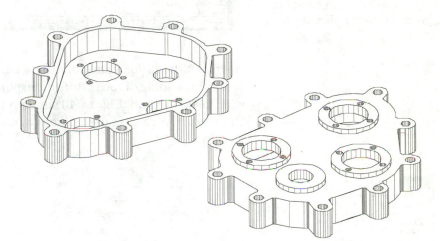

Fig. 14.34 A 3D model of a gear case cover – two views from top and from underneath

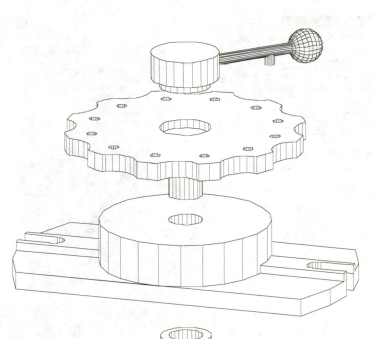

Fig. 14.35 A 3D model of the parts of an indexing device

The tool DView

Left-click on **3D Dynamic View** (3dview) in the **View** pull-down menu (Fig. 14.37). The Command Line changes as shown in Fig. 14.36. The reader is advised to experiment with the various pictorial

Fig. 14.36 The Command Line prompts when **Dview** is called

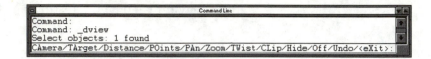

views available for manipulating a 3D model. Figures 14.38 and 14.39 show some of the results of responding to prompts associated with the command. Fig. 14.40 shows a **Dview** perspective view of a bungalow which is ready to have windows and doors fitted.

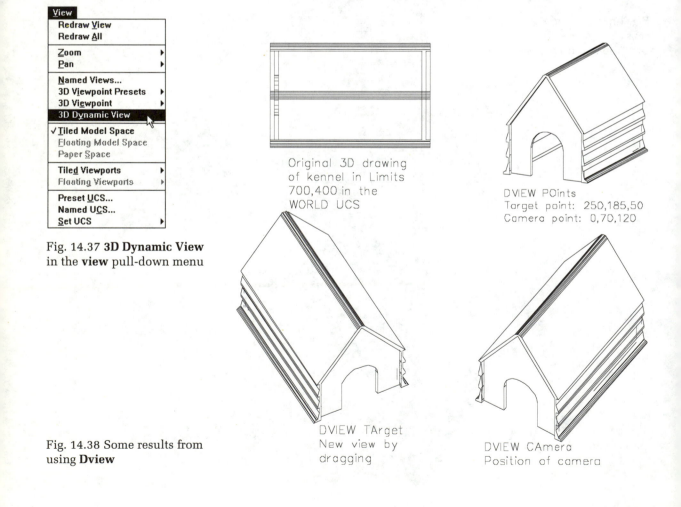

Fig. 14.37 **3D Dynamic View** in the **view** pull-down menu

Original 3D drawing of kennel in Limits 700,400 in the WORLD UCS

DVIEW POints
Target point: 250,185,50
Camera point: 0,70,120

Fig. 14.38 Some results from using **Dview**

DVIEW TArget
New view by dragging

DVIEW CAmera
Position of camera

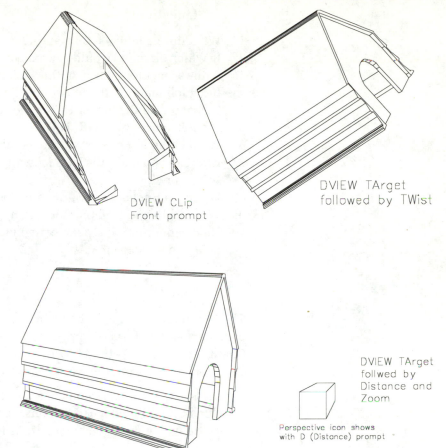

DVIEW CLip
Front prompt

DVIEW TArget
followed by TWist

DVIEW TArget
follwed by
Distance and
Zoom

Perspective icon shows
with D (Distance) prompt

Fig. 14.39 Further examples of
using **Dview**

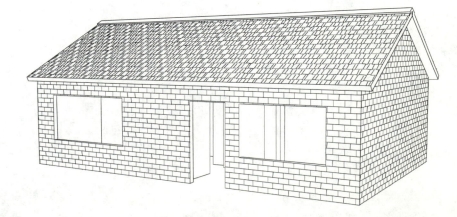

Fig. 13.40 A **Dview**
perspective view of a
bungalow

Questions

1. What do the letters **UCS** stand for?
2. In which direction would you expect to find a positive *x* coordinate with respect to the face of the screen?
3. In which menu will you find the **Preset UCS...** command?
4. Can you find the **Preset UCS...** tool in a toolbar?
5. What is meant by **WORLD UCS**?
6. What is the importance of the variable **UCSFOLLOW**?
7. How can you make the UCS icon appear at an origin point in a 3D solid drawing?
8. What is a **Boolean operator** in AutoCAD R13?
9. Where will you find the Boolean operator tool icons?
10. How can a pictorial, perspective view of a 3D solid drawing be obtained on screen?

Exercises

The following exercises are to construct 3D models of the drawings produced as orthographic projections for Exercises 4,6,7,8 and 9 of Chapter 8 – pages 139 to 141. Dimensions for the following exercises should be taken from the exercises on those pages.

1. Fig. 14.41. From Chapter 8 Exercise 4. There are many methods by which this 3D model can be constructed. It is left to the reader to decide which methods he/she finds most suitable.

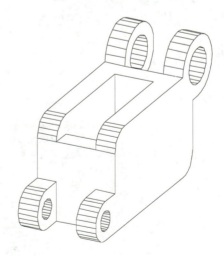

Fig. 14.41 Exercise 1

2. Fig. 14.42. From Chapter 8 Exercise 6. Again, the reader should choose their own method of construction

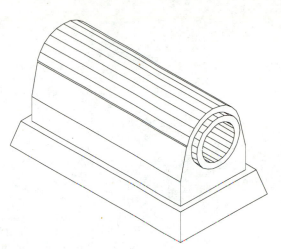

Fig. 14.42 Exercise 2

3. Fig. 14.43. From Chapter 8 Exercise 7. Construct the 3D model shown.

Fig. 14.43 Exercise 3

4. Fig. 14.44. From Chapter 8 Exercise 8. This 3D model has been constructed from extrusions of **Polar Arrays**. Contruct the model shown.

Fig. 14.44 Exercise 4

5. Fig. 14.45. From Chapter 8 Exercise 9. Part extrusions and part boxes. Construct the given model.

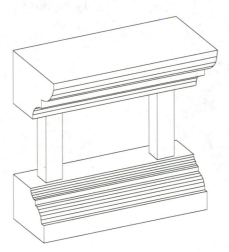

Fig. 14.45 Exercise 5

CHAPTER 15

More about 3D model construction

Introduction

All previous work described in this book has been constructed in what, in AutoCAD R13 terms, is known as **Model Space** . In Model Space all drawing is in a 3D coordinate system – with X, Y and Z axes. It is convenient at times to place 3D models in a 2D graphics window known as **Paper Space**.

Viewports

Left-click on **Layout...** in the **Tile Viewports** sub menu of the **View** pull-down menu (Fig. 15.1). A dialogue box appears showing the variety of viewport layouts available. Fig. 15.2 names the layouts as they appear in the dialogue box. They are called **tiled** because the viewports are fitted one against the other as if they were tiles. Note that there is a tick against **Tiled Model Space** in the **View** menu showing that **Model Space** is active.

View	
Redraw View	
Redraw All	
Zoom	▶
Pan	▶
Named Views...	
3D Viewpoint Presets	▶
3D Viewpoint	▶
3D Dynamic View	
✓ Tiled Model Space	
Floating Model Space	
Paper Space	
Tiled Viewports	Layout...
Floating Viewports	1 Viewport
Preset UCS...	2 Viewports
Named UCS...	3 Viewports
Set UCS	4 Viewports
	Restore
	Delete
	Join
	Save

Fig. 15.1 The **Tiled Viewports** sub menu from the **View** pull-down menu

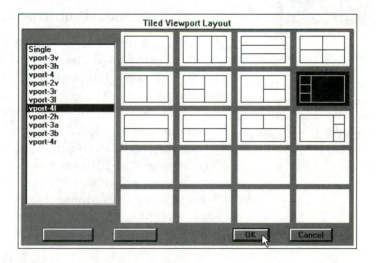

Fig. 15.2 The variety of viewport layouts

Model Space and Paper Space

The graphics window is in **Model Space**. To switch to **Paper Space** either *left-click* on **Paper Space** in the **View** menu or, at the Command Line:

Command: *enter* tilemode *Return*
New value for TILEMODE<1>: *enter* 0 *Return*
Command:

and the graphics window changes to the **Paper Space** 2D system with the **Paper Space** icon at the bottom left-hand corner of the window (Fig. 15.3).

To switch back to **Model Space** either *left-click* on **Tiled Model Space** or, at the Command Line:

Command: *enter* tilemode *Return*
New value for TILEMODE<0>: *enter* 1 *Return*
Command:

Fig. 15.3 The **Paper Space** icon

and the graphics window changes to the 3D model space window showing the **UCS** icon at the bottom left-hand corner.

Notes

1. 3D models can only be constructed in **Model Space**.
2. Viewports are tiled in **Model Space**, but not in **Paper Space**, even though it looks as if they are.
3. Instead of selecting these two tools from the **View** menu you may prefer to select from the tool icons (Fig. 15.4).

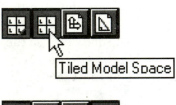

Fig. 15.4 The **Tiled Model Space** and **Paper Space** tool icons in the **Space** flyout of the **Standard** toolbar

3D model construction in four viewports

Left-click on **Tiled Viewports** in the **View** pull-down menu (Fig. 15.1). In the **Tiled Viewport Layout** dialogue box, *left-click* on **vport-4l** (viewport 4 left), followed by a *left-click* on the **OK** button of the dialogue box. The graphics window changes to the four-viewport layout shown in Fig. 15.5, which includes the 3D model Fig. 15.6 under construction. The value of working in such a four-viewport window is that the drawing can be constructed in the largest viewport and different views in the other, smaller, viewports allow the operator to check whether what is being constructed is correct as regards its three-dimensional shapes.

Before commencing the drawing, the viewports are given different **3D Viewpoint Presets** (Fig. 15.7) and **UCSFOLLOW** settings:

Main viewport: **UCSFOLLOW** set to 1 (ON). **UCS** set to **WORLD**, but the construction of this example was carried out in three preset **UCS** positions – **WORLD**, **FRONT** and **RIGHT**.

Top left viewport: **UCSFOLLOW** set to 0 (OFF). **3D Viewpoint Preset – Viewpoint SW**.

Middle left viewport: **UCSFOLLOW** set to 0 (OFF). **3D Viewpoint Preset – Front**.

Bottom left viewport: **UCSFOLLOW** set to 0 (OFF). **3D Viewpoint Preset – Viewpoint NW**.

It is particularly important that the **UCSFOLLOW** settings are as shown, otherwise the main viewport would not respond to the **WORLD**, **FRONT** and **RIGHT UCS** presets and the other three viewports would change with the **UCS** changes of the main viewport if the **UCSFOLLOW** setting was on.

All drawing additions in any one of the four viewports will be reflected in the other three, but changes in the **UCS** will only affect the large one.

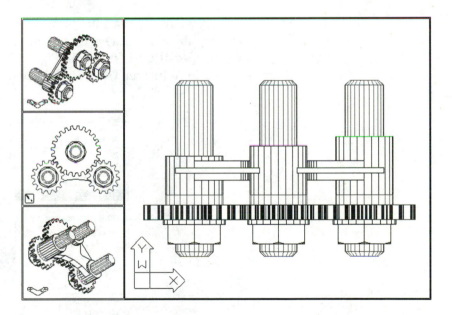

Fig. 15.5 The four-viewport window in which Fig. 15.6 was constructed

Now switch to **Paper Space** with a *left-click* on **Paper Space** in the **View** menu.

The screen empties except for the **Paper Space** icon. In order to recover the drawing:

Command: *enter* mview *Return*
ON/OFF/Hideplot/Fit/2/3/4/<First point>: *enter* 4 *Return*
Fit/<First point>: *pick* near bottom left of window
Second point: *pick* near top right of window
Regenerating drawing.
Command:

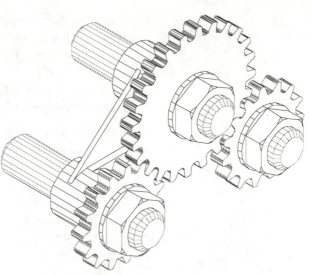

Fig. 15.6 The 3D model worked in the four-viewport graphics window shown in Fig. 15.5

The drawing reappears in a **view-4** viewports window with the same view in all four viewports. To change each viewport to a suitable viewing position as shown in Fig. 15.8, switch back to **Model Space** with a *left-click* on **Tiled Model Space** in the **View** menu.

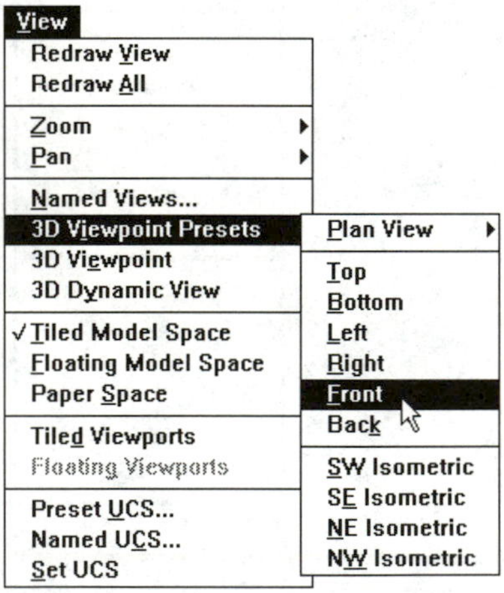

Fig. 15.7 Selecting a **3D Viewpoint Preset** from the **View** menu

Then set **all** viewports to **UCSFOLLOW** off and the **3D Viewpoint Presets** to:

Top left viewport: **Front View**.
Top right viewport: **Left View**.
Bottom left viewport: **Top View**.
Bottom right viewport: **SW Isometric View**.

Then switch back to **Paper Space** with a *left-click* on **Paper Space** in the **View menu**.

The viewports with their contents can now be moved by:

Command: *enter* m (for Move) *Return*
Select objects: *pick* an edge of a viewport **1 found.**
Select objects: *Return*
Base point of displacement: *pick* a point
Second point of displacement: *pick* a point
Command:

and the viewport and its contents are moved. Fig. 15.8 shows the four viewports moved to positions as if the views were in first angle orthographic projection with a pictorial view in the bottom right-hand corner of the window.

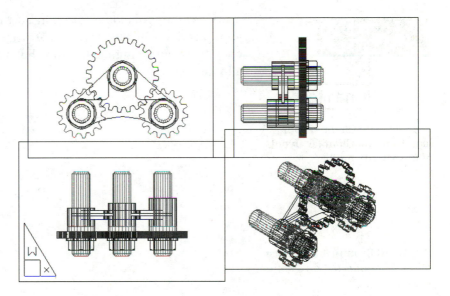

Fig. 15.8 The same 3D model in a four-viewport **PaperSpace** window after the viewports have been moved

The Mview prompts

When in **Paper Space** in order to place an **MSpace** drawing in the graphics window, the command **Mview** must be called. The prompts which show at the Command Line are:

ON/OFF/Hideplot/Fit/2/3/4/<First point>:

The **Fit/2/3/4** prompts are for 1, 2, 3 or 4 viewports. The **Hideplot** prompt allows printing or plotting of all viewports onto a single plot sheet with all hidden lines removed. This is achieved by calling the **Hideplot** prompt by *entering* **h**, followed by *picking* the edges of the viewports in which the drawing is to be printed or plotted with hidden line removal. Don't worry if nothing appears to happen, but the hideplot data is stored with the drawing data when the drawing is saved to file and/or plotted. In any case the viewport outlines will not be plotted with the drawing.

The **ON/OFF** prompts allow the contents of any viewport to be hidden from the graphic window. Call **OFF** by *entering* **off**, followed by *picking* the edge of a viewport. The contents of the selected viewport disappear, but can be made to reappear by *entering* **on**, followed by *picking* the edge of the viewport from which the drawing was removed by off.

Solid model drawing tools

The Chamfer tool

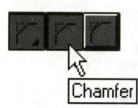

Fig. 15.9 The **Chamfer** tool icon from the **Chamfer** flyout of the **Modify** toolbar

The **Chamfer** tool icon is found in the **Modify** toolbar – the same tool as is used when chamfering 2D drawings. Fig. 15.10 shows the chamfering of a single edge and the chamfering of several edges in a **loop**.

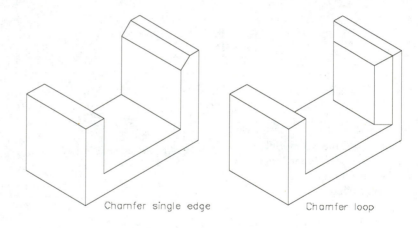

Chamfer single edge   Chamfer loop

Fig. 15.10 Examples of the use of the **Chamfer** tool on a solid model

Left-click on the **Chamfer** tool icon in the **Modify** toolbar (Fig. 15.9). The Command Line shows:

Command:_chamfer
(TRIM mode) Current chamfer Dist 1 = 10, Dist 2 = 10
Polyline/Distance/Angle/Trim/Method/<Select first line>: *enter*
    d (Distance) *Return*
Enter first chamfer distance: *enter* 15 *Return*
Enter second chamfer distance: *enter* 15 *Return*
Command:
(TRIM mode) Current chamfer Dist 1 = 15, Dist 2 = 15
Polyline/Distance/Angle/Trim/Method/<Select first line>:

Loop/<**Select edge**>: *pick*
Loop/<**Select edge**>: *pick*
Command:

If a **Loop** chamfer effect is required *enter* **l** (Loop) in response to:

Loop/<**Select edge**>: *enter* l (Loop) *Return*
Edge/<**Select edge loop**>: *pick*
Loop/<**Select edge**>: *pick*
Loop/<**Select edge**>: *pick*
Loop/<**Select edge**>: *pick*
Loop/<**Select edge**>: *pick*
Loop/<**Select edge**>: *Return*
Command:

for as many edges as are to be chamfered in the loop.

The Fillet tool

A similar series of prompts occurs at the Command Line in response to the **Fillet** tool being called, except that a **Fillet** requires a single radius and the prompt **Chain** is used instead of **Loop** for a series of fillets. Examples of a single fillet and a chain fillet are given in Fig. 15.12. *Left-click* on the **Fillet** tool icon (Fig. 15.11), which is on the **Chamfer** flyout. The Command Line shows:

Command:_fillet
(TRIM mode) Current fillet radius = 5
Polyline/Radius/Trim/<Select first object>: *enter* r (Radius) *Return*
Enter radius <5>: *enter* 15 *Return*
Chain Radius/<Select edge>: *pick*
1 edges selected for fillet
Command:

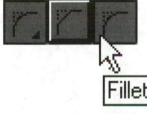

Fig. 15.11 The **Fillet** tool icon from the **Chamfer** flyout of the **Modify** toolbar

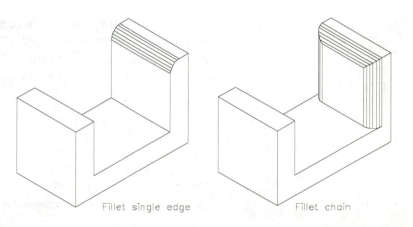

Fig. 15.12 Examples of the use of the **Fillet** tool on a solid model

Fillet single edge   Fillet chain

If **c** (Chain) is *entered* in response to:

> **Chain Radius/<Select edge>:** *enter* c (Chain) *Return*
> **Edge/Radius/<Select edge chain>:** *pick*
> **Edge/Radius/<Select edge chain>:** *pick*
> **Edge/Radius/<Select edge chain>:** *pick*
> **Edge/Radius/<Select edge chain>:** *Return*
> **3 edges selected for fillet**
> **Command:**

for as many edges as are to be filleted. An example of the application of chamfering and filleting to a simple solid model drawing is given in Fig. 15.13.

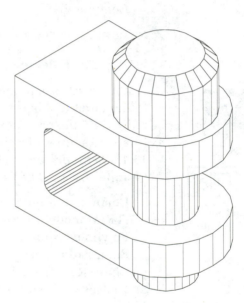

Fig. 15.13 A solid model which includes a chamfer and fillets

The Slice tool

Fig. 15.14 The **Slice** tool icon from the **Solids** toolbar

Fig. 15.15 shows the sequence of constructing a solid model drawing using the **Revolve** tool from the **Solids** toolbar and then cutting it in half with the aid of the **Slice** tool (Fig. 15.14). When the **Slice** tool is selected, the Command Line shows:

> **Command:_slice**
> **Select Objects:** *left-click* on the solid **1 found**
> **Select objects:** *Return*
> **Slicing plane by Object/Zaxis/View/XY/YZ/ZX/<3points>:** *pick*
> **2nd point on plane:** *pick*
> **3rd point on plane:** *enter* .xy *return*
> **of** *pick* 1st point again **(need Z):** *enter* 1 *Return*

Both sides/<Point on desired side of plane>: *point*
Command:

Fig. 15.15 shows: **Stage 1** – Polyline to be revolved; **Stage 2** – The solid of revolution; **Stage 3** – The action of **Slice**; **Stage 4** – the sliced solid.

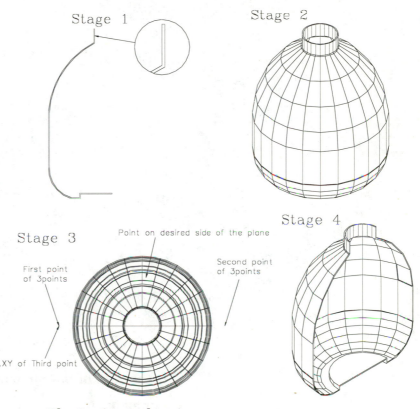

Fig. 15.15 Stages in constructing a solid model, followed by **Slice**

The Section tool

The action and command line prompts for this tool are similar to those for the **Slice** tool, except that a sectional view is formed along the plane chosen for the sectioning. Fig. 15.16 shows stages in producing a sectional view with the aid of this tool. After constructing the solid model from a polyline with the **Revolve** tool:

Fig. 15.16 The **Section** tool icon from the **Solids** toolbar

Stage 1: *left-click* on the **Section** tool icon from the **Solids** toolbar and, following the prompts select the three points on a cutting plane as for the **Slice** example. Two cuts were made, one for the body, the other for the bung.

Stage 2: When the section plane has been selected, the model in a **SE Viewpoint** position shows the sectional view.

Stage 3: The sectional view moved out of the solid model.

Stage 1

1st point
of 3points

2nd point
of 3points

3rd point
of 3points
with .XY of

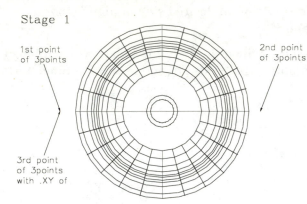

Stage 2 – The section plane
showing in the solid model

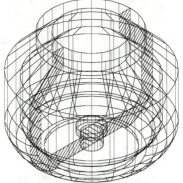

Stage 3 The sectional view removed
from the solid model

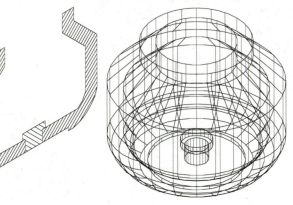

Fig. 15.17 Using the **Section**
tool on a solid model

Further use of the Slice and Section tools

Example 1

This example consists of a 270° solid of revolution from a polyline outline and an extrusion from part of a polygon. The two parts were joined with **Union**. The sections were constructed with the aid of the **Section** tool used twice. Each of the sections were exploded and half of each then erased. Fig. 15.18 shows the polyline outline from which the lower part of the solid was revolved, together with the final solid with its sections.

Example 2

This example, somewhat more complex than the first, is included here to show how a sectioned Front view of a solid model can be used as part of an orthographic projection. Figures 15.19 to 15.21 show the three stages by which the resulting Front view was obtained:

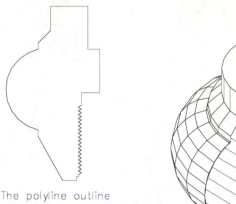

The polyline outline
on which the lower
revolved part of the
solid model was
based

Fig. 15.18 Example 1

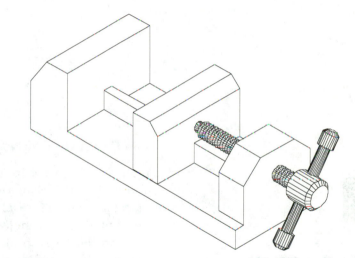

Fig. 15.19 Example 2: Stage 1

Stage 1: Fig. 15.19. The complete solid model was constructed from extrusions, boxes and solids of revolution using the **Extrude**, **Revolve** and **Box** tools.

Stage 2: Fig. 15. 20. The **Slice** tool was used to slice the body and vice jaw in half. Note that the screw, its handle and the slide in which the vice jaw moves were not sliced – because such parts are shown in outside views in a sectional view.

Stage 3: Fig. 15.21. The **Section** tool was used, first on the body, then on the vice jaw to produce the required hatching.

Note: The **UCS Presets** were changed several time during each stage of the constructions.

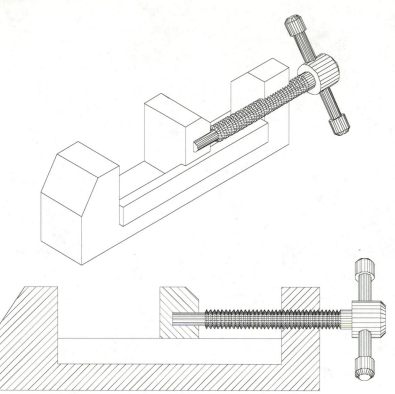

Fig. 15.20 Second example.
Stage 2

Fig. 15.21 Second example.
Stage 3

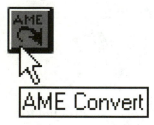

Fig. 15.22 The **AME Convert**
tool icon from the **Solids**
toolbar

The tool AME Convert

Solid model drawing files from AutoCAD Releases 11 or 12, in
which solid modelling was performed in the Advanced Modelling
Extension, can be loaded into R13. If you wish to add further details
to these solid models they must first be converted to the R13 solid
data form. Load the AME solid model, then *left-click* on the **AME
Convert** tool icon in the **Solids** toolbar (Fig. 15.21), *left-click* on each
part of the loaded drawing and follow the prompts at the Command
Line. When the converted drawing is saved it will be in R13 drawing
data format.

Other solid models tools

The Elev command

At the Command Line *enter* elev as follows:

Command: *enter* elev *Return*
New current elevation<0>: *Return* (to accept)
New current thickness<0>: *enter* 50 *Return*
Command:

Any objects now drawn in the graphics window will assume a thickness — some examples are given in Fig. 15.23. The **elev** command is of value for setting a UCS plane at height different to the plane when the UCS is first called. For example setting the elevation at 100 and its thickness to 0 allows anything drawn in the UCS to be on a plane 100 units above the original UCS plane level.

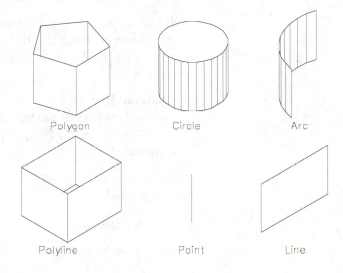

Fig. 15.23 Objects drawn with **elev** set to thickness of 50

The Purge command

I find it advisable to occasionally purge a drawing under construction because the use of this command destroys unwanted data features

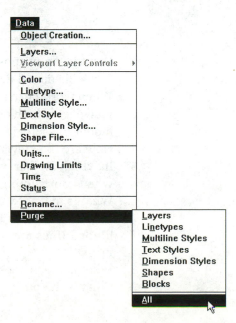

Fig. 15.24 Selecting **Purge** from the **Data** pull-down menu

and unwanted data from memory before a drawing is saved to file. Considerable saving of disk space can be achieved by the use of **Purge**. Either select the command from the **Data** pull-down menu (Fig. 15.24) or *enter* **purge** at the Command Line. Then follow the prompts appearing at the Command Line.

The Zoom command

It will be found that it is frequently necessary to **Zoom** All or 1 after each change of the **UCS** and each change of a **Viewpoint**, when constructing solid model drawings. The easiest way of doing this is as follows:

Command: *enter* z *Return*
All/Center/Dynamic/Extents/Left/Previous/Vmax/Window/<Scale (X/XP)>: *enter* a (All) *Return*
Command:

You may also find it necessary to zoom to 1 (Scale 1/1) as well as zooming to All.

A reminder

If in doubt as to the action to be taken, quite apart from the prompts in the Command Line, every tool and/or command brings up a short description of the use of the tool or command in the bottom left corner of the graphics window. This description replaces the bar containing the **Grid**, **Snap**, **Ortho**, **Time** windows at the bottom of the screen.

Questions

1. What is the purpose of the **Tilemode** command?
2. Can a 3D model drawing be constructed in **Paper Space**?
3. When working in a graphics windows arranged for more than one viewport, which command is used to set different views of a 3D model in each viewport?
4. How are the views in viewports moved when in **Paper Space**?
5. In which toolbar would you expect to find the **Chamfer** tool icon when constructing a chamfer in a 3D model drawing?
6. What is meant by a **Chain** when using the tool **Fillet**?
7. When working in **Paper Space** how can an operator ensure that hidden lines are removed from a drawing when it is plotted or printed?
8. What is the purpose of the **Slice** tool from the **Solids** toolbar?
9. What is the purpose of the **Section** tool from the **Solids** toolbar?

10. Why is it necessary to use the **Zoom** tool when changing to a new UCS?

Exercises

1. The graphics puck shown in the 3D solid model in Fig. 15.25 has been constructed to the dimensions given with Exercise 4, Fig. 10.24 on page 162. Construct the solid model drawing to the sizes given with that exercise.

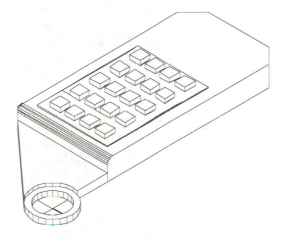

Fig. 15.25 Exercise 1

2. Another puck is shown in Fig. 15.26. Using you own discretion about sizes, construct a similar 3D solid model drawing.

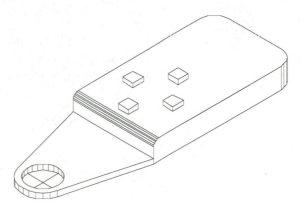

Fig. 15.26 Exercise 2

3. Using your own discretion concerning the sizes of your drawing construct a 3D model drawing of the simple calculator shown in Fig. 15.27.

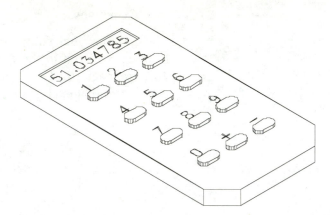

Fig. 15.27 Exercise 3

4. Two rectangular pipes 80 mm by 30 mm are joined to a bend as shown in Fig. 15.28. Working to a convenient scale, construct the 3D model shown.

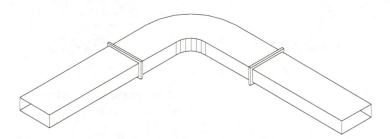

Fig. 15.28 Exercise 4

5. Fig. 15.29 is a 3D model drawing of a dustbin constructed mainly from solids of revolution. Construct a similar 3D model drawing working to sizes according to your own judgement.

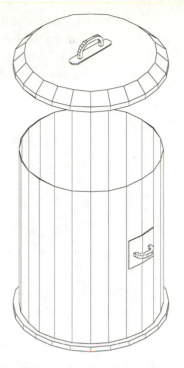

Fig. 15.29 Exercise 5

6. Fig. 15.30 is a 3D solid model drawing of a wooden box with a lid. Working to a design of your own, construct a similar 3D model drawing of a box with a lid.

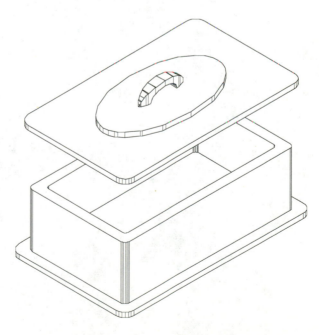

Fig. 15.30 Exercise 6

7. The left-hand drawing of Fig. 15.31 shows the polyline used when forming the solid of revolution shown on the right-hand side of Fig. 15.31. Note the closed nature of the polyline. Construct a similar drawing of a 'bottle' as that shown.

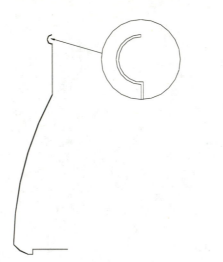

Fig. 15.31 Exercise 7

CHAPTER 16

The Render toolbar

Introduction

3D solid model drawings can be *rendered* in AutoCAD R13 to produce realistic, photo-like images with the aid of tools from the **Render** toolbar (Fig. 16.1). Fig. 16.2 includes the names of the tools in the toolbar. Examples of the rendering of 3D solid models from previous chapters are given in this chapter. Colour plates of renderings are also included in the colour section (see plates X–XVI).

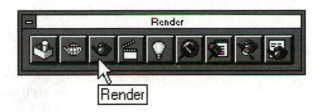

Fig. 16.1 The **Render** toolbar

Fig. 16.2 The names of the tools in the **Render** toolbar

Bringing the Render toolbar on screen

To bring the **Render** toolbar into the graphics window, either *left-click* on **Render** in the **Toolbars** sub-menu of the **Tools** pull-down menu (Fig. 16.3) or, at the Command Line:

    Command:
    Toolbar name (or All): *enter* render *Return*
    Show/Hide/Left/Right/Top/Bottom/Float: <Show>: *Return*
    Command:

and the **Render** toolbar appears on screen.

Use of the Render tools

A first example is included here to show basic methods of rendering. From then on the examples show a progression of difficulty to include the various options using the **Render** tools. If the reader has

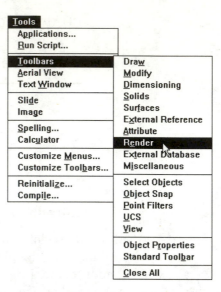

Fig. 16.3 Selecting **Render** from the **Toolbars** sub-menu of the **Tools** pull-down menu

saved work from earlier chapters, 3D model drawings for the renderings in the examples should be available for experimentation with renderings.

Example 1

Fig. 16.4 shows the rendering of the model resulting from Exercise 3, Chapter 8 (page 139). The stages to produce the rendering are:

1. **Open** the drawing file. When the 3D model drawing appears on screen, place it in a **3D Viewpoint Preset** of **SW Isometric**, **Zoom** to All.
2. *Left-click* on the **Render** tool icon (Fig. 16.5). The **Render** dialogue box appears on screen (Fig. 16.6).

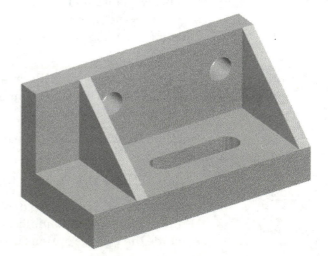

Fig. 16.4 Example 1

3. *Left-click on* the **Render** button of the dialogue box and the 3D model renders as shown in Fig. 16.4.

Fig. 16.5 The **Render** tool icon from the **Render** toolbar

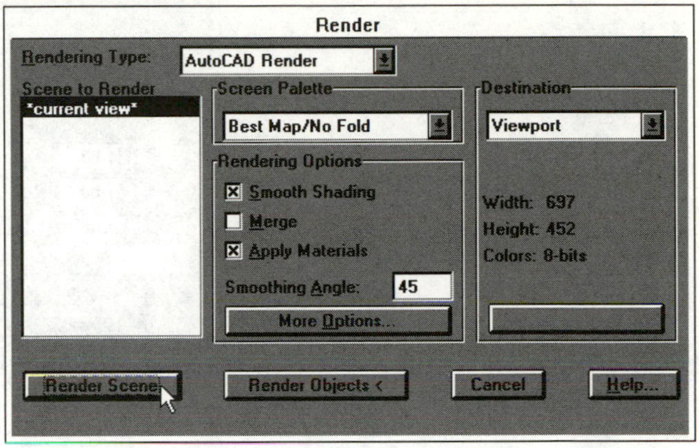

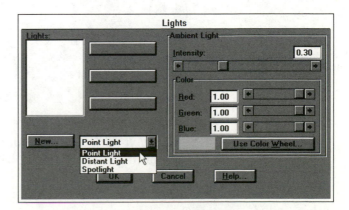

Fig. 16.6 The **Render** dialogue box

Example 2

The bracket with a pin shown in Fig. 16.7 is the 3D model for this example.

1. Place the model in the **WORLD UCS**.
2. *Left-click* on the **Lights** tool icon in the **Render** toolbar – Fig. 16.8.
3. The **Lights** dialogue box appears (Fig. 16.9). *Left-click* on **Point Light** in the pop-up list of the dialogue box showing the types of lights, followed by a *left-click* on the **New...** button. The **New Point Light** dialogue box comes on screen (Fig. 16.10).
4. *Enter* a name in the **Light Name:** box – in the example given this is **UPPER**. *Left-click* on the **Modify** button. An icon for a point light appears in the graphics screen. In response to the prompts appearing at the Command Line, place the icon in a suitable position. In the example given in Fig. 16.11, this is above the 3D model drawing, giving a general light on to the model from above.

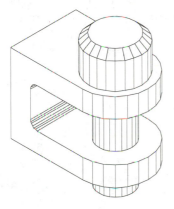

Fig. 16.7 The 3D model for Example 2

Fig. 16.8 The **Lights** tool icon from the **Render** toolbar

Fig. 16.9 The **Lights** dialogue box

New Point Light

Light **N**ame:	UPPER
Intensity:	197.25

Attenuation
○ N**o**ne
● Inverse **L**inear
○ Inverse S**q**uare

Position
[Modify <]   [Show...]

Color
Red: 1.00
Green: 1.00
Blue: 1.00

[Use Color **W**heel...]

[OK]   [Cancel]   [Help...]

Fig. 16.10 The **New Point Light** dialogue box

5. *Left-click* on the **OK** button of the dialogue box. The **Lights** dialogue box reappears. This time select **Distant Light** in the pop-up list and when the **New Distant Light** dialogue box appears (not illustrated here), name it **RIGHT** and modify its position in answer to prompts at the Command Line. Fig. 16.11 shows the positions of two **Distant** lights – one named **LEFT**, the other named **RIGHT**.

Point light
at 150,250,300

UPPER

Fig. 16.11 The arrangement of the three lights in Example 2

Distant light
at 20,80,150

Distant light
at 300,50,250

6. Now place the 3D model in a **3D Viewpoint Preset** of **SW Isometric** and *left-click* on the **Render** tool icon in the **Render** toolbar. The resulting rendering is shown in Fig. 16.12.

Fig. 16.12 The rendering of
the second example

Example 3

The 3D model for this example is shown in Fig. 16.13. The stages in
producing a rendering of the model were:

1. Place the model in a **WORLD UCS**.
2. Add suitable lights. In this example a **Point** light above and three
    Distant lights, front right, front left and behind (and below) were
    added.
3. *Left-click* on the **Materials Library** tool icon in the **Render** toolbar
    (Fig. 16.14). The **Materials Library** dialogue box appears (Fig.
    16.15).

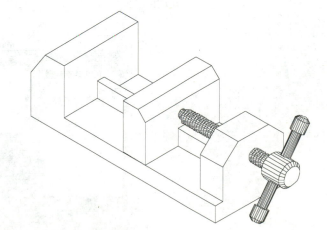

Fig. 16.13 The 3D model for
Example 3

Fig. 16.14 The **Materials Library** tool icon from the **Render** toolbar

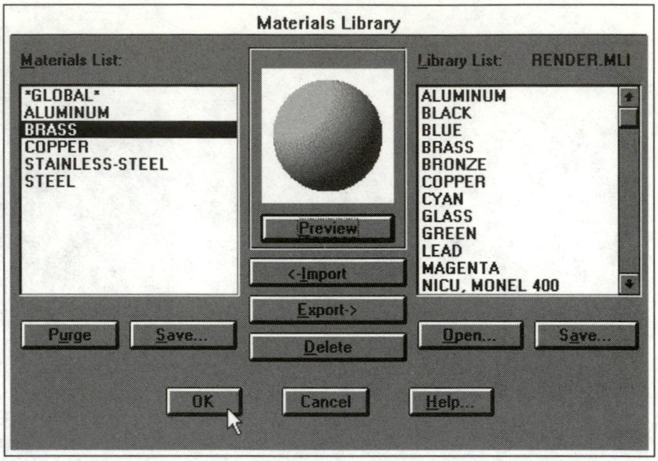

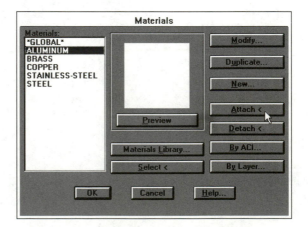

Fig. 16.15 The **Materials Library** dialogue box

4. *Left-click* on suitable material names in the **Library List:** list box of the dialogue box, followed by another *left-click* on the **Import** button. The name appears in the **Materials List:** box. Continue selecting suitable materials in this way until sufficient have been imported. Then *left-click* on the **OK** button of the dialogue box.

5. *Left-click on* the **Materials** tool icon in the **Render** toolbar (Fig. 16.16) and the **Materials** dialogue box appears (Fig. 17.17). *Left-click* on a material name in the **Materials list:** box, and another on the **Attach** button. The dialogue box disappears to allow selection by a *left-click* on that part of the 3D model to which the selected material is to be attached.

Fig. 16.16 The **Materials** tool icon from the **Render** toolbar

6. Continue attaching materials to parts of the 3D model in this manner until all materials have been attached as required. In this example the following materials were attached to parts of the 3D model:

Fig. 16.17 The **Materials** dialogue box

Aluminium   to the body
Copper   to the pin handle
Stainless steel to the screw
Brass   to the sliding part.

Note: These materials are not at all suitable for this particular clamping device, but are merely attached in this example to demonstrate the methods of attaching materials when working in **Render**.

7. The resulting rendering is shown in Fig. 16.18.

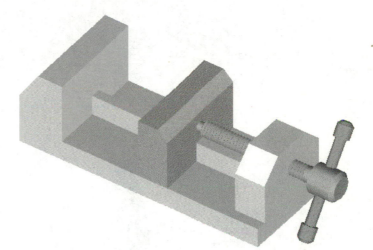

Fig. 16.18 The rendering of the Example 3

Example 4

Fig. 16.19 shows the 3D model constructed for this example and Fig. 16.20 the rendering. The model is a solid of revolution.

Example 5

This final example is a rendering of a more complex 3D model. The 3D model shown in Fig. 16.21 has been rendered to produce the rendering Fig. 16.22.

Note: Further examples of rendered 3D models are given in the colour section of this book in Plates X–XVI.

The Shade tool

Left-click on the **Shade** tool in the **Render** toolbar (Fig. 16.23). A 3D model in the graphics window changes colour. Fig. 16.24 is an example of what happens when the tool is selected. However, the

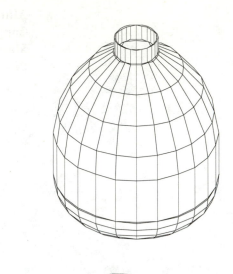

Fig. 16.19 The 3D solid model rendered for Example 4

Fig. 16.20 The rendering of Example 4

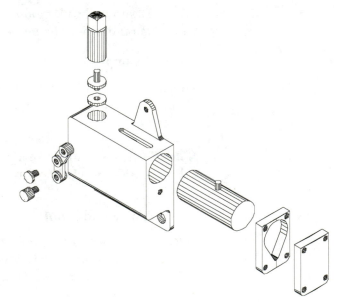

Fig. 16.21 The 3D model Example 5

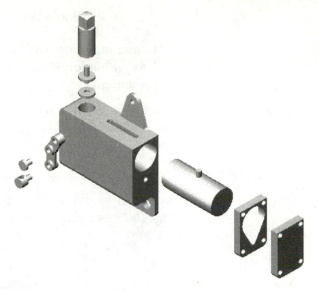

Fig. 16.22 The rendering for
Example 5

Fig. 16.23 The **Shade** tool icon
from the **Render** toolbar

method of shading depends upon the settings of the set variable
Shadedge as follows:

Shadedge set to 0 Faces shaded to the colour of the object.
  Edges not shaded.
Shadedge set to 1 Faces shaded. Edges in background colour.
Shadedge set to 2 Faces not shaded. Edges in object colour.
Shadedge set to 3 Faces shaded in colour of object. Edges in
  background colour.

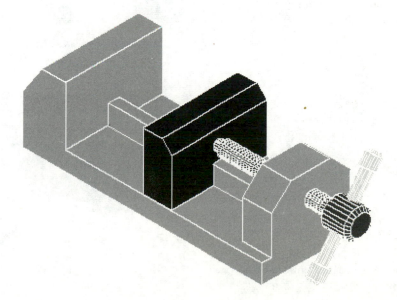

Fig. 16.24 An example of the
use of the tool **Shade**

To set Shadedge

Command: *enter* shadedge *Return*
New value for SHADEGE<3>: *enter* required figure *Return*
Command:

and the variable is set to the new figure. The default setting is 3 – Faces shaded in colour of object with edges in the colour of the graphics window background.

Further examples of renderings

Two more examples of renderings are given in Figs 16.25 and 16.26. Fig. 16.25 is a rendering of an exploded 3D model of an indexing

Fig. 16.25 A rendering of an exploded 3D model of an indexing device

Fig. 16.26 Two renderings showing top and bottom of a gear cover case

device and Fig. 16.26 consists of two renderings of a gear case cover showing top and bottom of the part.

Questions

1. What is meant by the term **rendering** as regards CAD work?
2. What is the difference between using the tool **Render** and the tool **Shade**, both from the **Render** toolbar?
3. Why do you think the tool **Hide** is in the **Render** toolbar?
4. What is the difference between a **Point** and a **Distant** light?
5. From which dialogue box are materials chosen?
6. Library files have an extension ***.mli**. In which directory will you expect to find the **Render.mli** file?
7. What do you think is the purpose of placing a light behind a 3D model when it is being rendered?
8. Look at Fig. 16.15 on page 252. One of the buttons is marked **Preview** and in the window above the button is a sphere which has been rendered. Experiment with the **Preview** button. What is its purpose?
9. *Left-click* on the **Render Preferences** tool icon in the **Render** toolbar. Can you explain the purpose of the various buttons in the resulting dialogue box?
10. *Left-click* on the word **Viewport** in the **Destination** area of the **Render** dialogue box. Having done that, can you explain how a rendered image in the R13 window can be saved to file?

Exercises

From your work with 3D solidsfrom previous chapters, attempt rendering the examples of 3D solids given in earlier chapters. You may be able to use your drawings made in answers to previous Exercises.

APPENDIX A

Printing and plotting

File	
New...	Ctrl+N
Open...	Ctrl+O
Save	Ctrl+S
Save As...	
Print...	Ctrl+P
Import...	
Export...	
Options	▶
Management	▶
1 FIG56H.DWG	
2 FIG55.DWG	
3 D:\CHAP16\LINKS\FIG13.DWG	
4 D:\CHAP16\LINKS\FIG07.DWG	
Exit	

Fig. A.1 *Left-click* on **Print...** in the **File** pull-down menu

Fig. A.2 The **Print** tool icon from the **Standard** toolbar

Introduction

Printing or plotting for a Windows applications is usually carried out through the Windows **Print Manager**. This involves a printer or plotter configured in the **Printers** dialogue box, from the **Control Panel** of the **Main** window of the Windows **Program Manager**. Although drawings constructed in R13 can be printed/plotted through the **Print Manager** of Windows, printers/plotters are more likely to be set so as to bypass the **Print Manager** having been configured with the other R13 configurations for video and digitiser. No matter whether the **Print Manager** is involved or not, once the printer/plotter has been configured for the computer onto which the R13 files have been loaded, sending a drawing to a printer or to a plotter is made very easy through the various tools and dialogue boxes within the AutoCAD R13 print or plot systems. The reader is warned not to attempt resetting the parameters for a printer or plotter, unless he or she has complete use of the computer being worked.

Printing from AutoCAD R13

To print or plot a drawing which has been constructed in the AutoCAD R13 graphics window, follow the procedure:

1. Either *left-click* on **Print...** in the **File** pull-down menu (Fig. A.1) or *left-click* on the **Print** tool icon (Fig. A.2). The **Plot Configuration** dialogue box appears (Fig. A.3).
2. In the **Plot Configuration** dialogue box, *left-click* on the **Window...** button, which brings up the **Window Selection** dialogue box (Fig. A.4), allowing the drawing to be windowed. What is within the window will be printed/plotted.
3. When a window has been selected around the required drawing, *left-click* on **Full**, and again on the **Preview** button and the drawing as it will appear when it is printed on the paper will come on the screen (Fig. A.5).

4. A *left-click* on **End Preview** in the preview screen brings back the **Plot Configuration** dialogue box. A *left-click* on the **OK** button will normally start up the print/plot. If some error in the connection of the printer or plotter occurs, the warning box Fig. A.6 will appear. Correcting the error in the system, followed by a *left-click* on the **Retry** button, should solve the problem.

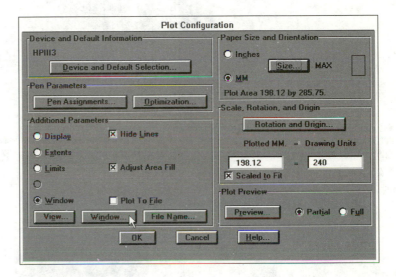

Fig. A.3 The **Print Configuration** dialogue box

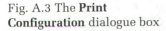

Fig, A.4 The **Window Selection** dialogue box

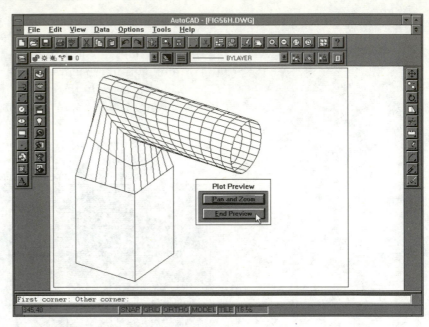

Fig. A.5 The **Preview** screen

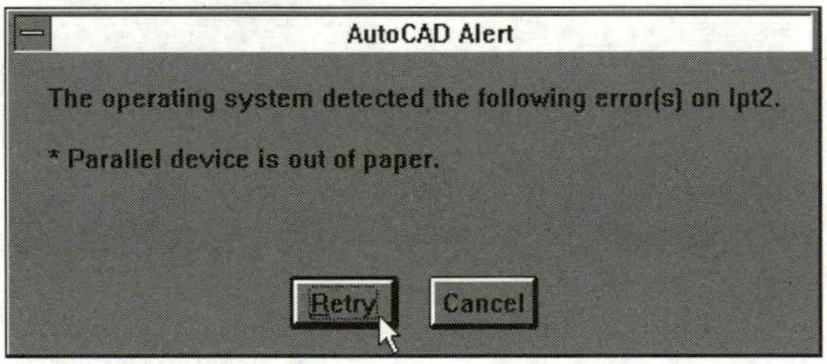

Fig. A.6 The **AutoCAD
Warning** box which appears if
there is an error in the printer/
plotter setup

Some of the new features in R13

Introduction

There are numerous features in R13 which are new to this release. In a book of this nature, which is only intended as an introductory text to those new to AutoCAD Release 13, only five of these new features are included in this appendix.

Drawing previews in the Select File dialogue box

When a drawing is saved in R13 and later opened, when the **Select File** dialogue box appears on opening a drawing, a preview of the drawing will be seen in the **Preview** box of the **Select File** dialogue box when the file name is selected by a single *left-click*. An example is shown in Fig. B.1. If one is doubtful as to which drawing file name to select, a *left-click* on the **Find File...** button of the dialogue box brings up another dialogue box showing small pictures of all files in the directory in which the drawing files are held. Fig. B.2 shows the result of a *left-click* on **Find File...** when the directory **c:\book** had been chosen in the **Select File** dialogue box.

Fig. B.1 A preview of a drawing showing in the **Preview** box of the **Select File** dialogue box

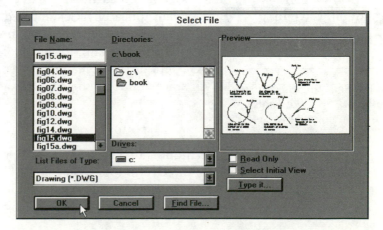

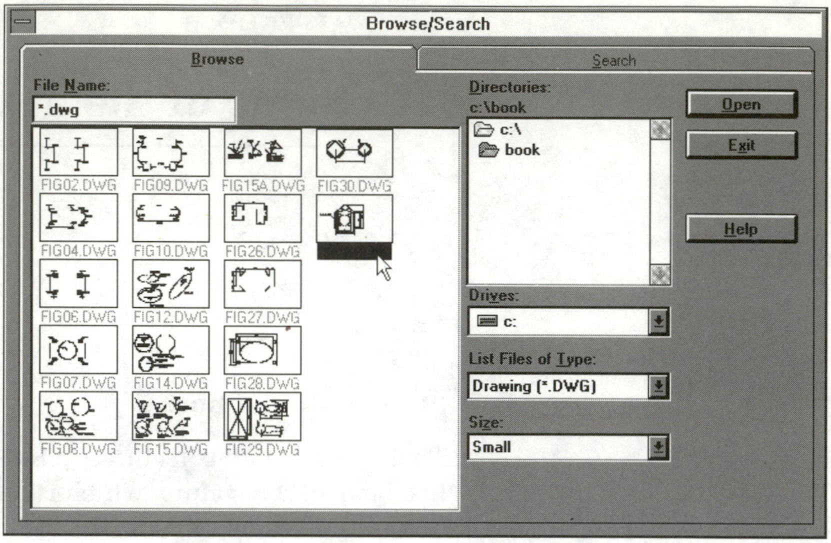

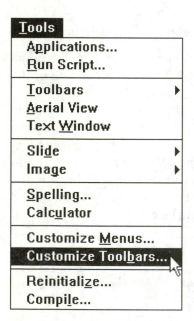

Fig. B.2 The **Browse/Search** dialogue box showing all files in **c:\book**

Fig. B.3 Selecting **Customize Toolbars...** from the **Tools** pull-down menu

Customising a toolbar

If you wish to make up your own toolbar in which the tools you most frequently use are held, follow the procedure as below:

1. *Left-click* on **Customize Toolbars...** in the **Tools** pull-down menu (Fig. B.3). The **Toolbars** dialogue box appears (Fig. B.4).
2. *Left-click* on the **New...** button in the dialogue box. The **New Toolbar** dialogue box appears.
3. *Enter* a suitable name in the **Toolbar Name** box of the dialogue box – in the example shown in Fig. B.4, the name is **My toolbar**.
4. *Left-click* on the **OK** button of the **New Toolbar** dialogue box and a new toolbar will appear at the top of the screen with the name **My toolbar** in its title bar.
5. A *left-click* on a toolbar name in the **Toolbars** list box of the **Toolbars** dialogue box and the tool icons in the selected toolbar name appear in a **Customize** dialogue box (Fig. B.5).
6. Drag a required tool icon from the toolbar in the **Customize** dialogue box into the new toolbar of name **My toolbar**.
7. Continue in this manner until all the required tool icons have been dragged into the new toolbar as shown in the example Fig. B.5.

Groups

A number of objects on screen can be grouped together with the aid of the **Group** tool (Fig. B.6). When grouped, all objects within the group can be acted upon by tools from the **Modify** toolbar as if they were a single object. There are several methods by which the tool can be called:

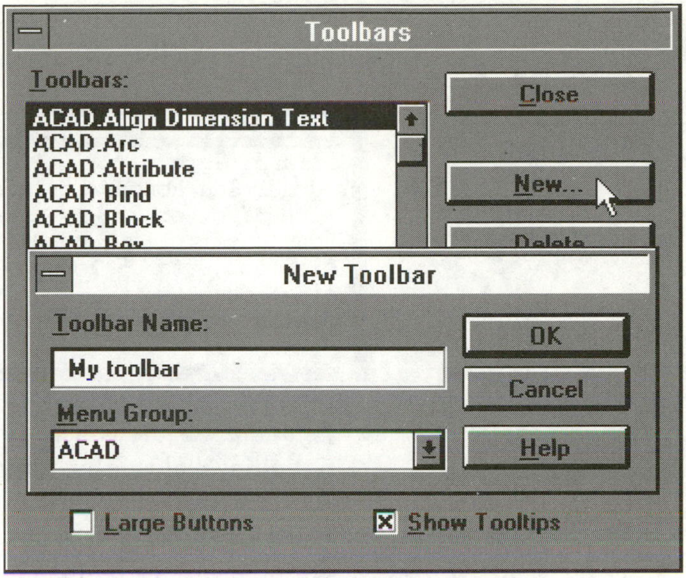

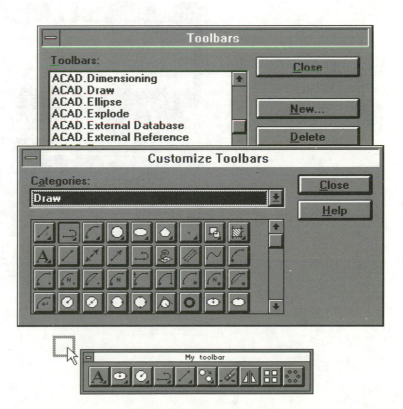

Fig. B4 *Entering* a new toolbar name in the **Toolbar Name** box

Fig. B5 The **Customize Toolbars** dialogue box with the **Draw** tool icons

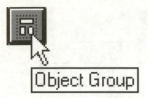

Object Group

Fig. B.6 The **Object Group** tool icon from the **Standard** toolbar

Fig. B.7 The prompts at the Command Line when **–group** is *entered*

1. *Enter* **–group** at the Command Line and follow the prompts which appear – Fig. B.7.

```
AutoCAD - Command Line
Command: -group
?/Order/Add/Remove/Explode/REName/Selectable/<Create>:
Group name (or ?): my_array
Group description: new01
Select objects: 5 found, 1 group
Select objects:
Command: Regenerating drawing.
Command:
```

2. *Left-click* on the **Object Group** tool icon (Fig. B.6). The **Object Grouping** dialogue box appears (Fig. B.8). The group shown in Fig. B.9 (**ARRAY**) has already been formed and a second group (**ARRAY02**) is about to be formed. The reader should experiment with the various buttons in the **Object Grouping** dialogue box to learn their various functions.

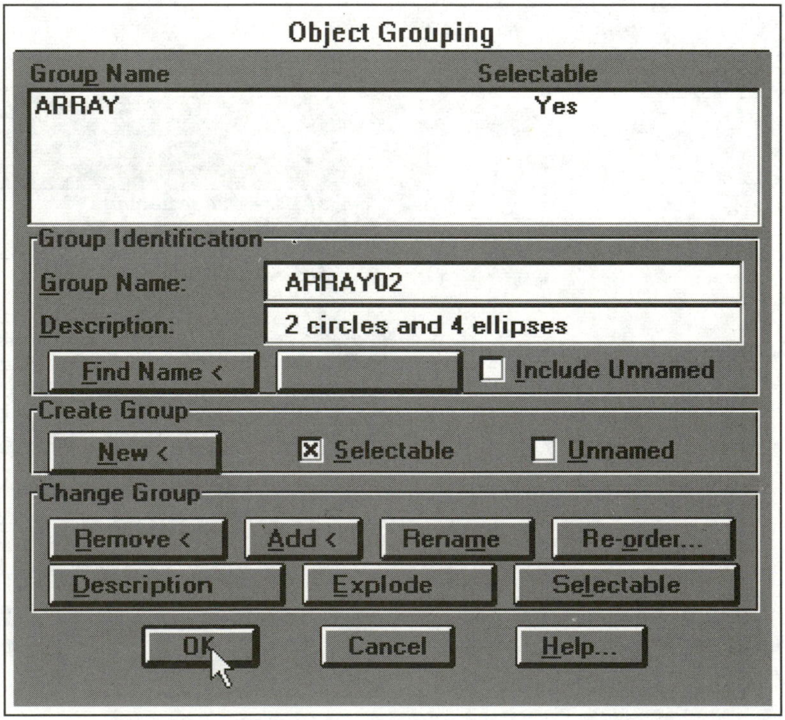

Object Grouping

Group Name	Selectable
ARRAY	Yes

Group Identification

Group Name: ARRAY02

Description: 2 circles and 4 ellipses

Find Name <   ☐ Include Unnamed

Create Group

New <   ☒ Selectable   ☐ Unnamed

Change Group

Remove <   Add <   Rename   Re-order...

Description   Explode   Selectable

OK   Cancel   Help...

Fig. B.8 The **Object Grouping** dialogue box

3. *Enter* **group** (i.e. without the – in front of the name) at the Command Line. This also brings up the **Object Grouping** dialogue box.

Fig. B.9 shows the effect of using **Copy** on a group. The group acts as if it were a single object.

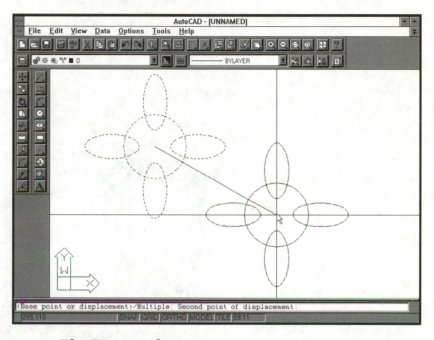

Fig. B.9 The effect of **Copy** on the group **ARRAY**

The Purge tool

Purge can be used at any time during a work session on a drawing in the R13 graphics window to purge from memory any unwanted data. When the drawing data is saved to a file, a purged file will usually be smaller than an unpurged one – sometime considerably smaller. This is unlike using the command in earlier releases when it could only be used immediately after a drawing had been opened to the screen. To use the tool:

Command:
Purge unused Blocks/Dimstyles/LAyers/LTypes/STyles/APpids/ Mlinestyles/All:

The most common response will be **a** (for All) which will produce a number of requests such as:

Purge shape file SIMPLEX<N>: *enter* y (Yes) *Return*

Entering **y** (Yes) at subsequent requests will purge all unwanted data in the drawing.

Saving in AutoCAD R12 format

If a drawing is to be saved so as to allow it to be opened in AutoCAD Release 12, with the drawing in the graphics window of AutoCAD R13:

Command: *enter* saveasr12 *Return*

and the **Save release 12 drawing as** dialogue box appears. *Enter* a suitable name in the **File Name:** box, followed by a *left-click* on the **OK** button of the dialogue box and the drawing is saved in the R12 ***.dwg** format to that filename. Note that the drawing, once saved as an R12 drawing, will not appear in the **Preview** box if it is opened in R13.

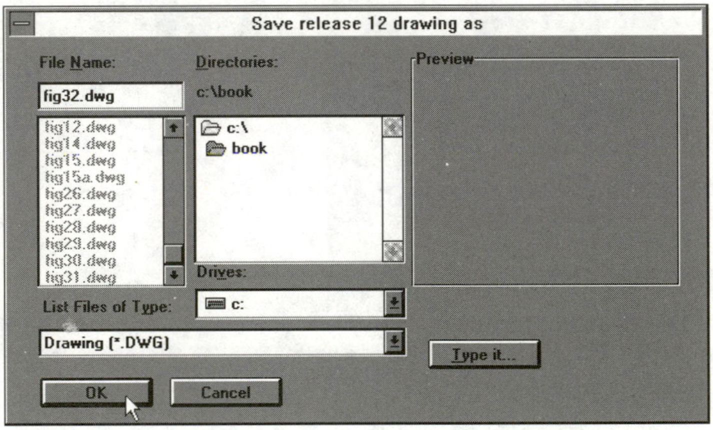

Fig. B.10 The **Save release 12 drawing as** dialogue box

Glossary

This glossary contain some of the more common computing terms.

Application – the name given to software packages that perform tasks such as word processing, desktop publishing, CAD etc.

ASCII – american national standard code for information interchange. A code which assigns bits to characters used in computing.

AT – advanced technology. Applied to PC's which have an 80286 processor (or better).

Autodesk – the American company which produces AutoCAD and other CAD software packages.

BASIC – beginner's all-purpose symbolic instruction code. A programming language.

Baud rate – a measure of the rate at which a computer system can send and received information (measured in bits per second).

BIOS – basic input/output system. The chip in a PC that controls the operations performed by the hardware (e.g. disks, screen, keyboard etc.)

Bit – short for binary digit. Binary is a form of mathematics that uses only two numbers: 0 and 1. Computers operate completely on binary mathematics.

Block – a group of objects or entities on screen that have been linked together to act as one unit.

Booting up – starting up a computer to an operating level.

Bus – an electronic channel that allows the movement of data around a computer.

Byte – a sequence of 8 bits.

C – a computer programming language.

Cache – a section of memory (can be ROM or RAM) which holds data that is being frequently used. Speeds up the action of disks and applications.

CAD – computer-aided design. Should not be used to mean computer-aided drawing.

CAD/CAM – computer-aided design and manufacturing.

CD-ROM – compact disc read only memory. A disk system capable of storing several hundred Mb of data – commonly 640 Mb. Data can only be read from a CD-ROM, not written to it.

CGA – colour graphic adaptor. A screen display with a resolution of 320×200 in four colours. Not used much with modern CAD systems.

Chips – pieces of silicon (usually) that have the electronic circuits that drive computers formed on their surface.

Clock speed – usually given in megahertz (MHz) – this is a measure of the speed at which a computer processor works.

Clone – refers to a PC that functions in a way identical to the original IBM PC.

CMOS – complementary metal oxide semiconductor. Often found as battery powered chips which control features such as the PC's clock speed.

Command Line – in AutoCAD R13 the Command Line is a window in which typed commands are entered, and which displays the prompts for, and responses to, these commands.

Communications – describes the software and hardware that allow computers to communicate.

Compatible – generally used as a term for software able to run on any computer that is an IBM clone.

Co-processor – a processor chip in a computer that runs in tandem with the main processor chip, and can deal with arithmetic involving many significant figures ('floating-point' arithmetic). Often used in CAD systems to speed up drawing operations.

CPU – central processing unit. The chip that drives a PC.

Data – information that is created, used or stored on computer in digital form.

Database – a piece of software that can store, handle and organise large amounts of information.

Dialogue box – a window that appears on screen in which options may be presented to the user, or which requires the user to input information requested by the current application.

Directories – the system used in MS-DOS for organizing files on disk. Could be compared to a folder (the directory) containing documents (the files).

Disks – storage hardware for holding data (files, applications, etc.). There are many types: the most common are hard disks (for mass storage), floppy disks (less storage) and CD-ROMs (mass storage).

Display – the screen allowing an operator to see the results of their work at a computer.

DOS – disk operating system. The software that allows the computer to access and organise stored data. MS-DOS (produced by the Microsoft Corporation) is the DOS most widely used in PC's.

DTP – desktop publishing. DTP software allows the combination of text and graphics into page layouts, which may then be printed.

EGA – enhanced graphics adaptor. A screen display with a resolution of 640 × 350 pixels in 16 colours.

EMS – expanded memory specification. RAM over and above the original limit of 640Kb RAM in the original IBM PC. PCs are now being built to take up to 64 Mb RAM.

Entity – a single feature or graphic being drawn on screen, e.g. a line, a circle, a point, etc. Sometimes linked together with other entities to form a block, where the block then acts as a single entity.

File – a collection of data held as an entity on a disk.

Fixed disk – a hard disk that cannot usually be easily removed from the computer; as distinct from floppy disks which are designed to be easily removable.

Floppy disk – a removable disk that stores data in magnetic form. The actual disk is a thin circular sheet of plastic with a magnetic surface, hence the term 'floppy'. It usually has a firm plastic case.

Flyout – in AutoCAD R13, a flyout is a number of tool icons which appear when a main tool icon (which shows a small arrow) is selected.

Formatting – the process of preparing the magnetic surface of a disk to enable it to hold digital data.

Gigabyte (Gb) – in computing terms 1 Gb is 1,073,741,824 bytes (not 1,000,000,000).

GUI – graphical user interface. Describes software (such as Windows) which allows the user to control the computer by representing functions with icons and other graphical images.

Hardcopy – the result of printing (or plotting) text or graphics on to paper or card.

Hard disk – a disk, usually fixed in a computer, which rotates at high speed and will hold large amounts of data (up to 1 gigabyte).

Hardware – the equipment used in computing: the computer itself, disks, printers, monitor, etc.

Hertz (Hz) – the measure of 1 cycle per second. In computing terms, often used in millions of hertz (megahertz or MHz) as a measure of the clock speed.

IBM – International Business Machines. An American computer manufacturing company – the largest in the world.

Intel – an American company which manufactures the processing chips used in the majority of PCs.

Joystick – a small control unit used mainly for computer games. Some CAD systems use a joystick to control drawing on screen.

Kilobyte (K) – in computing terms 1 K is 1,024 bytes (not 1,000).

LAN – local area network. Describes a network than might typically link PCs in an office by cable, where a distance between the PCs is small.

LED – light-emitting diode.

Library – a set of frequently used symbols, phrases or other data on disk, that can be easily accessed by the operator.

Light pen – stylus used to point directly at a display screen sensitive to its use.

Megabyte (Mb) – in computing terms 1 Mb is 1,048,576 bytes (not 1,000,000).

Memory – any medium (such as RAM or ROM chips) that allows the computer to store data internally that can be instantly recalled.

Message box – a window containing a message for the user which appears when certain tools or commands are selected or executed.

MHz – megahertz. 1,000,000 hertz (cycles per second).

Microcomputer – a PC is a microcomputer; a minicomputer is much larger and a mainframe computer is larger still. With the increase in memory capabilities of microcomputers, the term seems to be dropping out of use.

Microsoft – an American corporation which produces Windows and MS-DOS software.

MIPS – millions of instructions per second. A measure of a computer's speed – it is not comparable with the clock speed as measured in MHz because a single instruction may take more than a single cycle to perform.

Monitor – a computer's display screen.

Mouse – a device for controlling the position of an on-screen pointer within a GUI such as Windows.

MS-DOS – Microsoft disk operating system.

Multi-user – a computer that may be used by more than one operator simultaneously.

Multitasking – a computer that can carry out more than one task at the same time is said to be multitasking. For example, in AutoCAD R13 for Windows, printing can be carried out 'in the background' while a new drawing is being constructed.

Networking – the joining together of a group of computers, allowing then to share the same data and software applications. LANs and WANs are examples of the types of networks available.

Object – a term used in CAD to describe an entity, or a group of entities that have been linked together.

Operating system – software, and in some cases hardware, that allows the user to operate applications software and organise and use data stored on a computer.

PC – personal computer. Should strictly only be used to refer to an IBM clone, but is now in general use.

Pixels – the individual dots of a computer display.

Plotter – produces hardcopy of, for instance, a drawing produced on computer by moving a pen over a piece of paper or card.

Printer – there are many types of printer: dot-matrix, bubble-jet and laser are the most common. Allows material produced on computer (graphics and text) to be output as hardcopy.

Processor – the operating chip of a PC. Usually a single chip, such as the Intel 80386 or 80486 chip.

Program – a set of instructions for the computer that has been designed to produce a given result.

RAM – random access memory. Data stored in RAM is lost when the computer is switched off, unless previously saved to a disk.

RGB – red, green, blue.

RISC – reduced instruction set chip. A very fast processor.

ROM – read only memory. Data and programs stored in a ROM chip are not lost when the computer is switched off.

Scanner – hardware capable of being passed over a document or drawing and reading the image into a computer.

Software – refers to any program or application that is used and run on computer.

SQL – structured query language. A computer programming language for translating and transferring data between an application such as AutoCAD and a database.

Tool – in AutoCAD R13, a tool represents a command which may be executed by selecting an on-screen icon.

Tool tip – a tool tip appears when the mouse cursor is moved over a tool icon – a small box appears carrying the name of the tool.

Toolbar – a toolbar contains a number of icons, each representing a different tool.

UNIX – multi-user, multitasking operating system (short for UNICS: uniplexed information and computing system).

VDU – visual display unit.

Vectors – refers to entities in computer graphics which are defined by the end points of each part of the entity.

VGA – video graphics array. Screen displays with a resolution of up to 640 × 480 pixels in 256 colours. SVGA (Super VGA) allows resolutions of up to 1024 × 768 pixels.

Virtual memory – a system by which disk space is used to allow the computer to function as if more physical RAM were present. It is used by AutoCAD (and other software), but can slow down a computer's operation.

WAN – wide area network. A network of computers that are a large distance apart – communication is often done down telephone lines.

Warning box – a window containing a warning or request which the user must respond to, which appears when certain circumstances are met or actions are made.

Weitek – makers of maths co-processor chips for 80386 and 80486 computers. Important for AutoCAD users, because the addition of a Weitek co-processor chip speeds up drawing construction processes considerably.

WIMP – windows, icons, mice and pull-down menus. A term that is used to describe some GUIs.

Winchesters – hard disks. Refers to the company which made the first hard disks. An out-of-date term.

Window – an area of the computer screen within which applications such as word processors may be operated.

Workstation – often used to refer to a multi-user PC, or other system used for the purposes of CAD (or other applications).

WORM – write once, read many. An optical storage system that allows blank optical disks to have data written onto them only once.

WYSIWYG – what you see is what you get. What is on the screen is what will be printed.

XMS – extended memory specifications. RAM above the 1Mb limit.

XT – extended technology. Was used to refer to the original 8060- to 8088-based computers.

Index

%% calls 159
**** 20, 55
. 8
*.3ds 172
*.bmp 172
*.dwg 8
*.eps 172
*.pcx 172
*.pfb 118
*.shx 118
*.ttf 118
*.wmf 172

2D
  drawing 98
  Modify tools 73
  Solid 105
3D
  construction 184
  Face 191
  Mesh 196
  Mirror 199
  models 220
  Polar Array 198
  Rectangular Array 198
  Rotate 199
  solid models 184
  Studio files 172
  surface meshes 191
  tools 74
  Viewpoint Presets 186
  Viewpoint Presets 232
3Dview 224
80386 23
80486 23

A3 drawing sheet 2
abbreviations 13
absolute coordinates 43
acad.dwg 62
acad.pgp 70, 130
acadiso.dwg 62
acadr13.bat 15
accurate drawing 43
adding text 119
ADS xi
Advanced Modelling
    Extension 208
advantages of CAD 24
Aerial window 108
Align 89
Alt/Tab 58
AME 208
  Convert 240
Annotation dialogue box
    67, 155
Arc 38
arrays 87
arrow cursor 3
associative hatching 143
attach materials 252
AutoCAD
  Development System xi
  Windows Colors 27
AutoCAD 13
  for DOS 15
  icon 2
AutoLisp xi
Automatic Save 114
AutoSketch 168
AutoVision xi

batch file   15
Bitmap files   172
Blips   10, 29
Block   174
Boolean operators   217
boundary hatch   146
Box   187, 212
Break   82
break lines   127
building plan drawing   179
buttons   7

C:\> prompt   16
cabinet drawing   122, 132
Cancel button   8
CD-ROM drive   xi
centre lines   127
Chamfer   83, 234
Change System Settings   5
check boxes   8
Check Spelling dialogue box   121
Circle   37, 46
circuit drawing   174
Clipboard   164
colon after command name   20
Color
    dialogue box   11
    icon   5
Command Line   3, 55
common computing terms   267
Cone   189, 214
configuration   4
Configure   4
configuring
    plotter   6
    printer   6
Construction Line   99
construction lines   128
Control Panel   5
coordinate system   29
coordinates window   4
Copy   75, 166
Copy View   165
copyclip   166
Create New Drawing dialogue
    box   62, 70
current drawing   2
cursor   1
customising toolbars   262
Cut   167

Cylinder   213

Data pull-down menu
    10, 67
dd calls   10, 17
dialogue box   6, 9
    title bar   7
digitiser   3, 6
digitising tablet   6
Dimension Styles dialogue
    box   67, 152
dimensioning   158
Dimensioning toolbar   12
dimensions   152
disadvantages of CAD   25
Dish   190
display   23
Divide   102
Dome   190
DOS
    and Windows compared   21
    on-screen menus   17
    pull-down menus   17
    version   xi, 15
double-click   1
drag   1
dragging   26
Draw
    toolbar   3, 11
    tools   98
Drawing Aids   9, 30
drawing limits   31
drawing previews   261
Dtext   119
Dview   224
DXF files   169

Edge   192
Edgesurf   195
Edit menu   163
Edit Polyline   90
electric circuit drawing   178
electronics circuit drawing
    178
Elev   240
Ellipse   50, 103
Elliptical Cylinder   213
embedding   164
end views   126
enter   1

entering commands   13, 21
environment   28
Environment dialogue box   11
EPS files   172
Erase   74, 85
Esc key   58
Explode   74, 146
Export   170
Extend   81
Extrude   215
Extruded Surface   193

F1 key   56
fence   76
File pull-down menu   113
file types   169
files   25
Fill   106
Fillet   84, 235
filters   185
first angle projection   123
floating toolbar   33, 73
flyouts   12, 33
fonts   27
Format dialogue box   67, 154
front view   126
function keys   57

geometric tolerances   156
Geometry dialogue box
        67, 153
graphic window   2
graphical interface   25
Grid   10, 29
Grips   111
groups 262
GUI   25

hair lines   3
hard disk   23
hardware   23
Hatch   142
hatching   142
    in engineering drawings   144
    text   146
Help   55
    window   57
hidden detail lines   127
Hide   32
Hideplot   233

Hijaak   xi
horizontal plane   123

icons   25, 32
Import   171
Insert Block   175
Insert Object   167
insertions   174
Intel chip   23
Intersection   219
isometric drawing   122, 131
Isometric presets   186
isoplanes   132

key combinations   57
keyboard
    commands   10
    short-cuts   57

languages   xi
Layer Control dialogue box   63
layer state   64
layers   2, 15, 63
left-click   1
libraries of files   174
Lights   249
Limits   29
Line   34, 43, 48
    tool   13
lines in technical
    drawings   127
linking   164
list boxes   7

Main window   5
materials   252
Mbytes   23
Measure   102
menu bar   2
message boxes   6
metafiles   172
metric A3 sheets   29
Mirror   86, 112
Model Space   3, 229
Modify toolbar   11
modify tools   91
monitor screen   4
mouse   1, 23, 25
Move   74, 112

MS-DOS
  Editor 130
  version 5.0 23
Multiline 12, 37, 100
Multiple Copy 76
Mview 233

number of views 126

Object Group 264
object linking and embedding
    164
Object Properties toolbar 2
Object Snap 52, 43
Offset 85
OLE 164
on-screen menu 55
oops 174
Options menu 2
  pull-down 4
Ortho 15
orthographic
  drawings 122
  projection 123
osnaps 20, 43
outlines 127

PageMaker xi
paint files 172
Pan 110
Paper Space 3, 229
Paste Link 165
Paste Special 167
pasting 164
pattern boxes 8
Pattern Type dialogue box 142
PC xi, 23
Pedit 90
pick box 1
plan 126
planometric drawing 122,
    136
Plot Configuration dialogue
    box 258
Plot Preview 258
plotting 258
pneumatics circuit drawing
    179
Point 101
Polar Array 88

Polygon 51
Polyline 35, 44, 49
  tool 12
pop-up lists 8
Precision box 30
Preferences dialogue
    box 11, 26
preview box 8
Printers dialogue box 6
printing 258
Program Manager 2
prompts 34
Properties 169
Prototype dialogue box 63
prototype drawing 65
  files 62
puck 23
Purge 241, 265
Pyramid 188

R13 icon 2
RAM 23
Ray 100
Rectangle 104
Rectangular Array 87
Redo 163
Redraw 113
Regen 113
relative coordinates 48
Render toolbar 247
renderings 256
Return 1
Revolve 216
Revolved Surface 192
revsurf 192
right-click 1
Rotate 77, 112
rotation angle 77
Ruled Surface 194
rulesurf 194
running object snaps 54

Save 113
Save As
  dialogue box 69
  R12 266
Save Drawing As dialogue
    box 113
Savetime 114

saving work   113
Scale   79, 112
screen
  limits   31
  size   23
scroll bars   8
Section   237
select fence   77
Select File   6
Select Font Style dialogue
    box   118
Select Objects toolbar   73
selected grip   111
SERVICE   21
setting osnaps   54
settings   xi
Shadedge   256
Shift+right-click   185
short-cuts   57
Single-Line Text   119
Slice   235
slider box   8
Snap   10, 15, 29
software   23
Solids toolbar   184, 208, 212
spelling checker   121
Sphere   189, 213
Standard toolbar   3, 163, 186
start-up   2
Stretch   78, 112
Styles   118
Subtract   218
Surfaces toolbar   184
Surftab   193
symbol libraries   174

tablet overlay   21
tabsurf   194
technical drawings   122
Text   118, 120
Text
  tools   119
text editor   120
Text Style dialogue box   68
third angle projection   123
  orthographic   127
Tilemode   3, 229
tool
  abbreviations   70

tips   11, 33
toolbars   3, 11, 32
tools   11
Tools pull-down menu   12
Torus   190
Trim   80
TrueType fonts   118
types of drawing   122

UCS   208
  icon   4, 209
  prompts   211
UCSFOLLOW   209
Undo   163
Union   217
units   29
Units Control   10
unselected grip   111
user coordinate system   208

variables   xi
vertical planes   123
VGA   23
video   4
View pull-down menu   229
viewport constructions   230
Viewports   229
Vpoint   96

warning boxes   6, 9
WCS   208
wildcard   8
WIMP   25
window frame   7
windows   25
Windows
  Clipboard   164
  Setup   5
  version 3.1   23
WORLD UCS   208

x,y coordinates   4, 15, 29
x,y,z coordinates   29
xline   99

Z axis   184
Zoom   31, 107, 242
  previous   110
  window   110